The Jewish Feminist Movement in Germany

Contributions in **Women's Studies**

The Chains of Protection: The Judicial Response to Women's Labor Legislation
Judith A. Baer

Women's Studies: An Interdisciplinary Collection
Kathleen O'Connor Blumhagen and Walter D. Johnson, editors

Latin American Women: Historical Perspectives
Asunción Lavrin

Beyond Her Sphere: Women and the Professions in American History
Barbara J. Harris

Literary America, 1903-1934: The Mary Austin Letters
T. M. Pearce, editor

The American Woman in Transition: The Urban Influence, 1870-1920
Margaret Gibbons Wilson

Liberators of the Female Mind: The Shirreff Sisters, Educational Reform, and the Women's Movement
Edward W. Ellsworth

MARION A. KAPLAN

The Jewish Feminist Movement in Germany
THE CAMPAIGNS OF THE JÜDISCHER FRAUENBUND, 1904-1938

Contributions in Women's Studies, Number 8

GREENWOOD PRESS

WESTPORT, CONNECTICUT ● LONDON, ENGLAND

Library of Congress Cataloging in Publication Data

Kaplan, Marion A
  The Jewish feminist movement in Germany.

  (Contributions in women's studies ; no. 8 ISSN
0147-104X)
  Bibliography: p.
  Includes index.
  1. Jüdischer Frauenbund. 2. Jew in Germany—
Politics and government. 3. Women, Jewish—Germany.
4. Pappenheim, Bertha, 1859-1936. 5. Germany—
Politics and government—20th century. I. Title.
II. Series.
DS135.G33K29   301.41'2'06243   78-67567
ISBN 0-313-20736-4

Library of Congress Catalog Card Number: 78-67567
ISBN: 0-313-20736-4
ISSN: 0147-104X

First published in 1979

Greenwood Press, Inc.
51 Riverside Avenue, Westport, Connecticut 06880

Printed in the United States of America

10 9 8 7 6 5 4 3 2 1

To JAY

Contents

Illustrations   ix

Acknowledgments   xi

✓ **1. Introduction**   **3**

     Germans, Jews, and Women   3

     Emancipation: The Goal of Jews and Women   8

     Jewish Feminists in a Man's World   11

     Double Jeopardy: Jewish Women in German Society   14

✓ **2. Bertha Pappenheim**   **29**

     "Only a Girl": Pappenheim's Early Years and the Story
       of Anna O   29

     The Author and Activist   40

3. Woman's Sphere   **59**

     The Feminist Aspirations of the Frauenbund   59

     "For Women's Work and the Women's Movement":
       The Goals of the Frauenbund   85

     The Organization's Structure   89

✓ **4. Prostitution, Morality Crusades, and Feminism**   **103**

     The White Slave Traffic and Its Opponents   103

     The Frauenbund's Attitudes Toward the Causes
       and Cures of White Slavery   113

     The National and International Campaigns Against
       the Traffic in Women   117

     Institutions and Programs to Prevent White Slavery   125

5. The Pursuit of Influence and Equality in Germany's Jewish Community   147

"And He Shall Rule over Thee": The Opposition
to Women's Suffrage   147

The JFB's Campaign for Women's Rights   151

6. Housework as Lifework   169

Marrying for a Living: Choices Available to
Middle-Class Women before World War I   169

Home Economics: The Attempt to Professionalize
Homemaking   173

Housekeeping for Survival: Depression and
the Third Reich   182

7. Conclusion   199

Selected Bibliography   209

Index   223

Illustrations

1. Bertha Pappenheim   28
2. JFB "Tree"   58
3. Front page of the JFB monthly, "Newspaper of the Jüdischer Frauenbund: For Women's Work and the Women's Movement"   102
4. Young women attending the JFB's girls' club in Breslau   128
5. A promotional picture for the JFB's program to provide dowries to needy brides   131
6. Children at the JFB's home in Isenburg   135

Acknowledgments

I wish to express my gratitude to those individuals who encouraged me in the preparation of this book. I would like to thank Fritz Stern for his helpful insights and suggestions regarding the content and style of the original manuscript. I am indebted to the guidance and friendship of Paula Hyman, who shared her knowledge of Jewish and women's history with me. Her probing comments and questions and her support were invaluable in the initial research and writing stages of this project. To the late Dora Edinger, I owe a special debt. A historian by training and a feminist by conviction, she was Bertha Pappenheim's first biographer and a devoted and loyal Frauenbund member. She shared her extensive files with me, read and criticized my work, and awaited the publication of this book with as much enthusiasm as I. My thanks are also due to Ismar Schorsch, who read the original manuscript and made important suggestions, as well as to Amy Hackett, whose pathbreaking work on the Bund Deutscher Frauenvereine provided a constant reference and whose incisive comments have been incorporated into the final text. Without the well-kept archives and extensive library of the Leo Baeck Institute in New York, this book would have been impossible. It is a pleasure to thank the staff of the LBI, particularly Helmut Galliner, Ilse Blumenthal-Weiss, and Sybil Milton, as well as my friend Monika Richarz, whose own research brought her to the LBI, for their helpfulness in guiding me through their rich collection. Finally, my unending thanks go to Jay Kaplan. He has read and commented upon all of these pages, in both their early and final versions. His gentle but rigorous criticism, intellectual vitality, moral support and love made an often exacting and frustrating process into an exciting, mutual experience. I hope this book merits, to some extent, the generous aid of those to whom I owe my sincere appreciation.

The Jewish
Feminist Movement
in Germany

chapter 1

Introduction

Germans, Jews, and Women

This study of the Jüdischer Frauenbund (League of Jewish Women), a German-Jewish feminist organization, focuses upon the convergent spheres of German, Jewish, and women's history. The Frauenbund (JFB) was a popular and articulate advocate of women's interests in twentieth-century Germany. Its visions, attitudes, and activities, as well as its successes and failures, reflected the broader political and social culture. The present work seeks to examine the goals of the JFB, to describe its charismatic leader, Bertha Pappenheim, and to assess the meaning of its three major campaigns: the fight against white slavery, the pursuit of equality in Jewish communal affairs, and the attempt to provide career training for women. Jewish women lived in a position of double jeopardy as a result of their religion and sex: as Jews and as women they endured discrimination in Germany, and as women they suffered from second-class citizenship in their own Jewish community. An appreciation of the efforts of the Frauenbund to combat women's inferior status can enrich our knowledge of the history of German Jewry and the women's emancipation movement.

Two frameworks may be applied to German-Jewish history, both of which are relevant to an understanding of the Jüdischer Frauenbund.[1] An "outer framework" encompasses the interactions of successive generations of Germans and Jews as well as their feelings, thoughts, and assumptions about each other. It is also concerned with political, social, and economic changes in Germany and their effect on Jews and other Germans. And, it deals with the actions of

Germans toward Jews and the varied reactions of German Jewry: the pursuit by some of full citizenship, and the decision by others to emigrate; the flight of some from religion, and the efforts on the part of others to defend and revitalize the Jewish community. This story of the Jüdischer Frauenbund is, in part, intended to cast light on these different aspects of relations between Germans and Jews. An "internal framework" concentrates on Jewish communal history. The Jewish community, or *Gemeinde*, was a legal entity, embracing all Jews in any one place of residence and empowered by the State to levy taxes on its members. Unless one took the extraordinary legal step of leaving it, one would be affected by the decisions of this corporate community. While influenced by its German environment, the Jewish *Gemeinde* had a life of its own which extended from the medieval, pre-emancipation era through the Nazi years: "its bearers and fashioners were conscious of their activity as Jews and motivated by Jewish considerations." The community had "its own wellsprings of energy and was shaped . . . in no small measure by internal and autonomous drives and purposes."[2] JFB members were conscious and observant Jews with strong communal feelings. The Frauenbund's activities and demands, its very existence, attested to the vitality of the German-Jewish community.

There was yet another Jewish community that has remained "hidden from history."[3] This group was made up of women, the majority of the German-Jewish community in the twentieth century. They had a story of their own, determined by their unique roles, aspirations, and achievements as well as by their relationship to the Jewish *Gemeinde*, the budding women's movement, and the German nation. Yet, their history has been largely unexplored. Students of German women's history have paid scant attention to Jewish women or the JFB. Historians of German Jewry, assuming that the history of women was subsumed in their studies, have succeeded primarily in portraying the lives of German-Jewish men. While scattered attention has been accorded a few famous ladies, most women were passed over silently. Of course, scholars of German-Jewish history are not guilty of a unique disregard of women. Remarkably little of substance has been written about the position and experiences of women in society prior to the recent growth of interest. American historian Gerda Lerner has noted that "the striking fact about the historiography of women is the general neglect of the subject by historians."[4] Mary Beard, in *Women as Force in History* (1946), criticized historians, who, being men, confined "their search for the truth to their own sex," thus exaggerating the force of men and missing "the force of women which entered into the making of history and gave it important direction."[5] Perhaps the reason men have omitted women from the histories they have written is due, in part, to the natural inclination of privileged or dominant groups in any society to identify and represent their ideas and interests as those of the community at large. Male norms have been set as the criteria by which to determine historical significance. These have included the exercise of "power over others,"[6] activity in the public sphere, and intellectual or creative genius. Women's public and private lives have been neglected as insignificant or outside of history. There is yet another explanation put forth by Virginia Woolf as to why men have overlooked the contributions of women: "Women have served all these centuries as looking-glasses possessing the magic and delicious power of reflecting the figure of man at twice its natural size." If woman "begins to tell the truth, the figure in the looking-glass shrinks. . . ."[7] Finally, interested historians have been hampered by a relative absence of documents, for women seem to have accepted men's standards as to what was worthy of note, and have left few records of their existence.

. Mary Beard encouraged the study of women in order to discover the necessary information and to develop the insight to write a more balanced history of the civilization of men and women. She observed: "Women have done far more than exist and bear and rear children. . . . Women have been a force in making all the history that has been made."[8] Historians have begun to follow her advice. Within the last decade, as a result of a renewed women's movement and the maturation of social history, women's history has developed into a new research area. Historians are placing women within their social context and demonstrating that they have a past worth knowing.[9] They are analyzing the reproductive sphere (that of the home and family) as well as the productive sphere (that of the work place), and they continue to uncover the public efforts and activism of women. Their studies raise new questions in an effort to go beyond traditional themes to find out what gave shape to women's lives. This examination of the Frauenbund addresses several of these issues. First, it considers how modern conditions have transformed the traditional roles and status of women. In particular, it traces the changing expectations and perceptions of women vis-à-vis their role in the Jewish community. Second, it explores the extent to which women shaped their own destinies and the extent to which they were constrained by circumstances beyond their control. Marx noted in the opening of his *Eighteenth Brumaire*: "People make their own history, but they do not make it as they please, they do not make it under circumstances chosen by themselves; but under circumstances directly encountered, given and transmitted from the past." One might argue that this statement is even more applicable to women than to men, for the former were more severely hampered by familial, economic, and political conditions. Yet, acknowledging the impediments to human agency is not enough: we must also analyze which circumstances shaped women's position, influenced their perceptions, goals, and strategies, and determined whether they succeeded or failed.[10] This study raises questions about the gender, ethnic/religious, and class determinants of women's history and illustrates areas in which women's goals reflected, reinforced, or transcended larger social developments.

Third, the role of cultural myths is examined, particularly those surrounding women's "nature." Did women actually believe in the altruism, superior morality, and self-sacrificing and empathetic maternal personalities that were ascribed to them? Or did they use these alleged attributes to extend women's sphere, or both? Fourth, the JFB's stress on duty and self-abnegation as well as its emphasis on social work raise the more general question of what constitutes "feminism." The Frauenbund provides a case study of a group whose "feminism" displayed a strange amalgam of internalized patriarchal values and woman-oriented concerns. A typical JFB member would be a housewife and mother who accepted her status in the private sphere and performed traditional voluntary social work in the *Gemeinde*; who demanded careers and educational opportunities for women, but for specifically "female" fields; and who insisted upon an equal role for women in politics and society, but did so in a most ladylike manner. In contrast to American and

British feminists, the German (and German-Jewish) tradition of feminism was built upon the assumption of certain natural differences between the sexes. It conceived of "equality" not in formal or inalienable terms but, rather, in terms of equal possibilities for the fulfillment of the unique potential of each sex.[11] To appreciate women as an active force in history, feminism ought not to be defined as merely an attempt to gain suffrage or legal equality; students of history must look for women's achievements and appraise their lives in a far broader context. Furthermore, an understanding of the variety of ideas and methods with which women tried to gain more control over the making of their own history suggests to us that feminism is a process rather than an ideology. While recognizable over time, it assumes different forms and expresses different historical goals.

Finally, this investigation also takes into account the relative importance of sex among the competing cleavages of class, religion, ethnic heritage, and nation. It points to the commonalities of experience among women across national, class, ethnic, or religious lines as well as to the divisions created by these same identities. Because the Frauenbund belonged to the middle-class women's movement, it can illuminate the sex-specific conditions which oppressed middle-class women regardless of religious affiliation. At all levels of twentieth-century German and Jewish societies the position of women was inferior to that of men. This created certain common bonds which enabled women of different religions to work with and for each other. Furthermore, because the JFB was organized along religious lines, it can highlight the political and social forces which induced Jewish women to act in solidarity with one another. Anti-Semitism in particular, making no distinctions between rich or poor, German or Eastern European Jew, subjected all Jewish women to the pernicious effects of racial and religious prejudice. Nevertheless, differences across class, religion, ethnic, and national loyalties were greater than the forces uniting women, imposing strict limits to sisterhood. Class and ethnic differences excluded the possibility of a union between Frauenbund members, most of whom were middle-class German Jews, and their proletarian Eastern European immigrant sisters. The latter, known as *Ostjuden*, remained recipients of, rather than collaborators in, the JFB's social work. Its middle-class motivations and sensibilities were perhaps most blatant in its campaign to train Eastern European girls to become domestic servants, but a distinctly maternalistic attitude pervaded all of its dealings with *Ostjuden*, both in Germany and in Eastern Europe. Moreover, Jewish women were divided between a minority of Orthodox and a majority of Liberal religious groups as well as between a small, but growing contingent of Zionists and those who insisted on loyalty to a German fatherland.[12] The latter, much to their chagrin, found that many middle-class German women did not accept them, either because of their consciously Jewish identity or because of their "racial" heritage. Thus, antagonism and conflicting experiences among women, just as among men, inhibited greater solidarity in the face of commonly experienced injustices.

Emancipation: The Goal of Jews and Women

Emancipation was the goal of activists among both German women and Jews in the nineteenth century. The period of legal emancipation of German Jewry, from approximately 1790 to 1871, overlapped the movement for women's rights, which began around 1848 and peaked in 1918. Both groups had suffered from prejudice and extensive discrimination, and both engaged in long, often bitter, struggles against oppressive restrictions based on sex or religion and in favor of equal rights for personal development. Their leaders believed that the first step toward a general amelioration in the status of these groups lay in the elimination of formal, institutionalized inequalities which contributed to social and professional segregation, political impotence, and ascribed social roles.

Jewish reformers identified their movement with the liberal-democratic ideals of the French Revolution. German feminists, while not eschewing these principles, stressed the need to defend women's interests, particularly their economic interests. Both movements were part of a larger power struggle, raging over the course of the century, between the upholders of feudal privileges and the bourgeoisie which demanded equality of opportunity. Furthermore, rapid industrialization in the second half of the nineteenth century was not matched by concomitant political and social modernization.

By this period, Jewish males had achieved considerable economic status as well as prominence in the professions. In these same decades some German women began to enter the field of teaching. Others demanded greater access to careers due to the "surplus" of women (*Frauenüberschuss*) in Germany which would result in large numbers of single women who had to earn their own livelihoods. Married women of the middle class, increasingly deprived of their domestic and child-bearing functions by servants, appliances, consumer products, and (by the turn of the century) birth control, became freer to develop new interests and to define themselves beyond household management and motherhood. Thus, both Jews and women intensified their campaigns to bargain for a status commensurate with their rising expectations.

When they met with little success, many Jews tried to "fit in" with German society by shedding their ethnic, social and, even, religious distinctiveness, and women, who could not disguise their uniqueness, argued that they were worthy citizens because of their special qualities. The emancipation of Jewish men had been accorded "occasional gestures of Christian solicitude" as early as 1781.[13] Despite piecemeal concessions dating from the reform era of Stein and Hardenberg, it was not until 1871 that Jewish men received full political and civil rights in all of Germany. Political rights for German women, whose claims to full participation in the life of the country dated from the revolutions of 1848, were denied until 1918. The hard-won gains of Jews and women formed part of the flawed and ephemeral emancipation of bourgeois society.[14] They disappeared in the undertow of anti-Semitism and antifeminism produced by the successive waves of inflation, depression, and Nazism.

German-Jewish women shared the disadvantages of their sex and of their people. They were, for example, disenfranchised in the German states as Jews, and when the vote was extended to Jewish males in the German Empire, Jewish women had to await the enfranchisement of German women. Even when female suffrage was granted in 1918, the victory of Jewish women was only a secular one; as women, they were still denied a political voice in Jewish communal elections. Similarly, when German women began to achieve modest advances as teachers, anti-Semitism blocked Jewish women from a share in this progress. Nevertheless, despite what might be called their "double jeopardy," German-Jewish women also benefited from the successes of Jewish men and from feminist inroads into the male sanctuaries of higher education, the professions, and, finally, politics. Whereas, before emancipation, Jews were among the poorest groups in Germany, by 1871 they had risen from an underprivileged position to one that was above average in wealth and education. Thus, the comfortable, middle-class status of most German Jews enabled women to afford household help and labor-saving devices. As a result of their economic position and their urban concentration, Jews were the first religious group in Germany to practice birth control widely by the turn of the century.[15] Thus, during the Second Empire, German-Jewish women were increasingly able to escape the confining responsibilities of domestic life. A few became outstanding leaders of German feminist thought and organization, while others became volunteers for Jewish charities. The latter donated their spare time to traditional, religious, benevolent, or burial societies, aiding poor or sick women, and preparing female corpses for interment. Such associations, which were generally limited in scope, proliferated in the second half of the nineteenth century. In 1904, the more progressive members of these societies, that is, those who were convinced of the virtues of German feminism and dissatisfied with the circumscribed nature of Jewish female charities, formed the nucleus of the Jüdischer Frauenbund. They decided to reform Jewish philanthropy and to establish a nationwide association of Jewish women.

The subtitle of the JFB's newsletter announced that Jewish feminists supported "women's work and the women's movement" (*für Frauenarbeit und Frauenbewegung*). The JFB concentrated on social work within the Jewish community while it also fought to raise the status of women, elevate their self-image, and improve the circumstances of their lives. It challenged religious as well as secular traditions as it tried to enlarge women's sphere and broaden opportunities for women in the Jewish *Gemeinde* and, through its relationship with the German women's movement, in the German nation. It demanded an end to sexual discrimination as it perceived it, arguing that only then would women be able to offer their unique and valuable contributions to their society. The Jüdischer Frauenbund grew to 35,000 women in its first ten years and to 50,000 women by the late 1920s. It played a vital role in the Jewish community until its dissolution by the Nazis in 1938.

The Frauenbund exemplified the dynamism of German-Jewish women, not only as helpmates in their community, but as independent forces. Its ideas, accomplishments, and failures reflected not only the position of women in Judaism, but also the situation of middle-class women and of Jews in Germany. Frauenbund members functioned within multiple, often overlapping, spheres: as feminists in a "man's world"; as members of a Jewish legal and social corporation, the *Gemeinde*; and as members of a religious and ethnic minority whose political, economic, and cultural advances in the twentieth century were not matched by social acceptance. These categories bear closer scrutiny and will introduce some of the themes and questions to be discussed.

Jewish Feminists in a Man's World

At the turn of the century, German and Jewish middle-class women shared with their Victorian counterparts in the United States and Britain a status and image riddled with contradictions. The genteel cult of "the lady" placed them on a pedestal where they could remain protected, respected, and powerless. Women had become "angels of the home," far removed from the frightful realities of the real world which men, naturally, controlled. Women were exalted as morally superior to men, but were subject entirely to male authority. They were charged with the preservation of religion and culture, but were denied equal religious or educational status. They were responsible enough to raise their offspring and manage their households, but were treated like children themselves and denied a responsible role in society. It was this sexual status quo with its political, economic, and social ramifications that feminists challenged.

As a feminist organization, the JFB was particularly successful in recruiting a large following. Its membership ranged between one-fifth and one-fourth of the eligible Jewish female population. In contrast, Germany's largest feminist organization, the Bund Deutscher Frauenvereine (BDF), had a membership of 132,000 in 1909, representing only .7 percent of all females over eighteen.[16] While its membership almost doubled by 1912 and was quoted at over 900,000 in the 1920s, the BDF still encompassed only a small minority of German women.[17] In fact, the Frauenbund was its largest organizational member.

Part of the reason for the JFB's appeal lay in the quality of its leadership. The JFB was founded and led by Bertha Pappenheim, a woman whose charisma, energy, and courage aroused widespread enthusiasm and support. Pappenheim, a dedicated feminist and a religious Jew, dominated the Frauenbund, first as its president and then as a member of its board of directors. She urged German-Jewish women to mobilize their womanly virtues in the service of the *Gemeinde* and applied German feminism to the situation of Jewish women. While direction came from above, restraint came from the grass-roots base of the organization. The feminism of the JFB was shaped by the tension between its members' needs for independence and their attachment to traditional values. Acting as initiators and guides, Pappenheim and the leaders of the Frauenbund worked to persuade their more traditional membership of the importance of women's equality. The leaders hoped to strike a balance between ideological purity and the attraction of a mass base, modifying their feminism in order not to alienate their followers.

There is yet another reason for the popularity of the JFB. Its growth reflected more general social and political developments. The late nineteenth century witnessed the rapid proliferation of pressure groups of all kinds after the Anti-Socialist Law had lapsed. The middle classes and proletariat tried to reform the political institutions and administrative practices of the State to conform with the changing nature of their roles in a society reaching industrial maturity. With the repeal in 1908 of the *Vereinsgesetz*, a law banning their participation in politics, women, whose opportunities for employment in the teaching and white-collar professions had expanded rapidly, followed the examples before them. They founded their own societies to protect their interests and to demand from men a political and social status commensurate with women's new roles in society. This phenomenon could be observed not only in Germany, but in the United States and England, to mention only the most prominent nations in which a women's movement developed. In both Anglo-Saxon countries Jewish women, too, organized themselves. While shying away from feminism, American

Jews founded the National Council of Jewish Women in 1893 and English Jews established the Union of Jewish Women in 1902. In Germany, women joined political, purity, and interest group associations. Protestant and Catholic women's associations were founded in 1899 and 1903, respectively. Thus the establishment of the JFB was the result of the efforts of determined women to expand the options available to their sex as well as of the prewar climate of demands for a more equitable society.

Charitable activities, in which women were traditionally active, provided a means for liberating them from an exclusive preoccupation with the home. Social work became the path of least resistance for Jewish women intent upon access to the public sphere. The result was "social feminism," a mixture of social work and feminism, moderate and motherly, but persistent and determined. Such feminism struck a responsive chord among bourgeois women whose new mobility, affluence, and growing consciousness of feminist demands made them amenable to a moderate feminism. It also appealed to those women whose ties to traditional charity work, community, and religion led them in the direction of social service. The JFB's campaign for the vote in the Jewish community was based as much on the need to have women serve the *Gemeinde*—both as active participants and as transmitters of Judaism to their offspring— as it was on women's rights. Its efforts to end white slavery and to provide careers for women combined its interests in raising women's status with Jewish social work and with attempts to become fully accepted members of German society. It supported tuberculosis care, youth homes, old-age homes, children's health and vacation facilities, and sanitaria, while it promoted feminist themes, concentrated on woman-related issues, and insisted on executing its own programs for and by women. Because the Frauenbund confined its feminist demands to areas it could combine with social work, it neglected more far-reaching women's issues, for example, women's situation within the nuclear family or sex role stereotypes. Such feminism added nothing new to ideas espoused by the mainstream of the German women's movement from which the JFB derived much of its feminist outlook. Nor did the Frauenbund go beyond the moderate tactics of its German sisters. Only in the Jewish community were its ideas frequently considered radical.

Both the content and style of social feminism, "subtle subversion" rather than a more militant approach, were appropriate to the JFB's German and Jewish surroundings. The Frauenbund was limited in its choice of goals and tactics by its position of weakness as an organization of women in a man's world, its social composition, and its members' inhibitions as Jews in Germany. The antifeminism of Jewish men and the aversion to radicalism of German feminists exerted a moderating influence on the JFB. Social composition, too, played a significant role in tempering its nature. Its service orientation was the result of middle-class leisure—only bourgeois women had the time and financial security to engage in voluntary social work—and its cautiousness was also consistent with the social status of its members.[18] Well-bred daughters of the bourgeoisie, both German and Jewish, were polite and self-denying. They shrank—as did their male counterparts—from a direct attack on the fundamental assumptions of their society. Jewish women, attempting to integrate more completely into this society, to "become bourgeois, and to become bourgeois quickly," were even more consciously restrained, civil, and moderate.[19] Anti-Semitism would also have inhibited any incipient radicalism that might have existed in JFB ranks. The insecurity of Jews made restraint and the acceptance of existing institutions a characteristic of most Jewish movements. In fact, it has been argued that their natural desire for acceptance and security in the face of an unrelenting anti-Semitism may have resulted in a "psychological disposition" among German Jews to defer to existing social and political institutions.[20]

Finally, the temperance of the JFB also resulted from the restraints it experienced due to its dual loyalties: to Judaism and to feminism. While its leaders insisted that the two were complementary, in fact they often stood in opposition. Yet, the JFB was as unwilling to sacrifice women's issues for Jewish solidarity as it was to forfeit Jewishness for feminist solidarity. Jewish feminists persisted in politely demanding both, while their campaign reflected the larger political and social forces which fettered Jews and women in Germany.

Double Jeopardy: Jewish Women in German Society

German Jews were bearers of liberalism in an illiberal society and of pluralism in a nation unsure of its identity. The primacy of order and unity in the hierarchy of German values led to divergent solutions to the "Jewish problem." Homogenization was counseled by the progressive, "friendly" elements of German society. Exclusion was the response of anti-Semites. The sense of identity of Germany's Jews and its Jewish community was determined by the extent of the pressures and opportunities for assimilation, the virulence of anti-Semitism, and the strength of Jewish tradition.

In the nineteenth century, many Jews and liberals assumed that nationalism—and, consequently, national unification—would bring Jewish integration into German society. Jews adopted German culture, supported liberal and progressive movements, and avowed their devotion and loyalty to the German states. After the formation of the German Empire, Jews did enjoy rapid economic and political successes, and they expect social integration to follow in the wake of these other triumphs. This occurred to a limited extent during the last prewar decades, with a resulting increase in Jewish patriotism. Zionism, therefore, did not make deep inroads among German Jews. Their confidence in a German homeland, despite recurring anti-Semitism, was strengthened when they compared their situation to that of their Eastern brethren, who were forced to endure pogroms and persecutions, and their French coreligionists, who had suffered the trauma of the Dreyfus Affair.

Yet emancipation had shifted the Jewish problem from the civic to the social field.[21] "Jews entered European society but did not merge with it."[22] They remained segregated in a religious and organizational subculture. Despite their seeming success, social acceptance was impeded by German attitudes ranging from Judaeophobia to a lingering anti-Jewish sentiment. Furthermore, a conservative and bigoted bureaucracy consistently refused to admit Jews to various branches of German and Prussian government employment. Jews were underrepresented in the most prestigious professions: Jewish access to the officer corps, federal and state civil services, the higher courts, university faculties, and the state primary and secondary schools was severely or entirely limited.[23] There were social clubs which snubbed Jews and private industries which refused to hire them. Anti-Semitic publications and sporadic outbursts of hostility poisoned the atmosphere. Thus a spirit of rejection was manifest which wounded and confused Jews. While a process of integration had gradually taken place from the beginning of the nineteenth century, and while this had succeeded to the extent that "Gentiles became increasingly indifferent to the fact that Jews lived in their midst, if and when their Jew-consciousness was not artificially stimulated," Jewish social acceptance by German society was far from complete.[24] There were, of course, exceptions: Jewish intellectuals found acceptance among the cultural elites (although, as mentioned, not in the universities), the Jewish "aristocracy" hobnobbed with Junkers, and some Jews participated in secular organizations, political parties, and movements.[25] Nevertheless, most of the aforementioned Jews relegated their Jewishness to a secondary or nonexistent status in order to belong, and, even then, some were not accepted. Bound by traditional ties and shared interests, and rejected by German society as well, most Jews were unwilling or unable to make this compromise. Their friends and close associates were primarily other Jews. Reflecting on her social relationships with non-Jews, one Frauenbund member (born in 1880) recorded: "Again and again I experienced the same thing: We lived among them, sat on the same school benches with them, met for social occasions—and remained complete strangers."[26]

German anti-Semitism was not confined to social relations. It was also tolerated by the government and most parties. Historians have pointed to a variety of interrelated causes for the rise of a virulent, racist, and political anti-Semitism in the 1880s and 1890s. Jews were seen as an alien, cosmopolitan element in a newly created, national society, whose self-identity, shaky at best, was rooted in an organic conception of the *Volk*. This German idea of nationhood did not welcome the possibility of an ethnically heterogeneous society. In the 1870s and 1880s, Germans experienced the economic and social dislocations associated with modernity. Rapid industrialization and a lingering depression (1873-1896) fostered an era of "cultural despair" in which anti-Jewish feelings were transformed into racism.[27] The inability of certain socioeconomic groups, the lower middle classes in particular, to compete in an industrial capitalist economy led to deep dissatisfactions.[28] "Jewish liberalism" and "Jewish capitalism" were blamed for the breakdown of security and old values: Jews were harangued as threats to an effective German community. Although "anti-Semitism . . . was only to a small extent the result of a real tension between Jews and Gentiles," Jews were held responsible for the real or imagined ills of modernity.[29]

In the late 1870s, an anti-Semitic political party organized by Adolf Stoecker, court chaplain to Emperor William I, attracted lower middle class members by blaming Jewish materialism for Germany's problems. In 1881 and 1892, anti-Semitic riots were violent enough to require intervention from a government, which, except in rare circumstances, did not hinder anti-Jewish actions. During the 1880s and 1890s, delegates running on specifically anti-Semitic platforms were elected to the Reichstag. In 1893, sixteen anti-Semites and seven emphatically anti-Semitic conservatives won seats. Together they had an estimated following of 400,000 or a 450 percent increase from the elections of 1890.[30] Boycotts were organized against Jewish merchants, protests were launched against kosher methods of animal slaughter, and there were ritual murder trials (Xanten, 1891, and Konitz, 1900) which inflamed rumors that Jews were engaging in their alleged ancient rite.[31] Nevertheless, the racist right remained on the fringe of German society. Parliamentary anti-Semitism declined by the turn of the century and anti-Jewish excesses were not widespread.[32] Yet, by the 1890s, resurgent anti-Semitism shocked Jews into an awareness of their undeniably marginal status and stimulated defensive measures based upon an assertion of the very Jewishness many had previously sought to deny.[33]

For at least one hundred years, Jews had been moving toward the adoption of German culture. In the nineteenth century, religion lost some of its hold on the European urban middle classes, although they did not abandon it altogether. Jews, in addition to experiencing the same secular trends as Germans, encountered pressure to repress their Jewishness, their ethnic and spiritual "otherness," in order to achieve German citizenship. This was in accordance with the expectations of liberal emancipators who hoped for the absorption of Jewry into society. While "no one . . . demanded that the Jews should become Christians, yet it was expected that they would cease to be Jews."[34] However, the assumptions of Germans and Jews—sometimes articulated, but often unspoken—seemed to clash. Whereas most Jews believed that acculturation could coexist with Jewish group survival, most Germans assumed that Jews would pay for their emancipation and subsequent entry into German life by rejecting their separate religious identity. Liberals, in particular, were ultimately "the most implacable enemies of a genuine and dignified Jewish presence in Germany . . . who no less than conservatives and populists were simply incapable of shedding the widespread German postulate that Jews were ultimately unassimilable, if not legally, at least socially."[35]

By the 1890s most German Jews considered themselves to be "assimilated," particularly when they compared themselves to recent Jewish immigrants from Eastern Europe. "Assimilation," however, connoted something different to each individual. All professed loyalty to the German nation. Yet, in their pursuit of full political, legal, economic, and social status, their relationship with their heritage differed. Some attempted to preserve their religious and communal distinctiveness by adapting outwardly and suppressing external signs of their Jewishness. Many of these individuals tried to placate anti-Jewish sentiment by modernizing their religion. Other Jews were bound to their own community less by the positive attachments of faith and culture than by their exclusion from German society. They retained only a mechanical allegiance to their faith and were tied to their culture only by birth. Finally, still others purchased what Heinrich Heine called a "ticket of admission to European culture" by converting to Christianity.[36]

Much has been written about the last two groups and about the centrifugal forces disrupting Jewish life. We have learned of the "large numbers of talented young men and women" who began to "desert their ancestral tradition" as well as of the "departure of those for whom personal Jewishness had become an inconvenience and an embarrassment."[37] Complaining about the dilution of Jewish communal life, historians of German Jewry have written that German Jews did

. . . their best in order to assimilate themselves, and . . . made every effort to make their Jewish denomination be felt as little as possible. . . . Not a small number of successful persons . . . renounced even their religion, and took care that their grandchildren should not be born as Jews.[38]

Contemporary critics also observed and decried the temptation of Jews to adopt Christian mores or to become lax in their concern for Jewish ritual. Some Jews feared the "death" of Judaism as a result of hasty absorption into German society.[39]

While it is undeniable that Jews sought entrance into the state and society and that religion became less central to their universe, there were large numbers of Jews who tried to preserve the best of both worlds. Male-centered, elite-centered, and Berlin-centered histories of German Jewry have tended to neglect the attachments of culture, religion, and tradition felt by this "silent majority" of Germany's Jews.[40] It is evident by the extent of the JFB's religious interests—it stressed religious observance far more than most of the major male-dominated German-Jewish organizations of its day— and its Jewish communal activities that the overwhelming majority of its 50,000 members were drawn from women who felt proud ties to the Jewish community. Most were observant Jews themselves who mixed primarily with other Jews. Jewish feminists who were not affiliated with either the religious or social institutions of German Jewry tended to join the Bund Deutscher Frauenvereine in preference to the JFB. They were considered *too* assimilated by JFB members who avowed their patriotism, but assumed that feeling an allegiance to Germany did not mean that they had to deny a strong, positive bond with their religion and *Gemeinde*. Most of them accommodated to the majority culture while remaining faithful to a Jewish way of life. Many gave their youngsters religious schooling, observed the Sabbath and holidays, followed Jewish dietary laws, attended Frauenbund lectures and discussions on Jewish history, culture, and religion, and participated in Jewish communal affairs. Jewishness, the practice of their religion as well as a strong sense of solidarity with other Jews, defined their identity more than has been recognized by many historians and more than they may have realized themselves. Thus, a study of the JFB may lead to a more balanced understanding of the process of assimilation and Jewish consciousness in Germany.

The strong sense of Jewish identity among Frauenbund members— most of whom were socialized during the Second Empire—indicates the strength and the continuity of tradition and community in the face of rapid social change in late nineteenth-century Germany. The daughters of wealthy Jews in the ghetto had been the first to learn the language, literature, and social graces of their neighbors. In the early nineteenth century, some of those with access to enlightened culture converted. Nevertheless, the images of the apostate Salon Jewess and the newly rich, bourgeois woman who neglected her religion in the pursuit of material pleasures were dramatic, but exceptional.[41] Most remained tradition-bound by family, class, and community ties as well as by the hostility of the non-Jewish world. Secularization seemed to affect women later than men. As small-town or city housewives they were responsible for the family's maintenance of Jewish tradition, from the observance of the dietary laws to the lighting of the Sabbath candles and the preparation of the household for Jewish holidays. Whereas husbands might neglect Sabbath or dietary rules due to the circumstances of their business or career, wives could fulfill their obligations more easily. Yet, their Judaism was not confined to religious observances: their entire social life revolved around the special dates on the Jewish calendar. Also, whereas men had the occasion to meet and associate with non-Jews, wives kept close ties with other family members and with Jewish friends. It was housewives and their daughters who, throughout the nineteenth century, formed large groups of volunteers for Jewish communal organizations, and, in a few cases, ran the organizations. Viewing themselves as "culture bearers" responsible for the furthering of Judaism, many women remained more traditional, more Jewish-centered than their husbands. While some customs and beliefs may have been altered to complement other forms of modernization, women maintained a continuity with past traditions and remained more consciously Jewish than men who, at least outwardly, were forced to adapt to Christian surroundings.

Jewish feminists acknowledged the positive attachments of faith, culture, and destiny that they shared with Jewish men. Also, they recognized more negative bonds. Like Jewish men, they were outsiders: both sexes were the objects of an anti-Semitism which spurred them to join forces in self-defense. While the formation of the Frauenbund stemmed from traditional sources of Jewish identity, it was also part of a more general Jewish reaction to the rise of anti-Semitism. The formation in 1893 of the Verband der Vereine für jüdische Geschichte und Literatur (Union of Associations for Jewish History and Literature), an association for adult Jewish education, was an attempt by Jews to equip other Jews with knowledge of, and pride in, their history, in order to withstand the pressures of anti-Semitism.[42] That same year, the founding of the Centralverein deutscher Staatsbürger jüdischen Glaubens (the Central Union of German Citizens of the Jewish Faith), the major Jewish defense organization in Germany, "embodied a repudiation of concealment as the price for equality."[43] Founded by acculturated Jews whose self-conscious return to Jewishness was inspired by disappointment, apprehensiveness, and pride, the CV attempted to revive the self-image and self-esteem of Jews as it fought for their place in German society. It sought a German-Jewish symbiosis and argued that the unique characteristics of Jews did not compromise their authentic Germanness.

The JFB shared the concerns of the defense organization and was, in part, an outgrowth of such efforts to revive Judaism. Pappenheim's background included an interest in the Verein für jüdische Geschichte and Literatur, and many of her coworkers belonged to the Centralverein. But the JFB also drew upon the traditional Jewish-centeredness of many whose greatest fear had been the total loss of a Jewish identity. These Jews hoped to use the new self-consciousness to impede or halt the disintegrating tendencies of Judaism. Many of them, like Pappenheim and her associates, had long participated in Jewish organizations and were eager to encourage the growth of national organizations which would revive the national life of German Jewry.

The differences in motivation for the founding of the CV and the JFB led to a difference in the orientation of each. Although, in the years between its creation and World War I, the CV moved from a purely defensive orientation to a more positive assertion of pride, it was primarily concerned with proving the German identity of Jews to other Germans. For many members of the Centralverein, according to Ismar Freund, a leader of the organization, "the battle against anti-Semitism in Germany was one of the strongest means for Jewish identity." Franz Rosenzweig agreed: ". . . it is true . . . the CV takes the place of Judaism for its members."[44] Thus, the CV provided a "surrogate Judaism" for many who had lost their faith.[45] The Centralverein considered itself an *Abwehrverein* (defense organization) until 1928 when it began to describe itself as a *Gesinnungsverein* (association of those sharing similar convictions).[46] The Frauenbund had from the beginning been a *Gesinnungsverein* whose social isolation from German feminists was due to its primary emphasis on "Jewish mindedness."[47] A central concern was the development of Jewish religious life and the Jewish community. That is why, despite the fact that the German women's movement welcomed all feminists, many Jewish women joined the JFB.

The JFB recognized the need to combat anti-Semitism directly and this became one of its official goals after World War I. It joined the Verband der Deutschen Juden (the Association of German Jews), a Jewish defense organization, in 1911 and the Centralverein in 1918.[48] Before the war, it also won the cooperation of the Bund Deutscher Frauenvereine in fighting anti-Semitism among women's organizations.[49] Between 1914 and 1918, the Frauenbund participated actively in the war effort, sensitive to the allegations of anti-Semites that Jews were shirkers. Both during and after the war, it urged Jewish women to wear conservative and unostentatious clothing in a campaign of "self-discipline" intended to lessen anti-Semitism. In the early 1930s the Frauenbund began "enlightenment work," by which it hoped to teach non-Jewish women about Jews and Judaism.

Even after Hitler came to power, the JFB, like most German Jews, believed that Jews had a place in Germany and that a synthesis of *Deutschtum* and *Judentum* was possible. Pappenheim and most of her colleagues placed their faith in the preservation of the *Rechtstaat.* As late as September 1935, when Hitler's Nuremberg Laws had stripped Jews of their citizenship and more, the JFB, like the major Jewish organization in Germany, the Reichsvertretung der Juden in Deutschland (the Central Association of Jews in Germany), saw a need for emigration but still assumed that there would be a place for some Jews in Germany. Even then, their attachment to their vision of a more tolerant and liberal Germany and their roots in that country made many overlook the warnings of danger. Despite their Jewish-centeredness, which might have made them more sensitive to German anti-Semitism than Jews who had looser ties to their religion and community, the members of the Frauenbund clung tenaciously to the hope that a Jewish future was possible in Germany. In December 1935, less than a week before he committed suicide, Kurt Tucholsky wrote a letter to Arnold Zweig in which his frustration and anger sharpened his normally acid pen. He decried the tendency of Jews to deny what they saw around them as "not the real Germany": "how they squint—how they feel like

Germans," he complained bitterly, "but, damn it, the Germans don't want you!" Referring to the Jews, he observed, "They don't even notice."[50] Frauenbund members, like other German Jews, noticed, but they were trapped by their hopes, by their fears, and by their successes.

Notes

1. Gerson Cohen, "German Jewry as Mirror of Modernity," LBIYB (1975), pp. ix-xxxi.

2. Ibid., p. xix.

3. This phrase is borrowed from the incisive title of Sheila Rowbotham's book, *Hidden from History* (New York: Random House, 1974).

4. Gerda Lerner, "New Approaches to the Study of Women in American History," *Journal of Social History* 3 (1969), p. 53. Until recently, this was true of nonelite men as well.

5. Mary R. Beard, *Woman as Force in History* (New York: Collier Books, 1973), p. 282.

6. See Adrienne Rich, *Of Woman Born* (New York: W.W. Norton, 1976), pp. 43-45.

7. Quoted by Joan Goulianos, ed., in *by a Woman writ* (Baltimore: Penguin Books, Inc., 1973), p. xvi.

8. Beard, *Woman*, p. 10.

9. Mary Hartman and Lois W. Banner, eds., *Clio's Consciousness Raised* (New York: Harper Colophon Books, 1974), introduction.

10. Renate Bridenthal and Molly Nolan raised this issue in their comments on three papers for the panel "German Women: The Pursuit of Influence and Equality," American Historical Association Convention, Dallas, 1977.

11. While most attention focuses on the suffrage movements, there were, at least in the United States, two other types of feminism, often described as "social feminism" and "domestic feminism." See, for example, William O'Neill, "Feminism as a Radical Ideology," *Dissent: Explorations in the History of American Radicalism*, edited by Alfred F. Young (De Kalb, Ill.: Northern Illinois University Press, 1968); Kathryn Kish Sklar, *Catharine Beecher: A Study in American Domesticity* (New York: W.W. Norton & Company, Inc., 1973).

12. "Liberal" is the term used by Jews in Germany who followed the reforms of Rabbi Geiger who argued that Jewish law developed through a process of evolution and change. They approved of adapting Jewish tradi-

tion to accommodate to modern times. Orthodox Jews defended the divine origin and obligatory character of Jewish law. By 1900, the liberal branch of German Jewry was predominant, with the Orthodox making up about 10 to 15 percent of German Jewry. Reform Jews, a tiny minority, were the most modern of all. David Rudavsky, *Emancipation and Adjustment: Contemporary Jewish Religious Movements, Their History and Thought* (New York: Diplomatic Press, Inc., 1967), chaps. 7-9; David Philipson, *The Reform Movement in Judaism* (New York: Ktav Publishing House, Inc., 1967).

13. Howard Morley Sachar, *The Course of Modern Jewish History* (New York: Delta Publishing Co., Inc., 1958), p. 46.

14. Reinhard Rürup, "Jewish Emancipation and Bourgeois Society," *LBIYB* (1969), pp. 67-68.

15. John E. Knodel, *The Decline of Fertility in Germany, 1871-1939* (Princeton: Princeton University Press, 1974), pp. 139-41, 253.

16. Amy Hackett, "The Politics of Feminism in Wilhelmine Germany, 1890-1918" (Ph.D. dissertation, Columbia University, 1976), p. 200.

17. Ibid. See also Ilse Reicke, *Frauenbewegung und Erziehung* (Munich: Rösl und Cie Verlag, 1921), p. 74; Hugh Wiley Puckett, *Germany's Women Go Forward* (New York: Columbia University Press, 1930, AMS reprint, 1967), p. 157; and Richard Evans, *The Feminist Movement in Germany, 1894-1933* (Beverly Hills, Calif.: Sage, 1976), p. 194.

18. The social composition of the Frauenbund reflected the fact that in the twentieth century the overwhelming majority of German Jews belonged to the middle classes. In 1933, only 8.7 percent of German Jews classified themselves as "workers" compared with 46.4 percent of Germans. *Volkszählung, Die Bevölkerung des Deutschen Reichs nach dem Volkszählung 1933*, Heft 5, Verlag für Sozialpolitik, Wirtschaft, und Statistik (Berlin: Paul Schmidt, 1936), pp. 25, 27.

19. John Murray Cuddihy, *The Ordeal of Civility, Freud, Marx, Levi-Strauss, and the Jewish Struggle with Modernity* (New York: Dell Publishing Co., Inc., 1974), p. 13.

20. Hans Morgenthau, *The Tragedy of German-Jewish Liberalism*, Leo Baeck Memorial Lecture, no. 4 (1961), pp. 8, 15-16.

21. Eva Reichmann, *Hostages of Civilization* (Boston: Beacon Press, 1951), pp. 22-30.

22. Jacob Katz, *Out of the Ghetto* (Cambridge: Harvard University Press, 1973), p. 216.

23. Ernst Hamburger, *Juden im öffentlichen Leben Deutschlands. Regierungsmitglieder, Beamten und Parlamentarier in der monarchischen Zeit, 1848-1918* (Tübingen: Paul Mohr, 1968).

24. Reichmann, *Hostages*, p. 236.

25. See, for example: Peter Gay, *Weimar Culture: the Outsider as Insider* (New York: Harper and Row, 1968), and "Encounter with Modernism: German Jews in German Culture, 1888-1914," *Midstream* (February 1975), pp. 23-65; Lamar Cecil, "Jew and Junker in Imperial Berlin," *LBIYB* (1975), pp. 47-58; Hannah Arendt, *The Origins of Totalitarianism* (New York: World Publishing Co., 1966), Chapter 3, book 2.

26. Rahel Straus, *Wir Lebten in Deutschland: Erinnerungen einer Deutschen Jüdin, 1880-1933* (Stuttgart: Deutsche Verlags-Anstalt, 1962), p. 266.

27. Fritz Stern, *The Politics of Cultural Despair: A Study in the Rise of the Germanic Ideology* (New York: Doubleday, 1965).

28. See, for example: Shulamit Angel-Volkov, "The Social and Political Function of Late 19th Century Anti-Semitism: The Case of the Small Handicraft Masters," in *Sozialgeschichte Heute: Festschrift für Hans Rosenberg*, edited by Hans Ulrich Wehler (Göttingen: Vandenhoeck und Ruprecht, 1974), pp. 416-31.

29. Reichmann, *Hostages*, p. 234.

30. Paul W. Massing, *Vorgeschichte des Politischen Anti-Semitismus* (Frankfurt/Main: Europäische Verlagsanstalt, 1959), p. 243.

31. Ismar Elbogen, *Geschichte der Juden in Deutschland* (Berlin: Erich Lichtenstein Verlag, 1935), pp. 290-93.

32. Richard Levy, *The Downfall of the Anti-Semitic Political Parties in Imperial Germany* (New Haven: Yale University Press, 1975). Levy notes that the political failure of these parties did not indicate a lessening of hostility toward Jews as much as it reflected political and economic changes. The Saxon population he investigated remained receptive to anti-Semitism.

33. Ismar Schorsch, *Jewish Reactions to German Anti-Semitism, 1870-1914* (New York: Columbia University Press, 1972), pp. 1-13.

34. Rürup, "Jewish Emancipation," p. 80.

35. Cohen, "Mirror of Modernity," p. xvi. See also, Uriel Tal, *Christians and Jews in Germany. Religion, Politics, and Ideology in the Second Reich, 1870-1914*, translated by Noah J. Jacobs (Ithaca, N.Y.: Cornell University Press, 1975).

36. For a comprehensive discussion of the problem of Jewish identity, see: Ruth Pierson, "German-Jewish Identity in the Weimar Republic" (Ph.D. dissertation, Yale University, 1970).

37. Sachar, *Modern Jewish History*, p. 158.

38. Elbogen, *Juden in Deutschland*, p. 294.

39. Rürup, "Emancipation and Crisis—The 'Jewish Question' in Germany, 1850-1890," *LBIYB* (1975), p. 17.

40. The attention accorded to "assimilationist" tendencies in German Jewry has not been matched by equal consideration of those Jews who maintained their group identity, communal structure, and common religious tradition. A shift in research to small-town Jews, nonelites, or Jewish women may indeed modify our perceptions regarding the speed and depth of acculturation and the strength of a Jewish consciousness. The smaller communities were the real upholders of piety (*Milieufrömmigkeit*), according to Leo Baeck. The few studies of small communities that do exist convey an atmosphere in which Jews did not forfeit their Jewishness. On small-town and nonelite Jews, see for example: Jacob Toury, "Neue Hebräische Veröffentlichungen zur Geschichte der Juden im Deutschen Lebenskreise," *LBI Bulletin* 4 (1961), p. 13; Utz Jeggle, *Judendörfer in Württemberg* (Tübingen: Tübinger Vereinigung für Volkskunde e. V., 1969); Werner J. Cahnman, "Village and Small-Town Jews in Germany, a Typological Study," *LBIYB* (1974), pp. 107-33. He includes several further bibliographic suggestions. At present, a three-volume study of nonelites based on memoirs and autobiographical material is in progress. Supported by the Leo Baeck Institute and edited by Monika Richarz, it is entitled *Jüdisches Leben in Deutschland: Selbstzeugnisse zur Sozialgeschichte*. Readily available sources on German-Jewish women do not exist at this time.

41. Selma Stern, "Die Entwicklung des jüdischen Frauentypus seit dem Mittelalter," *Der Morgen* (1925), pp. 496-516; (1926), pp. 71-81.

42. Schorsch, *Jewish Reactions*, pp. 111-12.

43. Ibid., p. 12.

44. Jehuda Reinharz, "*Deutschtum* and *Judentum* in the Ideology of the Centralverein Deutscher Staatsbürger Jüdischen Glaubens, 1893-1914," *Jewish Social Studies* 36, no. 1 (1974), p. 29.

45. Schorsch, *Jewish Reactions*, p. 207.

46. Reinharz, "Deutschtum," p. 37.

47. *AZDJ*, February 19, 1915, supplement, p. 1.

48. *IF*, January 19, 1911, p. 12; *IF*, February 7, 1918, p. 10.

49. *AZDJ*, December 26, 1913.

50. Kurt Tucholsky, quoted by Kurt Grossmann, "Deutsche Juden auf der Linken," in *Gegenwart im Rückblick*, edited by Herbert Strauss and Kurt Grossmann (Heidelberg: Lothar Stiehm Verlag, 1970), p. 101.

1. **Bertha Pappenheim.** *Courtesy Leo Baeck Institute, New York.*

chapter 2

Bertha Pappenheim

"Only a Girl": Pappenheim's Early Years and the Story of Anna O

The life of Bertha Pappenheim casts light on the place of women in late nineteenth-century society and on the origins and nature of German-Jewish feminism. The JFB was very much a product of her turbulent experiences and special leadership talents. Her sense of outrage at the injustices faced by women made her an indomitable fighter for their equality. The response she evoked was based upon her ability to use her distinctive attributes to tap the solitary, but common, experiences of German-Jewish women. Her anger against male dominance increased over the course of her career, as she tried to overcome the marginal status of women. At first, she attempted to advance the status of women in the traditional organizations of the German-Jewish community and to draw the attention of these organizations to issues which concerned women's rights and welfare. Despairing of rapid progress with this approach, she also forged new channels—women's channels—through which her followers could shape their own world.

Bertha Pappenheim was born in Vienna in 1859, the third daughter of wealthy, religious Jews. Her father, a merchant, was the son of an Orthodox Jewish family from Pressburg, Hungary (now Bratislave, Czechoslovakia) and was a cofounder of the Orthodox *Schiffschul* in Vienna. Her mother came from an old and wealthy Frankfurt family. As "just another daughter" in a strictly traditional Jewish household, Bertha was conscious that her parents would have preferred a male child. Years later she wrote that the "old Jews" considered a daughter of secondary importance:

This can already be seen in the different reception given a new citizen of the world. If the father, or someone else asked what "it" was after a successful birth, the answer might be either the satisfied report of a boy, or—with pronounced sympathy for the disappointment—"Nothing, a girl," or, "Only a girl."[1]

The Pappenheims finally had a son, Wilhelm (1860-1937), their fourth child. Bertha and Wilhelm, the only two children who lived to adulthood, did not get along very well. She may have been jealous of the special treatment accorded him, particularly the education that she was denied. Although this was an era in which most universities did not allow women to matriculate, she always felt that her lack of education was due to the Jewish prejudice which expected girls to marry and boys to achieve scholarly success.

Nothing is known of Bertha's childhood, except that she had been consistently healthy.[2] She attended a private Catholic school in Vienna and probably received her religious education from a private tutor.[3] After finishing high school, where she learned fluent French, Italian, and English, the attractive, imaginative, young woman was expected to settle down and await marriage. Bertha's life, in her own words, was "typical" of a *höhere Töchter* (a middle-class daughter of marriageable age), of the "religious Jewish middle class."[4] Her intellectual gifts were stifled as she, like her German (and Victorian) middle-class counterparts, trained to become a leisured lady. After completing school, *höhere Töchter* stayed at home and embroidered their dowries until they met suitable husbands. While most accommodated themselves to their situation, others considered such a life unbearable. Helene Lange, a leader of the German women's movement, wrote, "One can still feel a belated horror at the thought of the countless numbers of wasted possibilities and unused energies."[5] Bertha led a dull existence, often escaping into long daydreams that she called her "private theater."[6] She did some charity work, which was for her, like for many other girls and housewives of her class and society, the only acceptable diversion besides entertainment, reading, and embroidery. She later urged other *höhere Töchter* who were bored or unhappy with their meaningless lives to demand vocational preparation and higher education, as well as to pursue social work.

At twenty-one, after having nursed her dying father, Bertha experienced severe psychological disturbances.[7] Josef Breuer, whose reputation as a physician and scientist was widespread, was called upon to help the young woman. Breuer treated her in Vienna between 1880 and 1882 and told her story to Sigmund Freud in November 1882. Thus, her life during her early twenties is more carefully and intimately documented than that of most people. She was "Anna O," the patient most often discussed by Freud, although he never treated her. Her case became the best known and clearest example of what was then considered major hysteria. According to Breuer, she was "markedly intelligent, with an astonishingly quick grasp of things and penetrating intuition. . . . she had great poetic and imaginative gifts, which were under the control of a sharp and critical common sense."[8] She was "bubbling over with intellectual vitality," but her life was a boring one. This "left her with an unemployed surplus of mental liveliness and energy."[9] Breuer noted that while Anna was engaged in tatting lace (a hobby which she, unlike other feminists, always enjoyed), she "embellished her life in a manner which probably influenced her decisively in the direction of her illness, by indulging in systematic daydreaming. . . . While everyone thought she was attending, she was living through fairy tales in her imagination."[10] Freud suggested that women who did needlework, a popular pastime, were particularly prone to such daydreams.[11] A psychic trauma could shock them into a state in which their fantasies became their partial or total reality.

Although showing some symptoms during her father's illness, Anna O's real breakdown occurred after her father died. Breuer diagnosed "severe hysteria," the equivalent of what some psychiatrists today would label schizophrenia.[12] She suffered from disturbances of sight and speech, paralysis, a split personality, the loss of her native language and its replacement with English, hallucinations, the inability to eat or drink, and suicidal impulses. Breuer saw her twice a day with few exceptions, for one and one-half years. He hypnotized her and encouraged her to explain how certain symptoms first appeared. As her memories were revived, the symptoms disappeared. Patient and doctor shared the discovery of this surprising therapy. Anna called the process "chimney sweeping" or "talking cure," and, with her doctor's assistance, she actually treated herself.[13] Ernest Jones, Freud's biographer, called Anna O "the real discoverer of the cathartic method."[14]

As her symptoms receded, Breuer decided to bring the case to an end. He was summoned after his final visit to find Anna O in the midst of a hysterical childbirth. She was giving birth to "Dr. B's child."[15] Breuer's embarrassment, combined with his wife's jealousy of the attractive patient, convinced him to terminate the treatment. A year after discontinuing his visits, Breuer told Freud that Anna's condition was bad and that he wished she would die and be released from her suffering.

Breuer never interpreted Anna O's neuroses; thus she did not undergo psychoanalysis. Freud later surmised that the "childbirth" suggested the patient's transference of emotions to the doctor and, therefore, indicated the sexual etiology of psychoses. Breuer objected, noting in his report that "the element of sexuality was astonishingly undeveloped in her."[16] Investigations by later Freudians have corroborated the sexual element and criticized the limitations of Breuer's insight.

Little is known about Pappenheim's life for the seven years after Breuer's treatment. She had relapses, spent some time in sanatoria, traveled, and eventually regained her health. She moved to Frankfurt/Main with her mother in 1889 and remained in the Frankfurt environs for the rest of her life. Neither Freud nor Breuer ever commented on Anna O's later life, probably to protect her identity. Since her name was exposed by Ernest Jones, psychologists have turned with particular interest to the case of the hysterical woman who became a well-known feminist.[17] They have suggested that Bertha Pappenheim was sublimating the neuroses that Anna O had experienced, or, that her feminism was essentially her earlier illness in another form.

Such interpretations are typical of many psychologists and anti-suffragists who automatically associated feminism with mental illness. In 1918, H. W. Frink, a Freudian, wrote of feminists: "A certain proportion of at least the most militant suffragists are neurotics who in some instances are compensating for masculine trends, in others, are more or less successfully sublimating sadistic and homosexual ones."[18] It has, of course, always been easier for traditionalists to label those who challenge the status quo as "crazy" than to confront their arguments. In the United States, in fact, antisuffragists, finding comfort in psychology, concluded that suffragists all bordered on hysteria and, thus, their arguments could not be taken seriously.[19] While some Freudians, particularly Karen Horney, were sensitive to the social and cultural factors which impinged on women, shaping their personalities, by the mid-twentieth century "any questioning of women's place was readily equated with neurosis by the Freudian psychologists and their popularizers."[20] While psychoanalytic interpretations can offer a "general knowledge of the multiplicity of human motivation"[21] there is a danger of oversimplification. Analyses which focus only on the psychological causes for feminism while neglecting its social, economic, political, and cultural roots shy away from essential issues.

Among the Victorian bourgeoisie of Europe and America, female hysteria and nervous disorders, the "misunderstood" and "unhappy" woman, were commonplace, as doctors, psychologists, novelists, and historians have shown.[22] While most women accepted the "moralities" and "sentimentalities" that made them, in John Stuart Mill's words, "willing slaves,"[23] many suffered from monotony, others escaped through charitable work, and still others retreated from the Victorian norm by assuming hysterical maladies. Indeed, one might hypothesize that women who could not cope with the obvious injustices of their lot were psychologically "healthier" (that is, intent upon developing what Abraham Maslow has called "full humanness" instead of accepting "historically-arbitrary, culturally-local value-models") than those who reconciled themselves to second-class citizenship and inferior human status.[24] Furthermore, it could be speculated (as Erik Erikson's work suggests) that *recovery* from a psychological crisis, rather than its continuation or sublimation, might have given Pappenheim and her counterparts the inner strength to persevere in long, and often futile, battles in their later lives.[25] Testimonies of leading feminists lend credence to Maslow's and Erikson's interpretations. England's famous abolitionist, Josephine Butler, suffered recurring breakdowns from nervous exhaustion.[26] In America, Jane Addams had "nervous depressions and a sense of maladjustment" as a young woman.[27] She recognized that her distress was related to "a sense of futility, of misdirected energy." Elizabeth Cady Stanton, the American feminist leader, also struggled with her limited role: "I suffered with mental hunger, which like an empty stomach, is very depressing."[28] The German suffrage leader Hedwig Dohm described the anguish of womanhood which led her to feminism:

When, in the place of the knowledge and truth for which I was reaching out, they put into my hand the . . . cooking spoon,—they drove a human soul, which was created perhaps to live splendidly and fruitfully, into a desert of wild fantasies. . . . Whoever has thus felt in her own breast the whole misery of womanhood can measure, by the pain of wounds that never heal, the deadly injustice of the human order heretofore.[29]

Relief came only after these women rejected the typical life of young middle-class ladies.

Although psychological explanations may be of limited use in locating the source of Pappenheim's feminism, Breuer's description of Anna O's character traits is of value to the historian. Some of the young woman's feelings and personal characteristics remained strikingly similar to the adult personality of Bertha Pappenheim. Breuer recorded that during her illness she exhibited a sensitivity to injustice and a strong social consciousness. He reported that she was helped by caring for a number of poor, sick people, "for she was thus able to satisfy a powerful instinct."[30] Upon her recovery, these traits were reawakened by her female relatives in Frankfurt who were active in Jewish charities and, more importantly, by German feminism. Pappenheim read *The Woman*, a popular feminist periodical, first published in 1893. She admired its founder, Helene Lange, the president of the National Association of Women Teachers and the main theoretician of the German women's movement. The German movement's demand for educational and career opportunities for women appealed to Pappenheim, who also appreciated its call for political rights. Her interest in German feminism coalesced with her deeply felt identity as a Jew. The relative successes of German feminists encouraged her to attempt to right what she considered the injustices against women in Jewish customs and law and in the Jewish community. In 1924, after twenty-nine years of battle, she wrote:

Today I believe I have not completely done my duty. No one who knows that injustice is occurring anywhere may remain silent—neither sex, nor age, nor religion, nor party can be a reason to be quiet. To know of wrong and to remain silent makes one an accomplice.[31]

Her strong social consciousness compelled her to console and care for outcasts, as well as to goad the Jewish establishment to provide more adequately for its needy. In 1916 she wrote an article entitled "Woe to Him whose Conscience Sleeps," in which she demanded a national Jewish welfare association.[32] Such a body was created during the following year—the *Zentralwohlfahrtsstelle der Deutschen Juden* (the Central Welfare Office of German Jews)—and she was elected its deputy vice-president. The result of her crusading efforts, in part, was that she felt—and probably was—unpopular with Jewish leaders, particularly those in her home territory. In 1911, for example, she wrote a friend of her "flourishing unpopularity among the 'influential circles'" in Frankfurt.[33] Pappenheim was respected and even admired by many of the male authorities, but it is doubtful that she was liked by most, and it is certain that these feelings were mutual.

Breuer was as impressed with Anna O's willpower as later associates were with Bertha Pappenheim's. The very first paragraph of his case study concluded with a description of her willpower as "energetic, tenacious and persistent, sometimes it reached the pitch of an obstinacy which only gave way out of kindness and regard for other people."[34] It was Anna who decided that she would recover by a particular date. As her own deadline arrived, she arranged her room to resemble that of her father's, and was thus able to recall her most terrifying hallucinations which, Breuer felt, constituted "the root of her whole illness."[35] She had not recovered—and would not for several years—but the worst symptoms connected with this phase of her sickness had been overcome by her own strong resolve.

Bertha Pappenheim's tenacity and willpower are also well documented. Stubborn determination—often in the face of female indifference and male condescension—allowed her to organize the JFB and to persist, despite constant disappointment, in her battle against white slavery.[36] Only resoluteness (and self-righteousness) supported her in the face of severe criticism from Jews who refused to acknowledge the existence of Jewish vice.[37] Sympathetic associates described her as "absolutely uncompromising in causes she believed were just."[38] She was therefore "terribly uncomfortable for people who did not understand her,"[39] or, one might add, who did not agree with her. Not having her way—particularly with the male establishment—made her angry and sarcastic. A leader of the Frankfurt Jewish community in the 1930s wrote that every letter he received from Pappenheim contained at least one note of aggression.

Her impatience and strong will led to some conflicts even with colleagues in the JFB. She apologized to her friends for her impatience, explaining: "There is an impatience of youth which cannot wait to mature to do great deeds, and there is an impatience of age, which is harder to bear, because it fears that it will never see the completion of its work, of its life's duties."[40]

The inner strength which Breuer noted in Anna O was frequently an inspiration to Pappenheim's friends. She often "made the impossible possible," wrote Hannah Karminski, her closest associate. Pappenheim was aware that she could influence and inspire others. She commented: "I found it important to look for . . . people one could infect with one's own will, and . . . make them fit to be helpers."[41] Large numbers of women were attracted to the JFB by its determined, vigorous leader. They were influenced by her charisma as well as the goals she pursued. In fact, some of the more independent remained apart precisely because they disdained such powerful leadership.

Breuer remarked upon the intensity of Anna O's emotions. Co-workers were also impressed with the powerful, compelling nature of Pappenheim's feelings and her fiery eloquence. Cora Berliner, one of the JFB's vice-presidents, wrote:

A volcano lived in this woman; it erupted when she was angered. . . . But . . . she only fought about things that were directly involved in her goals. . . . She felt . . . the tragedy of these battles. . . . Her fight against the abuse of women was almost a physically felt pain for her. . . . Thus the passionate nature of her battle against white slavery.[42]

She approached all her crusades with vehement emotions.[43] In 1907, she wrote a friend, "my battle against white slavery consumes my thoughts."[44] She was aware of the volatile nature of her feelings and wondered if she enjoyed reading workers' newspapers so much because of their angry words which served an ideal they cherished.[45] Her happiness was also intense. She expressed her appreciation to one of her helpers in glowing terms: "What a stream of happiness and thankfulness comes from my heart to yours. . . . Please keep your strength to do good; plant it into the hearts of those with whom you work each day. In cordial love . . ."[46] Martin Buber's thoughts on Pappenheim also point to her passionate nature:

There are people of spirit, there are people of passion, both are less common than one might think; rarer still are people of spirit and passion, but the rarest is passion of the spirit. Bertha Pappenheim was a person of passionate spirit. Didn't she have to become severe, not hard, but strict, . . . and passionately demanding, because all was as it was . . .? She lived at a time which could not bear the white fire, . . . The white flame burned in our day. Now it is extinguished and only her image survives in the hearts of those who knew her.[47]

Breuer described Anna O's family as "puritanically minded." She was brought up in a Victorian, strictly religious setting. Pappenheim maintained exacting religious and moral standards in her adult life as well. She insisted that all JFB charitable homes and clubs maintain Jewish dietary laws, despite the fact that most members were not Orthodox. Pappenheim observed all Jewish holy days and tried to impart their meaning to the children under her tutelage. It is clear that her puritanical upbringing also affected her later attitudes toward moral matters. Her ideas were typically Victorian, but seasoned with sympathy and understanding. In her crusade against immorality, Pappenheim, like other reformers, never condemned the females involved in prostitution or sexual promiscuity. After meeting prostitutes in Alexandria, she accused the world's women of letting those lovely girls suffer.[48] Like most reformers of this period, she emphasized the distress of prostitutes. Only in one of her many speeches and writings did Pappenheim acknowledge that some girls actually chose this way of life of their own free will, without being forced or misled.[49] Isenburg, Pappenheim's pet project, was a home founded to help girls whose "physical, intellectual, or ethical" makeup had been damaged.[50] Her harsh moral condemnation was directed at a society which neglected them. When some of her charges at Isenburg became pregnant after careful warnings, attention, and "moral training," she treated them patiently despite her obvious disappointment. Her attitudes toward sex, although certainly not liberal, were compassionate. In a letter to a young female convict, she wrote: "It is not the worst thing to have made love with a boyfriend in adolescent passion."[51] Her plans for Isenburg specified the need for administrators who were not cloistered or ignorant of the world, women who would not feel morally superior toward "fallen girls." Pappenheim, who remained single, considered married women more qualified to run the institution because they "understand sex life and . . . therefore are neither too strict nor too lenient with the girls. Even the best intentioned unmarried woman might go to extremes one way or the other."[52]

A full picture of Pappenheim is incomplete without mentioning other personality features which Breuer did not note. Those who knew her commented on her charm and graciousness. She invited her coworkers at Isenburg to her nicely decorated home once a week for an evening of conversation and companionship. During these evenings she strung beads or tatted lace and often gave the finished product to a guest. She was fascinated by lace and enjoyed rummaging through secondhand stores to find old pieces of it. She considered her laces to be her greatest treasure, "documents of feminine artistry, taste, and culture,"[53] and she later donated her collection to the Museum of Arts and Crafts in Vienna.

Her sense of humor was remarked upon by friends and foes. She often joked at her own expense. In 1936, Pappenheim composed ironic and witty obituary notices for herself. Her obituary for the Zionist paper read: "An old and active enemy of our movement, though one cannot deny that she had Jewish consciousness, and strength. She believed herself a German, but she was an assimilationist. What a pity!" For the Frauenbund's own paper, she composed the following: "In 1904 she founded the JFB—its importance is not yet fully understood. The Jews of the entire world—men and women—owe her thanks for this social achievement. But they withhold it. What a pity!"[54] When the president of the JFB paid a sick call to the dying Pappenheim, the latter thanked her guest for the lovely yellow roses she had brought, remarking, "How very nice, they just match my complexion."[55] Pappenheim's humor informed her feminism, too. When a male acquaintance offered her one of his cigarettes, she declined the offer, commenting that several years earlier when it was still controversial for women to smoke, she would have had to accept.[56] She also exercised her wit on the topic of marriage as it applied to herself. In a letter to a friend, she wrote of an encounter in 1907 with an old woman in Lemberg who sold lace and antiques. The woman's first words to Pappenheim were, "Wouldn't you like to marry? I have a nice professor who is a widower." Pappenheim deftly maneuvered around the question, and commented to her friend, "and thus I escaped another *Shidduch* [arranged marriage]." She promised that if she passed through the city on her return trip she would check to see whether the antiques were still there and whether "the professor was still to be had!!"[57] While on a trip to survey conditions leading to white slavery in Eastern Europe, the attractive fifty-two-year-old Pappenheim found herself pursued by a lighthouse inspector who invited her to remain with him for a week. She wrote, "The most enticing thing he had to say was, 'I could show you much depravity.' You can imagine how much fun I had inside."[58] Pappenheim never mentioned regretting her unmarried status. In sacrificing a home life to help Jewish women, she drew support for her lifestyle from a prevailing Victorian norm which granted dignity and offered incentives to unmarried women engaged in social service.

Pappenheim did miss being a mother and openly admitted that much of her activity was surrogate motherhood. She wrote: "Motherhood is something that happens to a woman and may even make her unhappy. Motherliness is the primary feeling of a woman, it can be delightfully experienced even by one who has remained untouched."[59] She corresponded with her "daughter," a girl she had raised in an orphanage, and spoke of her "old motherly loyalty."

Her bouts of loneliness—"I am not necessary. For nothing and to no one"[60]—were counterbalanced by the pure joy she experienced with children:

> A child's hand in my hand
> My heart becomes a fairy land![61]

She was convinced that: "Women who have to miss the happiness of real personal motherhood may have an opportunity for spiritual motherhood, if they go the quiet way of helping children and adolescents whose actual mother may fail."[62] Pappenheim devoted her life to this spiritual motherhood. Not only did she remain the head of Isenburg for twenty-nine years, caring for and ministering to "her children," but her creation, the Jüdischer Frauenbund, was an institutional embodiment of this concept of motherhood. Through it, Pappenheim could shelter, educate, entertain, and protect young women and children. Like her German counterpart Helene Lange, she was deeply affected by her elevation of motherhood. On the one hand, she insisted that every female child be given the same educational and career opportunities as every male child and that every woman be allowed full participation in the political, cultural, and economic spheres. On the other hand, she believed in the sacredness of the family and insisted that every woman fulfill her responsibilities as a wife and mother first. She neither would, nor could, have asked that husbands or governments assume any of the traditional household or child-rearing functions; in fact, she probably would have opposed government intervention in the form of day care. Thus, she placed an insuperable burden on married women, particularly those with children, who responded to the lure of equality.

The Author and Activist

The first hint of Bertha Pappenheim as a mature adult came from a book of short stories she wrote in 1890 under the pseudonym Paul Berthold. Entitled *In the Second Hand Shop*, the book was a vehicle for Pappenheim's concern for the poor and her love of children.[63] Having embraced the ideals of German feminism, she next devoted an essay to the education of young middle-class women arguing that all girls should be prepared to provide for themselves, even those who might never have to work. Parents who pampered their daughters or refused to educate them were irresponsible. Pappenheim did not insist that wealthy girls absolutely had to earn their own living, but she reminded them of their obligation to society, and to themselves. Further, she implored Jewish families to cultivate their daughters' understanding of the real world:

Until now, an axiom of proper education was to keep girls from knowing anything that occurred beyond the confines of their homes. They studied history from books which were "rewritten for girls" but they remained cut off from the enormous demands of daily life. They do not understand the relationship of poverty, sickness and crime. To them, poverty is a street beggar or a scene in a play, sickness is disgusting, and crime is a sin. Under such circumstances we cannot be surprised when girls do not understand, or at best, feel fleeting pity for the tragedies of humanity.

Höhere Töchter could improve their own lives (as well as the lives of the needy) by volunteering to do social work.[64]

In 1899, Pappenheim published a play entitled *Women's Rights* and a translation of Mary Wollstonecraft's *A Vindication of the Rights of Women*.[65] The play stressed the political, economic, and sexual exploitation of women. The men in the drama were irresponsible seducers. The women—a poor, underpaid, unmarried mother who was arrested for attempting to organize other working women for self-protection, and her friend, a middle-class housewife whose husband legally controlled her property and would not allow her to give money to the poor woman—were victims of male society. A biography of Mary Wollstonecraft was published in Vienna in 1897.[66] This may have been the stimulus for Pappenheim's interest in the English feminist, whose original work had been published in 1792. The book that Pappenheim translated was a plea for the education of women. Wollstonecraft maintained that women should be men's companions, not their playthings. She sought equality of education for boys and girls, insisting that intellectual comradeship was the basis for a fulfilling relationship in marriage. Her main point was that women had human rights. Pappenheim, who would have shunned Wollstonecraft's unorthodox lifestyle and who found it too radical to insist on women's unequivocal "rights" without referring to their "duties," greatly admired the Englishwoman's charm and courage and hung a picture of Wollstonecraft in her living room.

Pappenheim's commitment to active social work also began in the 1890s. In the early years of the decade she worked in a soup kitchen for Jewish immigrants from Eastern Europe. Her interest in helping the needy, particularly women and children, gradually deepened. She organized a small Jewish nursery school, sewing classes, and a girls' club. In 1895 (the year Breuer and Freud published the case of Anna O in their *Studies on Hysteria*), Pappenheim accepted the position of housemother in an orphanage for Jewish girls. One of her charges wrote:

This period meant a complete revolution in her life . . . with total renunciation of her former habits—she was very spoiled in Vienna and lived the life of a *höhere Tochter*—she did justice to the many demands which this new sphere of activity imposed on her. She increased her manual skills, mingled with the children . . . and participated . . . in all kinds of housework.[67]

Pappenheim remained in this position for twelve years, gathering valuable experience as an administrator and educator.

In 1900, Pappenheim's feminism was influenced by her increasing awareness of the desperate situation of Jews in Eastern Europe, particularly Jewish girls. She wrote a short pamphlet, *The Jewish Problem in Galicia*, in which she maintained that their poor education ultimately led Jewish girls to poverty and vice.[68] She repeated her message in another pamphlet, *On the Condition of the Jewish Population in Galicia*.[69] The growing wave of Jewish conversions was the theme of a short story she wrote in 1902 for a Jewish literary publication. The main character in "A Weakling" was a Jewish boy whose religious father rejected him for choosing to be an artist. Conversion followed, but the young man missed his people and heritage. He met a Jewish woman who despised converts and told him: "Today, when we Jews are constantly under attack, Jews must stick together. . . . It is cowardly and dishonorable to defect to the side of the attacker."[70] Pappenheim stressed two minor, but important, themes in her story. The first was her fear that old-fashioned Jews were alienating young Jews by their insistence on total ignorance of the secular world. The second was her belief that Jewish girls desired better educations. Her heroine lamented: "I would have been interested in and enjoyed learning about art and politics, if I had been educated to understand them. I believe Christian girls know much more about these things."[71]

As a result of her concern for the welfare of Jews and women, Pappenheim founded the society Care by Women (*Weibliche Fürsorge*) in 1902. She turned exclusively to women, because she felt that "men always and in every situation follow their private interests."[72] Consciously attempting to transcend the image of the charitable lady, the "do-gooder," she sought to apply the goals of German feminism to Jewish social work. Although she did not stress social services as a "right" of the recipient as much as a "duty" of the donor, hers was still a more modern attitude than the sentimentality and narrowness of existing charities. She taught her followers new social casework techniques and set up special comittees which researched methods of child care, means of finding foster homes, and ways of providing travelers' aid. Her group founded vocational counseling centers and an employment service for women. As a delegate of Care by Women, Pappenheim attended her first conference on white slavery in 1902. Distressed by the number of Jewish girls who fell victim to the traffic in women, she traveled to Galicia and Western Russia intending to discover ways in which German Jews could aid their coreligionists. Thereafter, she took numerous study tours to the Middle East, Eastern Europe, and Russia. Her most well-known publication, *Sisyphus Work*, was a report on prostitution and white slavery in Eastern Europe and the Middle East. It was not intended to give a comprehensive description of the problem of white slavery, but to convince people—particularly Jews—that the problem existed and that the Jewish community had to act to remedy it.

In spite of, or perhaps because of, her success with Care by Women, Pappenheim called for larger, national Jewish social welfare organizations. The need for expanded services became apparent at the turn of the century, when Jewish refugees from czarist pogroms[73] flowed into Germany, overwhelming the traditional charities. Pappenheim remarked on the conspicuous absence of women in the leadership of those Jewish charities which did exist, and she accused the Jewish establishment of "underestimating the value of women's work and trifling with their interest by refusing to admit them as equal partners."[74] She argued that the leaders of Jewish community welfare boards were losing some of their best women, who were turning to German feminism as an outlet for their energies. Her demands met with either strong male resistance or attempts at co-optation. The B'nai B'rith, for example, asked her to form a women's auxiliary.[75] She refused, wanting nothing to do with an organization which would be no more than the "tail end" of the lodges (*Logen-schwanz*).[76] Pappenheim wanted a national women's organization that was equal to and independent of men's organizations.

By 1904, Protestant and Catholic women had their own organizations. This fact encouraged Pappenheim in her pursuit of a Jewish women's association. She envisioned an organization that would protect Jewish girls, extend modern social work techniques, and, most importantly, represent all Jewish women. The convention of the International Council of Women, which met in Berlin in 1904, provided the opportunity for Pappenheim to meet with several other Jewish activists. Together they founded the Jüdischer Frauenbund.

Pappenheim was elected the first president of the newly formed association, probably because of her intense interest in it and her leadership abilities. She held her post for twenty years and remained on the board of directors until 1934. To a large extent the history of the JFB is Pappenheim's story. It is often difficult to distinguish the JFB from Pappenheim, because she was the driving spirit and main personality in the organization. In fact, the JFB frequently stood in the shadow of its well-known president. Its members and leaders were generally more timid and cautious than its energetic, impetuous, and occasionally belligerent founder. Since most of Pappenheim's activities after 1904 were inseparable from her position in the JFB, they will be discussed in the chapters that follow.

Pappenheim expected women to volunteer their services to the JFB. A women's organization could not afford to pay professional social workers, of which, in any case, there were very few in the first decade of the twentieth century.[77] Also, Pappenheim distrusted professionals, fearing depersonalization, and warned that social work—which she described as a *Mitzvah*, the Hebrew word for blessing or commandment—would be dragged down to the level of a business. Furthermore, Jewish middle-class girls and women had leisure time and financial security (in the years when the JFB began), and would be educationally and socially enriched by their experience. In fact, since social work had been a welcome relief from the boredom of her youth, Pappenheim considered rescuing these women from an unfulfilling existence as an important goal in itself. If the field were monopolized by professionals, the volunteer would have been relegated to uselessness. While she was correct in seeing the widespread response evoked by the JFB as a result of the narrowness of the lives prescribed for women, who eagerly seized the opportunity to broaden their horizons, she did not understand that middle-class girls, who did not *have* to support themselves, nevertheless wanted to earn a living. They appreciated activity, but wanted economic independence as well. Only during the Weimar era did she finally begin to admit the need for trained workers, but even then she argued that their salaries should remain very low. She told a young social worker: "Many other girls do mechanical work, while you follow a profession from which you derive satisfaction: that is also worth something. Paid social workers should content themselves with an income considerably below that of a typist or a seamstress."[78]

Despite a gradual shift from volunteers to professionals in many of the JFB's homes, the majority of its locals and most of its counseling centers and railroad station posts were staffed by volunteers. Pappenheim's creation was rooted in a middle-class sensibility appropriate to the era in which it was founded. The JFB could alleviate the monotony faced by middle-class women by engaging them in a benevolent association which was not a threat to their class status or to their traditionalism. The Frauenbund reinforced the notion of women's supportive, maternal nature as it perpetuated social workers of its own class; with rare exception, the poor, Eastern Jewish immigrant remained at the receiver's end of the welfare chain.

Pappenheim worked tirelessly for the JFB, traveling frequently and lecturing widely on its behalf. She was also a prolific contributor to the JFB's newsletter, writing articles on Isenburg, women's education, white slavery, and the ethics of social work.[79] As the JFB grew in membership and established its own homes, schools, and clubs for girls, Pappenheim, encouraged by past successes and driven by her vision of the future potential of the JFB, urged the organization to broaden its scope still further. She pressed it to join the German women's movement and also initiated contact with international Jewish women's organizations.

Pappenheim tried to combine her feminism with her deeply felt religious identity by arguing that all of her activities were meant to strengthen the Jewish people. More alarmed than ever at the "epidemic of conversion" from Judaism, Pappenheim assigned the JFB the task of attracting women to the Jewish community.[80] Upset by formal renunciations, she was also disturbed by the tendency of assimilated Jews to find little meaning in their religion, observing it sporadically in a vague and superficial manner. Pappenheim believed women could transmit a love of religion to their offspring, thereby stemming intermarriage and preserving the Jewish family. However, she felt women were alienated from their community because they were not permitted to participate in it as equals. Therefore, the Jewish women's movement would prevent Judaism's decline by teaching women about their heritage and by fighting for women's rights within the Jewish community. Equality was an end, but it was also the means by which women would return to Judaism.

Pappenheim's participation in the Bund Deutscher Frauenvereine also reflected the symbiosis of her feminist and Jewish convictions. Her attitudes regarding women were derived from those of German feminists. Yet, despite her ten-year (1914-1924) membership on the board of directors of the BDF, her organization was part of, but separate from the German movement. She considered herself a fully acculturated German and fostered cooperation among Jews and Germans, but she hoped to preserve the communal and religious "otherness" of her people. Also, she was sensitive to anti-Semitism. She believed that if consciously Jewish women worked within the German movement, they would fight anti-Semitism through personal interaction. Her collaboration with German feminists was thus, in part, a means of combatting prejudice, but it was also proof to Pappenheim that there was a possibility for friendship among Germans and Jews. All her life, in fact, she tried to reconcile her German, Jewish, and feminist identities.

Even though Pappenheim insisted that feminism would strengthen Judaism, her Jewish faith and her feminist convictions frequently stood in opposition to one another. For example, she worried that Jews were not deeply enough involved in their religion and wrote Martin Buber: "Many Jews in terrible spiritual need reach for 'their Goethe' before 'their Bible.'" She wished Jews would emulate Christians for whom the Bible was "a path to God."[81] (She added, "to God not to HIM," a reference to Buber's use of the masculine pronoun in place of "God" in his translation of the Bible.) She criticized Buber's approach to the Bible as too intellectual. Jews, she maintained, should learn to love the Bible, not simply to read it as history.[82] Yet this literal and emotional view contradicted the rationalism of her attitudes toward the rights of women. To her dismay, she found that it was extremely difficult, if not impossible, to combine a literal and integral acceptance of the Bible with reformism. Orthodox Jews who agreed with her religious views were adamantly opposed to her feminism, while more progressive Jews accepted her feminist programs, but preferred Buber's conception of the Bible.

During these busy organizational years, Pappenheim, whose literary works were another part of her crusade, still found time to write. In 1910, she translated the *Memoirs of Glückl von Hameln* from Judeo-German into German.[83] She was a distant relative of Glückl (1645-1724), a German Jewess who married at the age of fourteen and bore thirteen children. A pious and strong women, she fulfilled her traditional role as a wife and mother. Yet, she was not a subordinate in the marriage partnership: her respect for her husband was clearly reciprocated, and she referred to him as her best friend. When he died she raised her large family and managed a business as well. Pappenheim was attracted by her efficiency, charm, and motherliness.[84]

In 1913 and 1916, Pappenheim published a three-act play and several short stories. The themes of the stories, anti-Semitism, Jewish life in Eastern Europe, and conversion, were areas of ever increasing concern to her. A subplot in all of the stories was the place of women in Judaism.[85] Her play, *Tragic Moments*, allowed Pappenheim to voice her continuing concern about anti-Semitism, white slavery, the needs of young mothers, and, most importantly, Zionism. Pappenheim treated the Zionist hero sympathetically, describing the pogroms he had experienced and his belief that Jews needed their own country. She depicted the hardships his family faced as colonists and noted—not as an aside, to be sure—that his wife died at a young age because of her double burden as a colonist and a mother. Yet, Pappenheim clearly identified with the son who could not face a future in Palestine. He explained that European culture was the inheritance of Christians and Jews, and pleaded:

I need the books, pictures, stages, newspapers, exchange of opinions and interests, city life . . . I can not play at being a farmer. . . . also as a Jew I should not follow the seductive call of Zionism. It is cowardly to leave the battleground with a few thousand and settle in a protected corner, to found a new ghetto, knowing full well that all other Jews, particularly the poorest and weakest, will not find a home there.

He blamed Zionists for dividing Jewish communities instead of telling Jews to "be patient, live righteously, learn the teachings of the religion and let no one rob you of them."[86]

Her travels to Eastern Europe and Palestine brought Pappenheim into contact with many Zionists. She welcomed them to the Frauenbund and organized "Palestine evenings" at Isenburg, but her identity as a religious Jew and a patriotic German left her with little patience for Zionism. She worried that its exponents, who were usually anti-Orthodox, did not respect the religious customs and traditions of Judaism, and her attachment to Germany convinced her that she already had a homeland. She also distrusted Theodor Herzl, the "latter-day Jewish saint," whose Jewishness she suspected to be of relatively recent vintage. In her circles, she wrote, "a man like him was considered an assimilationist—although that word had not yet been coined—and rejected."[87] Further, Pappenheim was unimpressed with Herzl's *Old New Land*, which she saw as a direct copy of the American author Bellamy's *Looking Backward*. Pappenheim was particularly dismayed by Zionists' seeming lack of concern for the problems of women: "In endless, irritating debates . . . I was repeatedly told Zionism is a purely political movement which can not be amalgamated with social or religious things; white slavery does not exist, prostitution is an international necessity, venereal disease is a personal misfortune,' and such arguments."[88] Furthermore, her independent feminist spirit resented the subordinate role to which Zionist women's organizations were relegated by the Zionist male establishment: "Women were only very hesitatingly accepted by Zionist men, and their activities were confined (primarily to money-raising)." This "absolute financial and spiritual dependence" was certainly not to Pappenheim's liking.[89] Finally, her antipathy to Zionism can be traced to her attitudes concerning motherhood. She feared that Zionists intended to break up families, and wrote: "Zionists . . . considered as negligible all those women's duties which I regard as absolutely essential."[90] She specifically disliked their "collective breeding and raising of children" and maintained that a healthy family should bring up its own offspring.[91] Her tenacious belief in the value of the nuclear family made her narrow and inflexible regarding Zionism. In the early 1930s, she fought Youth Aliyah, the Zionist effort to ship children to Palestine, which, she was convinced, was "exporting children" so that Zionists could populate their land.[92] Although her efforts to oppose Youth Aliyah were not effective, her distrust of Zionists made her exaggerate the risks of separating young people from their families in the face of the very real threat posed by the Nazis.

One gains the impression from Pappenheim's local, national, and international efforts that no matter how fast she ran, she was still in the same place: the poverty, exploitation, and inhumanity that she fought remained. As she aged, she consoled herself by achieving admittedly small victories—she called them "holy small deeds" (heilige Kleinarbeit). Pleased as she was with the girls' clubs, scholarships, health facilities, and cultural contributions of the JFB, she was "driven by fear" that she would "not . . . accomplish what she felt called upon to do."[93] In 1924, Pappenheim retired from the presidency of the JFB. Despite her failing health she continued to write for women and to work for the JFB, explaining that she could not tear herself away from any aspect of Jewish women's work without giving up a piece of herself.[94] In 1929, she translated the Mayse Bukh, a collection of medieval folk tales and

Biblical and Talmudic stories. In the eighteenth century this book, written in Judeo-German, was widely read by women. Pappenheim also translated the *Ze'enah U'Ree'nah*, or woman's bible, a popular version of the Five Books of Moses, the Five Megillot, and the Haftarot.[95] Her activities focused on the protection of children. In 1928 she proposed that a "world collective guardianship" be founded to care for all abandoned and neglected children. Collective guardianship would be the responsibility of one of the large Jewish agencies, which could provide every child with protection when their real or adoptive parents failed them.[96] Her idea was far too ambitious (and was never realized), but the JFB did consider her recommendation. In 1934, at the age of seventy-five, Pappenheim personally delivered several of her small charges to an orphanage in Glasgow.[97] She wrote two long essays that year in which she decried the historical role of Jewish women and pleaded for their education. Her anger at the "sin committed against the Jewish woman's soul and thus against all Judaism" had not abated.[98]

It might be supposed that her strong Jewish identity would have made Pappenheim more alert to the dangers of Nazism. But, it was precisely this self-conscious Jewishness—and her strong feelings for Germany—which clouded her perception of German anti-Semitism. Although not blind to the virulent anti-Semitism of postwar Germany, she did not appreciate its real danger until 1930.[99] Even then she guessed that it might be a "ghetto atavism" which made her suspect all Christians of harboring anti-Semitic feelings.[100] Like other German Jews, she relied on the constitution for her protection. Even when the Nazis destroyed the rule of law, Pappenheim's first reaction seems to have been that the forcible return of Jews to their faith was not an entirely negative phenomenon. Her short story, "The Inheritance," told the tale of a baptized professor who had been fired as a result of the first set of racial laws of 1933. He received a letter from America offering him an inheritance if he could prove his Jewish ancestry. The professor retrieved hidden documents in "unreadable characters" verifying his formerly well-kept secret, whereupon the inheritance arrived. It was a yellowed sheet of paper with religious commandments and prayers on it. Pappenheim concluded: ". . . the inheritance was great and it is to be wished that all discharged and baptized academics had received one."[101] Underestimating the nature of German fascism, Pappenheim discouraged mass emigration and argued that Jews still had a place in Germany. She did not admit her error until after the passage of the racial laws of 1935.[102] In this regard she displayed no less insight than most German Jews. In fact, the *Reichsvertretung*, the collective voice of Germany's Jews, maintained an ambivalent position even after Nuremberg, agreeing to the need for Jewish emigration, but also viewing the Nuremberg Laws as a *modus vivendi* for German Jewry.[103]

In the summer of 1935, Pappenheim was hospitalized for a tumor which later proved to be fatal. In the spring of 1936, she visited Isenburg for the last time. Desperately ill, she was summoned by the Gestapo to explain an anti-Hitler remark made by one of the children. After her encounter with the police, she never left her bed. Although she did not discuss her illness, she realized precisely how sick she was. Seven days before her death she dictated a prayer in which she declared her readiness to die and asked God to give her peace.[104]

Death spared her from the agony of the worst of the Nazi maelstrom. She died at Isenburg on May 28, 1936. At her request, the funeral was small and there were no eulogies. In her "last will," written in 1930, Pappenheim hoped that those who visited her grave would leave a small stone, "as a quiet promise . . . to serve the mission of women's duties and women's joy . . . unflinchingly and courageously."[105]

Notes

1. Dora Edinger, ed., *Bertha Pappenheim: Leben und Schriften* (Frankfurt/Main: Ner Tamid Verlag, 1963), p. 118. Pappenheim may not have been aware of the universality of this preference. Elizabeth Cady Stanton, the cofounder of the American suffrage movement, told a similar story: "The first event engraved on my memory was the birth of a sister . . . I heard so many friends remark, 'What a pity it is she's a girl,' that I felt a kind of compassion for the little baby." See "Excerpts from the Autobiography of Elizabeth Cady Stanton," in Eve Merriam, ed., *Growing Up Female in America* (New York: Dell Publishers, 1971), pp. 56-69.

2. Sigmund Freud and Josef Breuer, *Studies on Hysteria* (New York: Avon Books, 1966), p. 55. Pappenheim's biographer, Dr. Dora Edinger,

suggested that Pappenheim destroyed all records of her early years and later illness on her last trip to Vienna in 1935. Edinger, ed., *Bertha Pappenheim: Freud's Anna O* (Highland Park, Ill.: Congregation Solel, 1968), p. 20.

3. There were no Jewish high schools for girls in Vienna.

4. *BJFB*, July 1936, p. 11.

5. Lange, *Lebenserinnerungen* (Berlin: F. A. Herbig, 1921), pp. 87-88.

6. Joseph Breuer quoted by H. F. Ellenberger, "The Story of Anna O: A Critical Review with New Data," *Journal of the History of the Behavioral Sciences* (July 1972), p. 267.

7. Freud, *Hysteria*, p. 47.

8. Ibid., p. 55.

9. Ibid., pp. 56, 76.

10. Ibid., p. 56.

11. Ibid., p. 47. A popular novel written in 1895 corroborated Freud's theory. The heroine engaged in daydreams while doing her needlework. She imagined herself racing over Scottish heaths with Lord Byron, and she constantly returned to what she called her "second world." Gabriele Reuter, *Aus Guter Familie: Leidensgeschichte eines Mädchens*, 17th ed. (Berlin: S. Fischer Verlag, 1908), p. 102.

12. Richard Karpe, "The Rescue Complex in Anna O's Final Identity," *The Psychoanalytic Quarterly* 30 (1961), p. 23.

13. Karpe, "Rescue Complex," p. 8.

14. Ernest Jones, *The Life and Work of Sigmund Freud* (New York: Anchor Books by arrangement with Basic Books, Inc., 1960), p. 143.

15. Sigmund Freud, *Letters of Sigmund Freud*, selected and edited by Ernst L. Freud (New York: Basic Books, Inc., 1960), p. 413.

16. Freud, *Letters*, p. 413; *Hysteria*, p. 56.

17. See Karpe, "Rescue Complex"; Ellenberger, "The Story of Anna O"; Ellen Jensen, "Anna O—A Study of Her Later Life," *The Psychoanalytic Quarterly* 39 (1970), pp. 269-93. The latter includes a bibliography of psychoanalytic commentary on Anna O and on Bertha Pappenheim's later life.

18. Mary P. Ryan, *Womanhood in America: From Colonial Times to the Present* (New York: Franklin Watts, Inc., 1975), p. 276.

19. Mara Mayor, "Fears and Fantasies of the Anti-Suffragists," *Connecticut Review* 7, no. 2 (April 1974), pp. 64-74.

20. Ryan, *Womanhood*, p. 276.

21. Robert Waelder, "Psychoanalysis and History: Application of Psychoanalysis to Historiography," *The Psychoanalytic Interpretation of History*, edited by Benjamin B. Wolman (New York: Harper Torchbooks, 1971), p. 12.

22. Duncan Crow, *The Victorian Woman* (New York: Stein and Day, 1972), p. 62; Kate Millett, "The Debate over Women: Ruskin vs. Mill," in

Suffer and be Still: Women in the Victorian Age, edited by Martha Vicinus (Bloomington, Ind.: Indiana University Press, 1972), p. 137; Carroll Smith-Rosenberg, "Puberty to Menopause: The Cycle of Femininity in Nineteenth Century America," in *Clio's Consciousness Raised* (New York: Harper Colophon Books, 1974), pp. 23-37, and "The Hysterical Woman: Sex Roles and Role Conflict in Nineteenth Century America," *Social Research* 39, no. 4 (Winter 1972), pp. 652-78; Zinnecker, *Sozialgeschichte der Mädchenbildung* (Weinheim and Basel: Beltz Verlag, 1973), p. 98; Fanny Lewald, *Für und Wider die Frauen*, 2d ed. (Berlin: Verlag von Otto Janke, 1875), pp. 3-20; and Ann Douglas Wood, "The 'Fashionable Diseases': Women's Complaints and their Treatment in Nineteenth Century America," *Journal of Interdisciplinary History* 4 (Summer 1973), pp. 27-29, 35-36.

23. John Stuart Mill, *The Subjection of Women* (New York: Frederick A. Stokes Company, 1911), pp. 31-32.

24. Abraham H. Maslow, *Toward a Psychology of Being* (New York: D. Van Nostrand Company, Inc., 1962), pp. iii-iv, 190-91.

25. "The Problem of Ego Identity," in *Identity and the Life Cycle* (New York: International University Press, Inc., 1959), p. 133.

26. An abolitionist was someone who tried to abolish the regulation of prostitution.

27. Jane Addams, *Twenty Years at Hull House* (New York: James W. Linn, 1938; New York: Macmillan Co., 1910; New York: A Signet Classic from New American Library, 1938), pp. 64, 67.

28. Stanton in Merriam, *Growing Up Female*, p. 67.

29. Dohm in Katherine Anthony, *Feminism in Germany and Scandinavia* (New York: Henry Holt and Company, 1915), pp. 242-43.

30. Freud, *Hysteria*, p. 55.

31. Pappenheim, *Sisyphus Arbeit: Reisebriefe aus den Jahren 1911 und 1912* (Leipzig: Verlag Paul E. Linder, 1924), foreword.

32. The article, "Weh dem dessen Gewissen schläft!," appeared in the widely read *Allgemeine Zeitung des Judentums*, December 22, 1916, pp. 601-603.

33. Pappenheim, *Sisyphus*, p. 89.

34. Freud, *Hysteria*, p. 55.

35. Ibid., p. 75.

36. Certainly other leaders in the international fight against white slavery shared the same tenacious determination: Josephine Butler and Anna Pappritz are but two examples. Pappenheim particularly admired Butler's courage and social consciousness.

37. Rahel Straus, *Wir Lebten in Deutschland: Erinnerungen einer Deutschen Jüdin, 1880-1933* (Stuttgart: Deutsche Verlags-Anstalt, 1962), p. 151.

38. Werner collection, *Archives of the Leo Baeck Institute*, no. 3079 (35).

39. Ibid.

40. Straus, *Wir Lebten in Deutschland*, p. 258. See also Pappenheim, *Sisyphus Arbeit II* (Berlin: Druck und Verlag Berthold Levy, 1929), p. 49.

41. *BJFB*, July 1936, p. 12.

42. Ibid., p. 30.

43. See for example: Pappenheim, *Prayers*, translated by Estelle Forchheimer (New York: Arnold Stein Printing Company, 1946).

44. Pappenheim collection, ALBI, no. 33 (3).

45. Pappenheim, *Sisyphus*, p. 161.

46. Edinger, Pappenheim, *Freud's Anna O*, p. 29.

47. *BJFB*, July 1936, p. 2.

48. Pappenheim, *Sisyphus*, pp. 224-25.

49. *Israelitsches Familienblatt*, August 5, 1909, p. 11.

50. Else Rabin, "The Jewish Woman in Social Service in Germany," in *The Jewish Library*, edited by Leo Jung (New York: The Jewish Library Publishing Company, 1934), p. 300.

51. *BJFB*, July 1936, p. 16.

52. *BJFB*, June 1937, p. 2.

53. Edinger, *Freud's Anna O*, p. 95.

54. *BJFB*, July 1936, p. 28.

55. Edinger, *Freud's Anna O*, p. 21.

56. Ruth R. Dresner, "Bertha Pappenheim: The Contribution of a German-Jewish Pioneer Social Reformer to Social Work: 1859-1936" (master's thesis, Fordham University, 1954), p. 38.

57. Pappenheim collection, ALBI, no. 331 (9).

58. Pappenheim, *Sisyphus*, p. 90.

59. *BJFB*, July 1936, p. 16.

60. Pappenheim, *Sisyphus*, p. 161.

61. *Frankfurter Israelitisches Gemeindeblatt*, July 1936.

62. Edinger, *Freud's Anna O*, p. 60. These thoughts were common among unmarried women engaged in "social motherhood." In 1873, Catharine Beecher, a leader in the American home economics movement (and sister of Harriet Beecher Stowe), wrote that the "increasingly open avenues to occupations for women, [enable] them to establish homes of their own, where, if not as the natural mother, yet as a Christ-mother, they may take in neglected ones, and train future mothers, teachers . . . for the world." Kathryn K. Sklar, *Catharine Beecher: A Study in American Domesticity* (New York: W.W. Norton and Co., 1966), p. 167; Ryan, *Womanhood*, p. 235.

63. Paul Berthold (Bertha Pappenheim), *In der Trödelbude: Geschichten* (Lahr: Druck und Verlag von Moritz Schauenburg, 1890), p. 35.

64. Pappenheim, "Zur Erziehung der Weiblichen Jugend in den höheren Ständen," *Ethische Kultur*, February 1898, reprinted in *BJFB*, July/August 1936, p. 4. American reformers also shared Pappenheim's disgust with girls' education. Jane Addams wrote bitterly of "the assumption that the sheltered, educated girl has nothing to do with the bitter poverty and the social maladjustment which is all about her, and which, after all, can not be concealed, for it breaks through poetry and literature in a burning tide which overwhelms her." Jane Addams, *Hull House*, p. 65.

65. Paul Berthold (Bertha Pappenheim), *Frauenrechte; Eine Verteidigung der Rechte der Frau—Übersetzung aus dem Englischen* (Dresden: Verlag Pierson, 1899).

66. Helene Richter, *Mary Wollstonecraft, Die Verfechterin der Rechte der Frau* (Vienna: Verlag der Deutsche Worte, 1897).

67. *BJFB*, July 1936, p. 5.

68. Paul Berthold (Bertha Pappenheim), *Zur Judenfrage in Galizien* (Frankfurt/Main: Knauer, 1900).

69. Pappenheim, *Zur Lage der Jüdischen Bevölkerung in Galizien* (Frankfurt/Main: Neuer Frankfurter Verlag, 1904).

70. Pappenheim, "Ein Schwächling," *Jährbuch für Jüdische Geschichte und Literatur*, ed. Verbände der Vereine für jüdische Geschichte und Literatur in Deutschland (Berlin: Verlag von Albert Katz, 1902), V, p. 243.

71. Ibid., p. 242.

72. Pappenheim collection, ALBI, no. 331 (9).

73. The Kishinev pogroms occurred in April 1903 and October 1905.

74. Schönewald, unpublished memoirs, ALBI, no. 356, p. 16.

75. The Independent Order of B'nai B'rith, a fraternal society, was founded by German-Jewish immigrants to the United States in 1843. It was dedicated to Jewish education and welfare. The German branch, founded in 1882, supported orphanages, old-age and rest homes, and its own newsletter. It grew to over 100 lodges and 12,000 members by 1937.

76. Caesar Seligmann, *Erinnerungen (1860-1950)* (Frankfurt/Main: Erwin Seligmann, 1975), p. 133.

77. The first one-year course for a career in welfare work was offered in 1899. By 1902 a few trained social workers could be hired, but only with the opening of the Soziale Frauenschule, founded by Alice Salomon in 1908, did the fledgling profession begin to grow.

78. Livneh, unpublished memoirs, ALBI, p. 7.

79. Pappenheim led study groups on the ethics of social work at the Frankfurt Lehrhaus, an institute for Jewish education founded in 1919 by Martin Buber and Franz Rosenzweig.

80. *IF*, January 19, 1911, p. 12. Between 1901 and 1904, 8.4 percent of

Jewish men and 7.4 percent of Jewish women married out of their faith. Between 1910 and 1911 this figure increased to 13.4 percent of Jewish men and 10.3 percent of Jewish women. In 1915 intermarriage reached a high of 40.4 percent of Jewish men and 26.6 percent of Jewish women. By 1927, 25.8 percent of Jewish men and 16.1 percent of Jewish women married outside their religion. Rates of intermarriage were highest during the war years when fewer Jews married. In later years as the absolute number of marriages increased, intermarriage rates declined. It was estimated that about 22 percent of the children of mixed marriages were brought up to be Jews. Intermarriages presented a particularly thorny problem for Jewish women: since (as statistics indicate) more men than women intermarried, traditional Jewish women were deprived of potential husbands. For further statistical analyses of intermarriage, see: *ZDSJ*, 2, no. 7 (July 1906), pp. 107-108; (January/February 1924), p. 25; 5, no. 1 (July 1930), p. 14. See also, Erich Rosenthal, "Jewish Population in Germany, 1910-1939," *Jewish Social Studies* 6 (1944), pp. 233-73.

81. Letter from Pappenheim, March 18, 1936, in Martin Buber, *Martin Buber: Briefwechsel aus sieben Jahrzehnten II*, edited by Grete Schaeder (Heidelberg: Verlag Lambert Schneider, 1973), p. 587.

82. Ibid.

83. Judeo-German (*Judendeutsch*) was a language written in Hebrew characters. It developed out of Middle High German and contained some Hebrew (15 percent) and some Aramaic words. It was the forebear of modern Yiddish, although, in many cases, Judeo-German and Yiddish existed at the same time. Glückl von Hameln's memoirs were also translated into English. See *The Memoirs of Glückl of Hameln*, translated by Marvin Lowenthal (New York: Shocken Books, 1977).

84. George W. Pollack, "Bertha Pappenheim's Idealized Ancestor: Glückel von Hameln," *American Imago* 28 (1971).

85. Pappenheim, *Kämpfe: Sechs Erzählungen* (Frankfurt/Main: J. Kauffmann, 1916).

86. Pappenheim, *Tragische Momente: Drei Lebensbilder* (Frankfurt/Main: J. Kauffmann, 1913), pp. 84-85.

87. Edinger, *Leben und Schriften*, p. 112.

88. Ibid., p. 113.

89. Ibid., pp. 113-14.

90. Ibid., p. 112.

91. Ibid., p. 114.

92. *BJFB*, October 1936, pp. 6-7.

93. Edinger, "German-Jewish Feminist," p. 185.

94. Schönewald collection, ALBI, no. 3896 (III, 4), p. 8.

95. The Five Megillot consist of: The Book of Esther, The Book of Ruth, The Song of Songs, Ecclesiastes, and Lamentations. The Haftarot are biblical selections from the Book of Prophets.

96. Pappenheim, *Sisyphus II*, p. 61; *BJFB*, July 1936, p. 19.

97. Schönewald collection, ALBI, no. 3896 (V, 13).

98. Both essays, "The Jewish Woman" and "The Jewish Girl," are reprinted in Edinger, *Freud's Anna O*, pp. 77-90.

99. Edinger, *Freud's Anna O*, pp. 56-57.

100. *BJFB*, August 1930, pp. 7-9.

101. *Frankfurter Israelitisches Gemeindeblatt*, July 1936, pp. 277-78.

102. Edinger, *Freud's Anna O*, p. 21.

103. Karl A. Schleunes, *The Twisted Road to Auschwitz: Nazi Policy toward German Jews, 1933-1939* (Urbana: University of Illinois Press, 1970), p. 126.

104. Karminski, unpublished memoirs, ALBI, no. 301. The prayer was translated by Lucy Freeman, *The Story of Anna O*, p. 170.

105. *BJFB*, July 1936, p. 39. Jews traditionally leave a small stone when they visit a grave.

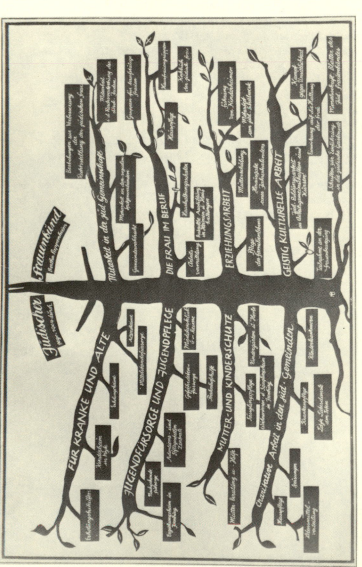

2. JFB "Tree" used as the front page of their prospectus. Each branch indicates a specific field of endeavor: care of the old and sick, of youth, and of mothers and children; participation in the Jewish community; educational and cultural work; support of careers for women. Among the minor braches are: votes for women; the battle against immorality; attempt to improve the legal status of Jewish women; and participation in the women's movement. *Courtesy Leo Baeck Institute, New York.*

chapter 3

Woman's Sphere

The Feminist Aspirations of the Frauenbund

PRECURSORS OF THE JFB

The JFB's conception of "women's place" derived primarily from the attitudes and experiences of German feminism. The Frauenbund supported German feminists' stand on the "woman question" and adapted their ideas to Jewish customs and circumstances. Pappenheim wrote: "The German women's movement gave the shy, uncertain advances of Jewish women direction and confidence."[1] A brief introduction to the historical development of the German movement will, thus, shed light on Jewish feminism.

The German women's movement was an outgrowth of the liberalism and idealism of the late 1840s. Louise Otto, credited by bourgeois and socialist feminists alike as its founder, attempted to ameliorate the economic, social, and political conditions of women. When Robert Blum, a leader of the revolution of 1848, asked whether women had the right to participate in the State, Otto responded with the founding principle of the women's movement: women had not only the right, but the duty to "concern" themselves with the fatherland.[2] She developed this theme further, by demanding an education for all women to prepare them for their responsibilities.[3] Both German and Jewish feminists repeated this refrain, adding that they were not selfishly demanding their rights, they were politely fulfilling their obligations.

Louise Otto and Auguste Schmidt founded the General German Women's Association (Allgemeiner Deutscher Frauenverein) in 1865. This was the nucleus of the bourgeois women's movement. It concentrated upon furthering the economic independence of women.[4] The social conditions which led women to demand jobs can only be sketched here. Feminists pointed out that industrialization made the upkeep of the household a less cumbersome task, thus depriving unmarried female family members of work. An imbalance in the sex ratio, what Germans called a "surplus of women" (*Frauenüberschuss*), made spinsterhood—and an impoverished one at that—inevitable for many middle-class women. Employment was their only salvation.[5] To allay fears of a female revolution, Otto reassured men that "the only emancipation which we demand for our women is the emancipation of their work."[6] This temperance was both tactical and genuine. These women sought to mollify male hostility, which expressed itself vociferously in journals, books, and organizations. In 1884, for example, the Conservative Party stated that women, with very few exceptions, were unable to teach.[7] In 1912, the Federation to Combat the Emancipaton of Women insisted that careers for women would destroy matrimony and that suffrage would bring about the denaturing of women. Even men who favored women's education warned that "no matter how much a woman may be mentally emancipated, she must not overstep the bounds of womanliness": her role was that of housewife and mother.[8] The leaders of the women's movement had accepted the values of their patriarchal society and were inclined to adopt this advice: they were not asking to replace men. In fact, few regarded men with the same hostility that they experienced from men.

In 1866, a second organization favoring women's employment was founded by Dr. Adolf Lette, with the aid of Crown Princess Victoria of Prussia. In an era in which, according to a Prussian census, approximately two million women had no means of earning a livelihood, the Lette Society supported a purely vocational movement to help unmarried, middle-class women. Traditionally, these women could only become governesses or seamstresses. The Lette institutes taught new occupations, including nursing, midwifery, engraving, pattern-making, telegraph operations, bookkeeping, and library skills. Most of these occupations were seen by Lette as extensions of women's motherly or housewifely functions, and he emphasized: "What we do *not* want, and never, even in the most distant centuries, wish nor aim for, is emancipation and equal rights for women."[9] Despite its patronizing approach, the Lette Society helped the feminist cause. It taught thousands of women skills and provided them with economic independence. Later, feminists would insist that this economic self-sufficiency made women ready for political independence, too.

A third major force in furthering German feminism and shaping its attitudes was the advent of the kindergarten. In the 1840s, Friedrich Fröbel conceived a radical approach to child development: play with instructive objects would lead to children's intellectual growth. Instead of receiving immediate, serious instruction, young boys *and* girls could grow naturally in his "garden for children." Conservatives looked askance at the substitution of play for drill, suspected that the institution of the family was threatened by the earlier removal of the child from parental tutelage, and distrusted the liberals and democrats who flocked to Fröbel's cause.[10] The women's movement, on the other hand, benefited from Fröbel's belief in the equal education of the sexes, and from his opinion that women's maternal instincts were ideally suited to the teaching profession. Responding eagerly to Fröbel's encouragement, young women entered teacher-training seminars, only to be stymied by the Prussian government. Labeling kindergartens as centers of socialism, atheism, and other types of destructive progressivism, it banned them in 1851.[11] After years of agitation and an increase in the numbers of needy spinsters among middle-class women, Prussia repealed the Anti-Kindergarten Law in the 1860s. Feminists popularized the kindergarten. Lina Morgenstern, who as the daughter of a wealthy Jewish family had become involved in social work, founded the first kindergarten association in Germany in 1859.[12] The mother of five and a board member of the General German Women's Association, she also served as the president of the kindergarten association and was responsible for establishing the first kindergartens in Berlin and the first institute for kindergarten teachers. In Leipzig, Henriette Goldschmidt, another elected official of the General German Women's Association, founded kindergartens and training centers for teachers and organized the Society for Familial and Popular Education to further Fröbel's teachings.[13] Like other feminists, she realized kindergartens were a boon to female employment and education. The wife of a rabbi, Goldschmidt left the dominant beliefs about women's roles intact. She fought for the establishment of the first girls' high school, but insisted that it be aimed consciously at the needs of women.[14] Like Fröbel, she believed these needs stemmed from women's motherly inclinations.[15] Yet she insisted that women join all aspects of German life and demanded the vote, higher education, and public posts for them.[16] She considered her demands to be "rights," but argued that these rights were not ends in themselves. They were means to an end— the participation of women in a "culture of humanity."[17]

Economic and demographic conditions were essential to the growth of the women's movement. For middle-class women, household chores were made less arduous by nineteenth-century inventions. Sewing machines (first used in Germany in the 1850s), incandescent lamps (1879), and gas lamps (1885) simplified the traditional tasks of women. By the 1890s, gas stoves and ovens could be found in most bourgeois homes.[18] Ready-made clothing, available in the 1840s, was widely purchased by the 1850s. Increasingly, toward the end of the nineteenth century, spinning, weaving, gardening, soap making, candle making, butchering, smoking, canning, and even baking were done outside the home. Urbanization also limited homemaking tasks. It was easier to care for smaller city residences. City homes lacked large gardens for planting vegetables and flowers and did not have storage room for preserves and other foods that were prepared in advance. Thus women were increasingly compelled to rely on store-bought products. Finally, the rising standard of living among the bourgeoisie in Wilhelminian Germany resulted in later marriages and fewer offspring. Thus, more women had the time to join organizations and a small but energetic number supported feminist causes.

In the 1870s and 1880s propagandists for women's rights maintained the restraint of the earlier associations. In 1870, Jenny Hirsch, a member of the Lette Society, but also a "closet-feminist," translated *On the Subjection of Women* by John Stuart Mill. This book, published in 1869, denounced the myriad discriminations suffered by the female sex, and Mill's liberalism offered some German women a philosophical rationale to accompany their economic demands. It was German liberalism, however, which provided German feminism with its basic philosophical underpinnings. Like the male-dominated liberal movement, feminists emphasized the necessity of earning equality rather than being accorded it as a natural right. Following their male counterparts, feminists accepted a corporately oriented definition of freedom which stressed duties rather than liberties, and which displayed an overriding concern with the national well-being. This resulted from the "peculiar speed" of German industrializaton, which allowed little time for an individualized society to develop between an era of corporatism and collective, large-scale organization.[19] It also reflected the German bourgeoisie's privileged position, and its consequent unwillingness to challenge the status quo head on. Furthermore, the "political reality of the authoritarian state"[20] forced feminists to emphasize "safe" issues, such as education, rather than provoke government repression.

This was in stark contrast to English and American feminists whose demand for equal rights focused on a struggle for the vote. Their emphasis on political improvements stemmed from a previous historical tradition (and, in the American case, from the antislavery campaign) and they attempted to persuade governments which were already representative and liberal to respond to the needs of the disenfranchised. In Germany, military, dynastic, agrarian, and bureaucratic elements from the old order dominated the most important positions of power in the petty states of the Germanic Confederation and in the German Empire. Bismarck's personal dictatorship and the paternalistic policies which bolstered his rule made political change far less likely to succeed than demands for educational or occupational opportunities. Furthermore, female suffrage was an issue which could hardly inspire great enthusiasm, even among women, in a nation where the question of preservation or reform of the discriminatory and undemocratic Prussian three-class franchise was a major issue of internal politics. One of the earliest historians of the German women's movement concluded that:

. . . woman suffrage as such has always aroused less enthusiasm in Germany than in any of the countries having an organized women's movement. The existence of popular governments has pushed the matter to the fore in England and America. In Germany, the vote has had little significance, even for the men, and political interests have yielded first place to social and economic problems.[21]

Finally, German governments enforced discriminatory laws (*Vereins-gesetze*) against the participation of women (and minors) in political organizations. Such laws of associations, instituted by Prussia and many other states in the mid-nineteenth century, made it illegal for women to engage actively in politics. Thus, until 1908, when a unified Imperial Law of Association finally permitted women's participation, German women's political activities were limited to the states of Baden and Württemberg and to the cities of Hamburg and Bremen. Even in Hamburg, the German Association for Women Suffrage (1902) first demanded educational reforms and the aboli-tion of the laws of association and assembly rather than the vote.

Ironically, American and English antifeminists always accused the suffragists of using the vote as a cloak for wide-ranging reforms in women's status, while in Germany, irate males insisted that behind the cry for educational and social reforms lurked the real goal of feminists—the vote![22] Both sets of critics, actually, were justified in their suspicions. Though their strategies differed, the ultimate aim of German as well as American and English feminists included a general expansion of the rights and welfare of women.

In 1894, some members of the General German Women's Associ-ation initiated the formation of an umbrella organization of feminist groups, the Bund Deutscher Frauenvereine (Federation of German Women's Associations). The BDF grew to be the strongest force in middle-class German feminism. It sought to secure higher education for women and to place them in social service jobs; to assist work-ing mothers by establishing day care centers; to help working women by obtaining better hours and working conditions; to improve public health and fight lax sexual morality.[23] Only in 1902 did the BDF begin to consider the cause of women's suffrage—it did not demand it officially until 1907, anticipating the end of the *Vereins-gesetz*. During World War I, feminists left the suffrage question in abeyance. Prepared to continue their struggle for gradual enfran-chisement, they were the startled beneficiaries of the revolutionary wave that engulfed Germany at the end of the war. They rejoiced over the vote that had "fallen in our laps," a vote that was a result of the revolutionary uprisings far more than the women's suffrage movement or women's wartime work.[24]

Helene Lange was the main theoretician of the Bund Deutscher Frauenvereine. Her ideas provided a common basis for much of German and Jewish feminism. She accepted, as her predecessors had, the view that women ought to contribute to the German state and culture rather than selfishly to demand equality. Also, she perpetuated the conventional notion that motherhood was the destiny of women, a cliché that went unchallenged in socialist feminist circles as well. In her first essay, "What We Want," she declared: "Motherhood is the most important career, because it includes the profession of educator of future generations."[25] The cult of motherhood applied to all women regardless of their marital status: for those who could not fulfill their domestic destiny, Lange suggested educational and social work, both of which she perceived as extensions of women's natural child-rearing functions. (This characterization of women reached an extreme during and shortly after World War I, when speakers—German and Jewish, bourgeois and socialist—emphasized that women were by nature against war, because they bore life. Such sentimentality preceded pro-war and pacifist lectures alike.[26]) Lange suggested that the increasing leisure of middle-class women freed them to lend a harmonious balance to male politics. She believed that women complemented masculine enterprise, boldness, and intellect. Her demands were always couched in terms of how women could complete the regime established by men, rather than in terms of women's rights. Also, she used economic arguments to bolster her cause. Economic necessity had created the German women's movement, and German women's contribution to the economy justified their desire for equality.

The only German woman who had the audacity as early as 1876 to engage in the unladylike behavior of demanding equality as a matter of simple justice was Hedwig Dohm. The militant Dohm refused to argue that women should be educated to help humanity. Instead, she shocked contemporaries by insisting: "Woman ought to study, because she wants to study, because the unhindered choice of a vocation is a main factor of individual liberty, of individual happiness."[27] A small, vocal group of radical feminists maintained the Dohm tradition, adopting more advanced ideas than those who followed Lange.[28] They enjoyed a brief heyday between 1898 and

1908, but the more conservative elements finally won control of the Bund Deutscher Frauenvereine. The radicals were pacifists, while the moderates were nationalistic; the former were influenced by a liberal individualism, whereas moderates favored a collectivist approach, stressing the importance of women to society; and both camps disagreed over women's rights and relationship to their own bodies. The radicals supported the *Mutterschutz* (protection of mothers) movement which advocated homes for unwed mothers, the dissemination of contraceptive information, legalized abortions, and the abolition of state regulation of prostitution on the basis of the indignity such regulation foisted upon women. Further, radicals criticized marriage and attacked the double standard without denying female sexuality. Moderates took a far more traditional stance. While supporting abolition, they linked all such issues with women's destiny as mothers. Finally, radicals wanted the women's organization to launch vigorous propaganda campaigns to enlarge women's rights and sought thorough reforms of the political and social systems, while moderates did not comment on general political issues and preferred to avoid public campaigns.

Socialist feminists, too, differed from the mainstream women's movement in their emphasis on sweeping change rather than sex-specific reforms. In 1894, socialist and middle-class women had parted ways. Lily Braun, a socialist spokeswoman, blamed the BDF's bourgeois narrowness for the split. Helene Lange argued that working women's clubs were invited to join, but that socialist organizations were legally barred because the Prussian Law on Associations forbade women from participating in "political" clubs. Socialist clubs would have given the BDF a "political" complexion and subjected it to legal problems. Probably class interests and loyalties, far more than legal impediments, dictated the split. Despite their revolutionary political and economic analysis and vision, socialist feminists, much like Lange, were influenced by an idealist-romantic tradition which regarded women as fundamentally different from men. Because they were not identical to men, women had unique contributions to add to society. And, as in the case of their middle-class sisters, they argued in collectivist terms: Clara Zetkin, one of the principal socialist theoreticians on the woman question, assured her male colleagues that she demanded rights for women not for selfish reasons, but "in the interest of the working class."[29]

The means that Lange and her associates chose to achieve their goals were timid in comparison to those of their English and American counterparts. The former renounced political agitation, opting for unobtrusive methods. They petitioned their government for changes in the status of women, published political handbooks for women, and educated women who did not belong to their organization about the goals of feminism. Organizers such as Helene Lange and Gertrud Bäumer were very proper bourgeois ladies who eschewed all radicalism. While a minority decried how "infinitely gentle and, unfortunately, so infinitely patient" German women were, Lange believed that "agitation" meant sacrificing real accomplishments for a lot of noise.[30] The moderation of the German movement, its attempt to gain power by working through accepted channels, was a legacy it left to its Jewish sisters.

Jewish women experienced both the inequalities from which German women suffered and the effects of Judaism's cultural and religious prejudices against women. The position of women in the Jewish faith rested upon an ancient role differentiation in which the characteristics of strength, initiative and intelligence were ascribed to men, while women were regarded as inherently close to the physical, material world, and were held responsible for the moral development of the family.[31] The highly esteemed activities of prayer, study, and the regulation of the Jewish community were male monopolies. While women did work outside the home in the late Middle Ages and the early modern period, they were expected, above all, to fulfill their natural, maternal roles. Many of these same attitudes were still commonplace among nineteenth and twentieth-century German Jews. Most Jewish women accepted the dictates of their patriarchal culture, performing their duties in the confines of the home.

One of the only forms of outside activity traditionally permitted women was religious charity work. In the nineteenth century Jewish women took part in the primitive social services of the Jewish community. Their activities, inspired and limited by religious customs, focused on poor relief and participation in burial societies (*Chevra Kadisha*). Women cared for the poor and made donations in money or in kind. Some provided the needy with rent money, others brought coal, bread, potatoes, wine, and milk, and still others gathered dowries for brides. Women also donated old clothing or sewed new garments for the indigent. Many societies maintained special holiday funds to supply poor families with ritual foods—for example, matzoth for Passover—and poor children with Purim gifts. Members of burial societies sewed shrouds and washed and dressed deceased women. They watched over the bodies before interment and offered aid and solace to the bereaved family.[32]

By the end of the nineteenth century, as their consciousness developed, some Jewish women began to demand greater control over their own lives. Many resented male-led women's charities. A Frauenbund member recalled her brief association with one such group: "The women sat quietly, while the male chairman read the annual report. Then they were allowed to nod their approval."[33] Women who joined the Frauenbund were also unhappy with coffee klatches, sewing circles, and the aimlessness (*Vereinsspielerei*) of existing clubs. The JFB gave them a sense of independence and purpose, as can be seen from the following testimony:

I too belonged to the large mass of women who did not have the faintest idea of what to do. I was a young woman from a religious family. My father had been a Liberal rabbi, my husband was active in the Jewish community. I had a deep desire to do something, but I did not know what. And I was afraid to open my mouth. In those days only men spoke up in the Jewish community, and women were more or less relegated to the house and family. Then Bertha Pappenheim . . . taught us through practical examples that women had as much right to be heard as men . . . she awakened our interest in Jewish social work.[34]

The JFB initiated woman-oriented and woman-defined projects, while respecting its members' religious orientation. It always remained aware of its "Jewish" (as opposed to a primarily feminist) base of support, carefully couching feminist demands in terms which would appeal to a traditional following. Its leaders, religious (although not Orthodox) Jews themselves, always connected the eradication of women's inequality with the reconstruction of Jewish society.

The Frauenbund derived aspects of its organizational structure, program, and attitudes from the Bund Deutscher Frauenvereine.

The rhetoric of the German movement glorifying the innate differences between man and woman appealed particularly to Jewish
women who had been brought up in this tradition. The JFB's earliest
statutes promised to amalgamate the goals of the German movement
with the moral and religious beliefs of Judaism. Its efforts to achieve
suffrage and educate girls came from similar concerns within the
German movement, and its concern for unwed mothers and prostitutes was an inheritance from the more radical feminist contingent.
They were unique only in their Jewish context.

THE PRIMACY OF MOTHERHOOD

The Frauenbund shared many of the prevailing bourgeois attitudes toward the reproductive sphere. Most Germans before the
war praised marriage, extolled motherhood, and linked sexuality
with reproduction, instead of acknowledging it as vital and natural
in itself. Even Social Democrats such as Lassalle, Wilhelm Lieb-
knecht, and Bebel, in spite of their attacks on traditional sexual
morality and marriage, voiced generally repressive sexual attitudes.
They regarded contraception as "offensive," "immoral," and "un-
natural" and encouraged their supporters to find an answer to the
sexual drive by marrying.[35] After the war, radical feminists, socialists, and communists openly supported birth control and abortion.
The former had become available during the Empire. The Com-
munist Party demanded the abolition of all laws which criminalized
abortion[36] and regulated personal sexual behavior, and called for
public sex education bolstered by public financing of contraception
and abortion.[37] Its slogan, "Your body belongs to you," appealed
to proletarian as well as some bourgeois women, but the mainstream
of German feminism as well as some leading socialist feminists
remained aloof from or hostile to the pro-abortion forces. Many
bourgeois feminists, in fact, considered birth control to be the lesser
of two evils. In 1928, the answer to unwanted pregnancies was still,
according to Agnes von Zahn-Harnack, president of the Bund
Deutscher Frauenvereine, "the education of our people to a restrained
sexuality." Clara Zetkin, too, refused to accept birth control or
abortion. Emphasizing the good of the whole over that of the individual, she argued that the solution to working-class women's
oppression was a redistribution of wealth, not family limitation.

The socialist leader saw birth control as an easy answer for egotists and those duped by Malthusian assumptions.[38]

From its founding until the Nazi years, Jewish women were continually exhorted by Frauenbund leaders to raise larger families. Mothers were "above all the educators of future generations"[39]; thus, the first responsibility of Jewish women was to bear children. The Frauenbund objected to birth control on religious grounds, although it clearly recognized its widespread use among Jews both before and after the war. Its newsletter and official statements opposed abortion. However, it did invite members to debate the subject during its 1930 summer school session.[40] Pappenheim (who objected to contraception as well) argued against the termination of pregnancy, while another JFB leader, a doctor, spoke in its favor. Linking sexuality to motherhood addressed a practical and pressing problem with which the JFB was acutely familiar, the decline in Jewish fertility. Between 1881 and 1909 the number of yearly births among Jews had dropped from 10,269 to 7,123.[41] The Jewish birth rate was equivalent to half the German one, which was also on the decline.[42] Although the Jewish birth rate approximately equaled that of the urban commercial bourgeoisie, Jews had fewer large families (five children or more).[43] Before 1907 the majority of Jews who married limited their families to one or two children, whereas the "two-child system" had made few inroads into German society.[44]

The topic of the declining birth rate made feminist organizations uncomfortably defensive, since male demographers and sociologists frequently pointed to the women's movement as the cause of the "birth strike." In 1918, in fact, a Reichstag committee report attributed the decline in births to women's "selfish wishes, . . . conceit, love of pleasure, aversion to domestic restrictions, . . . exaggerated concern about damage to their health."[45] Both German and Jewish feminists denied such charges and proved them inaccurate.[46] The real reasons for declining fertility had far more to do with a desire by couples to maintain their economic status, a decrease in religiosity, and an increased knowledge of birth control.[47] Yet, the pronatalism of these sister movements probably derived as much from concern for the vitality of their respective communities[48] as from the attacks upon feminism by those in favor of population growth.

The Frauenbund rarely alluded to sexuality, and when it did, such discussions were preceded by quotes from the Bible, references to Jewish sexual ethics, or reminders of the need to continue Judaism through offspring.[49] During the war, the Frauenbund sent leaflets to Jewish soldiers entitled "Be Holy!" They were told that intercourse was intended to produce life and that this "highest duty" was only allowed within marriage.[50] The JFB also published literature for German-Jewish youth which declared that Jewish ethics made them guardians of their instincts and lusts.[51] Within marriage, the JFB again tied sex to childbirth. Avoiding acknowledgment of the importance of human sexuality, the JFB actually departed from Jewish tradition which stressed the duty of procreation but also accepted female sexuality, even holding the husband responsible for his wife's sexual satisfaction. The husband's obligations to his wife were food, clothing, and sexual rights. Jewish law even stipulated how many times a week a husband had to have intercourse with his wife. The scholar, for example, had to satisfy his wife less often than the man of leisure. However, the husband had to be alert to his wife's desires beyond the minimum requirements in order to fulfill the *mitzvah* of domestic peace. His *duty* was to insure a peaceful home and to procreate, while his wife had a *right* to sex. This, then, was the opposite of the Victorian notion of marital sex as the husband's right and the wife's duty.[52] Thus, the JFB's position echoed much more the Victorian heritage of German Jews as well as a puritanical strain in German Protestantism and in German feminism. Helene Lange had also brushed aside the intrinsic importance of sexuality in her opposition to birth control: "People who do not want children should abstain from what produces them."[53]

The Frauenbund neither acknowledged any contradiction in its views on motherhood and feminism nor addressed the conflict between emancipation and increased fertility. It recognized that women were individuals who uniquely straddled public and private worlds. And, despite its desire for the participation of women in the public sphere, the private sphere held higher priority: women were wives and mothers first. Still, Jewish women were expected to take an interest in social work, communal politics, and careers. By stressing reproduction while encouraging careers and public activism, the JFB, as well as its German counterpart, assumed that women could take on a "double burden" (*Doppelbelastung*) which earlier feminists had recognized and rejected as too difficult a task.

Despite modern technology and occasional household help, the combined responsibilities of career, volunteer work, home, and hearth were—and are still—formidable, demanding exceedingly difficult physical and emotional commitments. Yet, the Frauenbund insisted that if women were more efficient, they could maintain the superior standards of the German *Hausfrau*, nurture their offspring, and find time for volunteer work or a career. Such a synthesis of the reproductive and productive spheres required "superwomen" who would juggle childbearing, childrearing, and the household while pursuing outside activities with energy and ambition. This may, unfortunately, have been the only real option available to women at the time (or, for that matter, for many women even today). No feminist organization then could have asked that men share the "natural" duties for which women were "intended." Nor, were feminists willing to accept a trade-off between family and career. Neither bourgeois feminists—or for that matter, socialists or communists—challenged the existing institution of the family in favor of collective or communal solutions to their dilemma. Jewish feminists, in particular, clung to the notion of the family. They suggested that the family was more important to an itinerant people, forced to move from country to country, with no history of permanence or belonging. Placed in a foreign culture, amidst different religions, the family provided roots and security to Jews.[54] Thus, the family was considered the very cornerstone of Judaism and women's emancipation could not come at its expense. Furthermore, the celebration of the family in Judaism—and in the JFB—helped Jewish housewives to rationalize their membership in an organization which encouraged younger women to embark on careers while they remained at home.

Jewish feminists (like their German sisters) placed further responsibilities on women by cultivating the Victorian idea of women as guardians of social and cultural values, "the mothers of civilization."[55] By exalting and perpetuating an image of themselves as transmitters of culture, and therefore, guardians of Judaism, the JFB accepted an awesome assignment for women. Yet, anything short of this would have been inconsistent with the upbringing of German-Jewish women and with their lives. In fact, this "solution" may have been the most rational response available to Jewish feminists at the time. They accepted and were trapped by the dominant ideology in which women were "educators." But, to some extent, they were also protected by this stereotype. In an age of disintegration, the traditional role of "culture bearer" may have been a means to preserve the respected position of women in the Jewish family and, thus, to secure future marriages for Jewish women (threatened by increasing rates of male intermarriage) and to open the public sphere to them.

SOCIAL MOTHERHOOD

Although the JFB and BDF shared the rhetoric of domesticity, their emphasis was different. German women stressed educational and career interests, whereas Jewish women were concerned primarily with social work. The JFB invoked "home and motherhood" to justify its concern with child welfare, unwed mothers, and the protection and education of girls. Its members were what William O'Neill, in his essay, "Feminism as a Radical Ideology," has called "social feminists," women who placed social reform above strictly feminist goals.[56]

The JFB was convinced that women's primal instincts to protect their young endowed them with special qualities for social work: while men fought for fame and power, women's natural compassion and love of humanity engaged them in a battle for social progress. Jewish feminists considered social work to be a form of "social motherhood."[57] Because the care of children—not just one's own— was a natural responsibility, the JFB appealed to women's maternal sentiments in its efforts to support orphanages, care for foster children, and help unwed mothers. Jewish feminists used exaggerated maternal rhetoric in their attempt to make "the consciences of mothers a pivotal factor in community life."[58] As late as 1934, the last leader of the JFB wrote: "Mothers, the carriers of life are called upon to protect . . . life . . . The united will of mothers is a force which . . . is capable of changing the ideas of the world."[59]

Social motherhood developed into social housekeeping.[60] It was women's "duty" to extend their salutary influence beyond their homes. The JFB proudly demanded a role in "the household management" of social welfare.[61] It was dissatisfied with women's limited functions as volunteer social workers and insisted that they participate on the decision-making boards of Jewish welfare organizations. Social work for women became one of the principal justifications for the JFB's feminism and was what many members admired about their movement. In fact, the JFB sometimes lost track of its feminism while it absorbed itself in social work. Such feminism clearly suffered from activities which drained off personnel from more political goals and caused ideological confusion, but it attracted members who might have been repelled by a single-mindedly feminist program. The attempt to prove that women should be granted full citizenship by stressing their social duties and maternal natures found the Frauenbund often more concerned with social efforts than with abstract rights. The latter, they believed, would follow from the services women rendered.

The care with which the Frauenbund articulated its goals was—like its devotion to social work and its choice of feminist issues—tactically deliberate, born of a position of weakness. Its language was a form of "subtle subversion," that is, a means to attain equality without alienating potential support.[62] Like German feminists, the JFB used maternal arguments to court public opinion and allay hostility. It suggested that the fulfillment of women's responsibilities to the *Gemeinde* merited and necessitated full citizenship. Thus, even this "right to vote" had the quality of a reward for good behavior attached to it. This "ladylike" approach was a necessary strategy because a strong conservatism regarding women's emancipation existed in the Jewish community. With very few exceptions, the rabbinical establishment was hostile or indifferent to the demands of women. Other Jewish males were only slightly less antagonistic than rabbis. They assured themselves that Jewish feminists had individual psychological problems and suffered from a group inferiority complex. One writer explained feminism as an attempt by a strange "type" of woman to lose her "will" in a mass movement.[63] Long after suffrage for women was an established fact in Germany, some Jewish men still assumed that women's demands were the fantasy or sport of a few individuals who had no other concerns. One admitted that women were "crassly" discriminated against in Judaism and suggested that this was a cause of the self-hatred which found its outlet in feminism and social work.[64] Finally, many Jewish women were also conservative, and the Frauenbund had to modify its arguments to appeal to new adherents. Even some of the leaders of the JFB retained surprisingly traditional self-images. When Ernestine Eschelbacher, a leader of the JFB for many years and the mother of five children, was hailed as a suffragist, she responded sharply that she was most certainly not, she was a rabbi's wife.[65] The JFB defended itself against the title "emancipated," which was used as an epithet in Germany.[66] As late as 1926, a JFB spokeswoman declared:

. . . we are not the so-called emancipated women, . . . We definitely do not want to be quasi-men and do not want to compete with men or displace them. On the contrary, we want to remain particularly womanly, particularly feminine women. We want to carry softness, warmth, love, and motherliness into life wherever we can.[67]

In all likelihood, JFB members were too imbued with such traditionalism to exploit it cynically. Yet, it is also obvious that they used traditionally ascribed attributes such as women's maternal solicitude in order to squeeze past the boundaries of a passive, private life and emerge into an active, public one. In private, JFB leaders reminded each other that "those who serve, really control."[68]

ATTEMPTS TO RAISE WOMEN'S CONSCIOUSNESS AND SELF-IMAGE

Despite the traditionalism of its philosophy, the Frauenbund sought to arouse a feminist consciousness and a feeling of female solidarity among Jewish women. The Frauenbund considered itself more than just a league of women, it was a "bond between women."[69] When Ottilie Schönewald was forced to disband the JFB, her farewell letter to her "sisters" expressed a sentiment that no doubt was shared by Frauenbund members of her generation and earlier: She was grateful to have participated in the JFB, which was not merely an organization, she wrote, but a "collective life [*Lebensgemeinschaft*] in which we were all united."[70] This sense of shared sisterhood may have been due to the fact that they all participated in what they considered an important movement, and (to some extent) an opposition one, in confrontation with the Jewish male establishment. Also, since these women did not have many outside interests (such as careers or jobs) and their children were grown, it is likely that the Frauenbund meant more to them than an analogous organization would have meant to men.

The JFB's leaders hoped to "awaken the forces that sleep in our women," and promised not to rest until "every community acknowledged and respected women's individual and collective effectiveness."[71] In their attempt to raise women's consciousness and appear nonradical at the same time, they often depicted a rosier version of women's state of progress than was accurate. In 1929, the JFB's newsletter proclaimed: ". . . today's . . . women have one immeasurable advantage . . . their life is free, not only of countless external prejudices, but of those which were part of their own feelings and beliefs. . . . The conscience of woman, freed from thousands of years of oppression, has become her own."[72] Certainly, the lot of women had improved in comparison to the mid-nineteenth century. Yet, overt discrimination existed against women in every area. Although the Frauenbund admitted that women had a long way to go, it preferred to emphasize the distance women had come, and hesitated to take a stand against all forms of discrimination. In fact, during the depression years it reluctantly accepted some economic discrimination, arguing that married men who supported families should be given more lucrative jobs than unmarried males or females. It asserted, however, that unmarried wage earners— male or female—should be treated equally and that the insidious myth that women could live on less money than men simply gave employers an excuse for paying women less for the same work.[73]

The JFB preferred the relatively safe path of raising women's consciousness of the public domain through their participation in a large movement. Leaders spoke of a "feeling of strength which arose from a community of women."[74] The Frauenbund maintained that women felt naturally close to each other, because they all shared similar physical and psychological feelings regarding birth and nurturing.[75] This sisterhood should be used to improve women's status and to alleviate problems which particularly affected women. For example, the Frauenbund encouraged women to lobby for suffrage and to support all measures which helped women. It never suggested an all-women's party, because it expected female representatives to support women's interests despite party affiliations.[76]

It also assumed female participation in all parties would lessen political acrimony. It did attempt to raise women's political consciousness by urging them to study political issues and (after 1918) to vote. But it insisted on its own German and Jewish political neutrality and ignored—or avoided—political issues. Several observations may explain this behavior. First, the JFB was formed in an era in which there were serious restrictions on women's political activities. Thus, it turned to social work as a way of improving women's lot and attracted followers who were primarily interested in welfare issues. After women were permitted to engage in politics, the JFB's members may have considered politics other than feminism a diversion from their concerns with women's welfare work. Second, since politics had been a male domain, even women who demanded participation may have felt uncomfortable with actual political involvement. Of the two generations which made up the JFB, only a tiny handful—often those trained in organizing and public speaking by a women's movement—were active in German or Jewish politics. Finally, the JFB's reluctance to invite political discussion was due to its fear of splitting feminist ranks. While most of its members—like most German Jews—belonged to a democratic party, there were some socialists among them. Yet, there is no evidence of political debates or discussions. And, only in the postwar years, when the Frauenbund, like many German-Jewish organizations, recognized that Jewish nationalism could no longer be ignored, did it encourage an "even-handed" debate between Zionists and non-Zionists. Emphatically, it reminded all participants of the need for "feminine conciliation."

Besides promoting a nonpartisan sisterhood to help improve conditions for women, the JFB also attempted to encourage a sense of female solidarity between married and unmarried women. It suggested that both groups could help each other. Married women who cared about reforming marriage laws needed the advice of women lawyers and politicians, who were frequently single. The former were also concerned about careers for their daughters and, sometimes, for themselves. The Frauenbund claimed that single women could learn home management from their married friends, and unmarried teachers shared a common involvement in child-rearing with married women. Feminists hoped that both groups would fight the prejudice against single women which, the JFB argued, was particularly intense among Jews who respected married men above married women, and wives who bore children above childless wives and unmarried women.[77] The Frauenbund insisted that marriage was not the only possibility for women; in fact, it was statistically impossible for some.[78] These women could still perform motherly tasks for the community. It is doubtful whether the JFB would have supported women who scorned marriage or who denied their "natural, motherly inclinations." With the exception of a few notable single women like Pappenheim, Hannah Karminski, and Cora Berliner, attempts to attract single women to the JFB before 1933 were generally unsuccessful. The JFB's glorification of motherhood probably doomed such efforts. Only after the advent of Hitler, when their professional organizations were aryanized, did single women turn to the Frauenbund.

The JFB tried to raise women's consciousness regarding their married state. It should be remembered that the Frauenbund consisted of members who had reached maturity before or shortly after World War I. While they were aware of the changes that affected women and were supportive of a greater role for women in the economy and society, they had been brought up to be—and most were—traditional housewives. Their progressive outlook regarding the new generation of women could not be matched by their relationship with their own spouses. Both German and Jewish culture reinforced the idea that women should be subservient to their husbands. In the Jewish tradition, the wife who was independent, self-assertive, and strong exhibited negative qualities. It was better to be submissive like Eve, who let Adam "rule over her" (Genesis 3:16), than aggressive like Lilith, Adam's legendary first wife who was punished for abandoning him.[79] The Jewish wedding ceremony was symbolic of the role each partner adopted: the groom took his wife, while she remained passive. German tradition was no less patriarchal. An Englishwoman visiting Germany in the first half of the twentieth century remarked on the tidy, thrifty, responsible *Hausfrau*, and then commented that German women

. . . have always been devoted to their homes and their families, and they are as subservient to their menfolk as the Japanese. They do not actually fall on their knees before their lords, but the tone of voice in which a woman . . . speaks of *die Herren* is enough to make a French, and American or Englishwoman think there is something to be said for the modern revolt against men.[80]

Despite the fact that its members maintained traditional marriages—even the last president of the JFB, an exceedingly energetic and active woman, was "thankful" that her husband was so understanding as to approve of her functions outside the home—the Frauenbund, by the late 1920s, began to discuss the companionate marriage, which implied a relationship between equals rather than between a subordinate and her superior. Speakers assured their listeners, however, that this was still a bourgeois idea. Husbands and wives still "belonged" to each other and sought secure, steady home lives, but they viewed each other as partners.[81] Frauenbund lecturers frequently discussed the history of the family, explaining that the roles of individual family members had evolved and would continue to change.[82] In these years the JFB newsletter presented new, often American, ideas on marriage in order to broaden the perspectives of Jewish women. At this time the JFB also became aware of new experiments in "trial" marriages. It condemned these, because it believed marriage, the "spiritual and physical union of man and woman," should lead to childbirth, and such temporary arrangements led to birth control or illegitimacy. The JFB was also concerned with women's future security. This was probably because of the traditional suspicion that in such relationships it was men who always left women, and because an abandoned woman (who had lost her virtue) might have difficulties finding a mate (who could presumably have his pick of the "surplus" of chaste young maidens). Interestingly, the JFB was concerned that both partners in a trial marriage might wind up "prostituting" themselves to each other, because neither had any security.[83] It never drew the same analogy to an unhappy marriage, a point made by other feminists.

The Frauenbund also supported German feminists' efforts to revise marriage laws. It recognized that women had become more independent due to higher education and careers, but that marriage remained an autocratic institution in which husbands could legally dominate their wives and children. But, while the JFB national leadership strongly supported German feminists, it assured members that: "Even if the law stresses equality, those who prefer hierarchical arrangements can continue privately, but at least a woman has her majority if her husband loses her trust."[84] Although it lauded the institution of marriage, the JFB called on women's solidarity to defend the rights of all mothers, even the unwed.[85] This was perhaps its most radical challenge to the norms of its community.

Its educational program was one of its most effective contributions to the cause of feminism. Local and regional associations offered lectures and summer school courses on such topics of contemporary concern as: women and politics, careers for women, women and the law, childrearing, abortion, and Jewish women in German social work.[86] In the 1930s (before and during the Nazi years), the JFB national ran a summer school which divided its offerings between Jewish and feminist topics. Because most of its members were middle-aged, the JFB's message was not to suggest that they enter careers, but to encourage them to be more than "just" housewives. Although the Frauenbund respected the job of housewife, even attempting to raise it to the status of a profession, it insisted that housewives rationalize their work and devote their extra time to their community. The Frauenbund's educational program attempted to "boost women's morale."[87] It demanded intellectual and spiritual equality for women. Its attitude toward motherhood also displayed concern for the mother's overall well-being. It encouraged women to maintain other interests, asserting that those who put their entire efforts into motherhood made their offspring too dependent: "The result is that children will hang onto their mother until she becomes the helpless one and switches roles with them."[88] Women who found added fulfillment beyond the home and whose self-image was thus not entirely that of a mother, would suffer less during menopause, according to articles reprinted in the JFB's newsletter. The Frauenbund challenged what it called "old wives' tales" about women's bodily functions.[89] It considered the problems of menopause to be due less to particular physical changes than to the attitudes perpetrated upon women by a male-dominated society which considered only those women who could bear children to be of any importance. The Frauenbund suggested that the later years allowed women more freedom to be creative in new ways, and it reminded women that men, too, went through changes in mid-life.

The JFB tried to make women proud of the accomplishments of their sex. In 1913, its members planned a "Jewish Women's Book" which would describe the literary, artistic, and scientific achievements of Jewish women.[90] Rather than confine themselves to reporting on a small elite which was already in the limelight, they hoped to ascertain what unknown Jewish women were doing. The JFB's newsletter frequently printed articles on early Jewish feminists, on historically prominent Jewesses, and on contemporary female artists and literary figures. It regularly carried book reviews and articles with materials intended to raise women's consciousness. Works by German feminists were discussed, and the Frauenbund showed particular interest in authors who "wrote for us," like the Jewish poet Frieda Mehler. Her collections praised motherhood and viewed women as strong and supportive.[91] The JFB also suggested that women analyze the Bible and Talmud from a woman's perspective in order to combat male interpretations.[92] This was a favorite theme of Pappenheim, who believed that men had an advantageous position in society because they made and interpreted the laws.

THE CONTRADICTIONS OF "JEWISH FEMINISM"
AND THE LIMITS OF SISTERHOOD

The Frauenbund's endeavor to reform Jewish society while conserving its religious foundations was difficult and contradictory. Despite Frauenbund rhetoric, Judaism and feminism most often stood in opposition to one another. Those Jews who shared the JFB's strongly held religious identity were often inveterate foes of feminism. Spokesmen for the religion refused to revise the legal position of women in Judaism, and the Jewish religious and communal establishment ignored the demand for women's representation until the 1920s, while a minority opposed it intransigently. Conversely, more progressive, secular Jews who might have welcomed the JFB's feminist stand were not attracted to its Jewishness. The conflict between Judaism and feminism was one the JFB could never solve to its own satisfaction. Although it did not achieve other than token power for women in Jewish communal affairs, the

JFB did succeed in equally important tasks: it made it possible for Jewish women to perceive their worth; to recognize their resourcefulness in areas beyond the home and family; and to contribute to their community.

The contradictory nature of the relationship of Jewish feminists to their religion was paralleled by their equally ambivalent relationship to German society. Feelings of success in a country which provided economic mobility clashed with feelings of insecurity in a society where Jews never ceased to be a "problem" or "question." Postures of superiority and ethnic assertiveness were often designed to mask hidden fears of inferiority and rejection. The reservation that the loss of a strong Jewish identity was too high a price to pay for social acceptance conflicted with the aspiration to become the sanitized Jews German liberals demanded. The JFB belonged to and maintained friendly relations with the Bund Deutscher Frauenvereine, with Pappenheim serving on its board of directors. Yet, few JFB rank and file participated in the German organization even though several of its well-known founders and a number of its prominent leaders were Jewish, or of Jewish origin. Henriette Goldschmidt cofounded the General German Women's Association; Lina Morgenstern organized the German Housewives' Association; Fanny Lewald propagandized for women's emancipation in her novels; and Jeanette Schwerin initiated the beginning of modern social work. After World War I, Henriette Fürth, who championed low-income housing; Camilla Jellinek, who fought for women's legal equality; Josephine Levy-Rathenau, who set up the National Women's Service (a wartime volunteer organization) and vocational guidance centers for girls; and Alice Salomon, who founded the first school of social work, were committed to the German movement along with other Jewish women. Some of them, particularly in the earlier generation, may have hoped to be accepted into German social circles. Others, like Salomon, were converts. Still others chose the BDF over the traditional Jewish charities which were not sufficiently stimulating. Jewish career women and single women also joined the BDF. Finally, some, like Fürth, divided their time between the German and the Jewish movements, both of which fulfilled different needs.

Jewish housewives were not attracted to the BDF for several

reasons. First, each organization emphasized different aspects of the women's movement: the JFB concentrated on social work; the BDF stressed improved educational, career, and political opportunities for women. The latter organization, founded and run by teachers and single, career women who cultivated a strictly nonsectarian outlook, may have intimidated Jewish housewives who lacked higher educations, career ambitions, and political interests and felt strong ties to their religion. (German housewives, too, often preferred the company of other nonprofessional and more religiously oriented women and found this in the Catholic and Protestant women's associations rather than in the BDF.) The self-conscious feminism of the BDF may also have discomfited Jewish women. For while the JFB gently embraced the motto "For Women's Work and the Women's Movement," it still bore a comfortable resemblance to traditional Jewish charities; if they needed it, Jewish women still had social work as an alibi for feminism. Most importantly, the women who joined the JFB identified positively with their Jewishness and sought the company of other Jews. They felt that the German movement preferred Jewish women who "fit in" (that is, who ignored their Jewish identity) rather than those whose Jewish consciousness was strong.[93] Pappenheim referred to those Jewish women who joined the German movement as "half-Jews" (*Halbe*).[94] Members of the JFB assumed that they were accepted by their liberal feminist sisters as feminists but not as Jews. When they acted as *Jewish* women, that is, with regard to issues which particularly interested or affected Jews, they did not feel as welcome.[95] Their perceptions were correct: the BDF avoided what it considered to be "sectarianism."[96] Like most German liberals, it invited Jewish integration at the price of Jewish identity and was decidedly uncomfortable in the face of Jews who resisted complete homogenization.

On occasion, the BDF also reflected the anti-Semitism of some of its members.[97] In 1913, an associate of the BDF, the Bavarian Provincial Association for Women's Suffrage, condemned kosher butchering. The JFB protested and was assured by the Prussian Association for Women's Suffrage that the latter rejected the stand of the Bavarian group.[98] Pappenheim was furious with Helene Lange in 1915, when the latter in a speech omitted the JFB while naming the Catholic and Protestant women's associations that belonged to the BDF. Gertrud Bäumer, the president of the BDF, told Pappenheim that she, Bäumer, could not censure a private member of the BDF. (Of course, Lange was well known and therefore not simply a private member.) Pappenheim angrily withdrew from the National Women's Service, accusing Lange and Bäumer of "hatefulness towards Jewish women and Judaism." Lange responded to a *Jewish* colleague: "It is a terrible pity that just now suddenly Jewish women too stress their religion, something from which they judiciously restrained themselves in the past."[99] Bäumer considered the JFB an organization which did social work among Jews, but did not acknowledge it as a religious women's organization. The JFB fought the idea of a united women's movement (that is, one in which there were no religious divisions), because it rightfully recognized that it would then have no reason to exist. Thus, this fight was not just over a religious issue; it was a jurisdictional dispute. The problem was not solved, but the disagreement ended when Bäumer sent an apologetic letter to Pappenheim. In the postwar era, anti-Semitism seemed to play a role in the denial of the BDF's top position to Alice Salomon. The leadership decided that in order to preserve the movement, a woman with a Jewish name could not be president.[100]

Thus, fears of anti-Semitism and a rejection of the assimilationist posture of some of the Jewish founders of German feminism kept most Jewish women from joining the BDF. Their reaction was not unlike that of Jewish men whose response to the rise of anti-Semitism in the 1890s was to form Jewish education societies and self-defense organizations to revive pride in Judaism and to fight anti-Semitism. Yet, lest the JFB's patriotism or adherence to feminism be questioned, it repeatedly assured its German sisters (as well as itself!) that its emphasis on Judaism made it a religious organization analagous to the Protestant and Catholic women's associations and did not prejudice its loyalty to the German nation or to its German sisters. It maintained that most Jewish women worked "in the spirit of the German women's movement," but as a result of anti-Semitism and the resurgence of nationalism (in this case, Jewish ethnic pride, not Zionism), they preferred to join their coreligionists in mutual endeavors on behalf of the Jewish community.[101] The JFB seemed to recognize (and in some ways epitomize) the ambivalent position of Jews in German society. On the one hand, it attempted to achieve a working relationship with the BDF in order to support the goals of German feminism, be accepted as part of a German movement, and stem the growth of anti-Semitism. On the other hand, the Frauenbund provided a congenial atmosphere for Jewish women who, while making the proper obeisances to their German heritage and to German feminism, enjoyed a feeling of ethnic community and preferred to work together on behalf of their own people.

"For Women's Work and the Women's Movement": The Goals of the Frauenbund

The aims of the JFB varied according to the changing political, economic, and social conditions which affected Frauenbund members as Germans, Jews, and women. Furthermore, its goals reflected the insecurities of German Jews, their desire to allay anti-Semitism and to conform to the majority culture. Finally, the JFB's interests were expressive of its constituency of middle-class housewives. Class barriers prevented working-class women from participating in and influencing the direction of the JFB. A Frauenbund which often saw them as the recipients of its social work, held little attraction for poorer Jews. And, there were ethnic differences between middle and working-class Jewish women: the former were German, while the latter were frequently *Ostjuden*, of Eastern European background. At best, these two groups maintained strained, but friendly relations and, at worst, they were often uninformed about and mistrustful of each other. Not only did the JFB fail to enroll working-class women, but younger women as well remained aloof and therefore failed to influence its goals. Organizations like the JFB were best suited to an era of middle-class prosperity such as had existed in Imperial Germany. With the economic downturn of the war and postwar periods, the JFB was unable to recruit young volunteers, since few had the option of becoming leisured ladies.[102] Also, the pool of potential young members shrank as a result of a decline in Jewish fertility after 1910. By the 1930s, only a few young faces could be found amidst the retired, widowed, and aging membership (at a time when more than 50 percent of German Jews were above the age of forty.)[103] Thus, the aims of the organization reflect the interests of approximately the same group of women over a period of thirty years.

In 1904, the JFB agreed upon the following goals: to fight white slavery; to "raise standards of morality"; to strengthen Jewish communal consciousness; to lighten the burdens of Jewish working girls and women; and to support efforts on behalf of better education for women. It also established special national commissions which focused upon the situation of Jews in Galicia, white slavery, female employment, juvenile welfare, travelers' aid, and the home for unwed mothers at Isenburg.[104] In 1914—perhaps as a result of its tenth anniversary and a lack of progress in women's rights—the JFB perceived the need for greater women's solidarity in order to achieve its aims. Pappenheim promoted sisterhood on three levels: between German and Jewish women's organizations; among Jewish women of all lands; and within a nondenominational, international framework. The JFB, a member of the Bund Deutscher Frauenvereine since 1907, agreed to support German feminists' demands for equal pay for equal work, a uniform standard of sexual morality for men and women, and the protection of women and children. In 1914, it also successfully initiated the first international Jewish women's convention, the result of which was the founding of the International Jewish Women's Federation. This organization attempted to eliminate the legal oppression of Jewish women under Jewish law, alleviate the poverty of women in Eastern Europe and Palestine, and facilitate communication between major Jewish women's organizations.[105]

The JFB's immediate concerns during World War I were related to the war effort, but it also expressed dismay over what it considered to be an anti-Semitic military survey of Jewish participation in the war.[106] After the war, the JFB showed increased interest in internal and international Jewish affairs. In the 1920s the Frauenbund described its goals as follows:

The association will . . . (a) strengthen Jewish communal consciousness; (b) encourage cooperation among Jewish women's clubs, as well as among Jewish organizations and those of other religions in order to improve the social and cultural life of German women, take part in the goals of the German women's movement and the reconstruction of Germany; (c) further conciliation among peoples by working with international organizations; (d) back efforts on behalf of the construction of Palestine; (e) seek equality for women in the Jewish community; (f) support healthy family life, promote juvenile welfare, marriage, etc.; (g) ease the lives of Jewish working girls and women; (h) fight all forms of immorality (white slavery, etc.); (i) combat diseases which affect the nation (venereal disease, tuberculosis, etc.); (j) campaign against anti-Semitism.[107]

Compared to its earlier platforms, the JFB had added two significant points: support of international conciliation and Palestine. These additions resulted, respectively, from the lessons of the war and the Balfour Declaration of 1917. The Jewish women's movement, like its German counterpart, assisted in the war effort. Later, however, it supported international peace movements, whereas the BDF maintained a more nationalistic stance. Leading members of the JFB were pacifists, and the JFB's newsletter regularly printed reports and announcements of the Women's International League for Peace and Freedom, a pacifist organization led by Jane Addams. In 1927, the JFB formally urged its members to join the WILPF, a radical step given the internationalism of the latter and the atmosphere of wounded German nationalism which surrounded the JFB. The Frauenbund also sent unofficial observers to disarmament conferences and circulated petitions in favor of disarmament.

Its attitude toward Palestine in the postwar era was sympathetic, but distant. The JFB reflected the leanings of most German Jews who maintained that they were German citizens of the Jewish faith and viewed Zionism as a threat to their painstakingly acquired status in Germany. They insisted on their authentic Germanness and their allegiance to the fatherland. At the first postwar national assembly of the JFB the topic of Palestine provoked a sharp debate between Pappenheim, who preferred to avoid it, and a small group of Zionist members,[108] who wanted the JFB to divert some of its efforts toward building a Jewish homeland.[109] A vote favored the recognition of the Palestine question, as one of "importance and great interest as a Jewish women's and a cultural question" (*Frauen und Kulturfrage*), but the JFB never accepted a Jewish-nationalist interpretation of Palestine.[110]

Another focus of Frauenbund attention in the postwar era was the plight of Jews badly hurt by years of economic chaos. It offered them extended health care, particularly for tuberculosis, setting up detection centers and supporting sanitaria. And, it began to care for aged women, providing cafeterias, clubs, and nursing homes for its impoverished, (formerly) middle-class coreligionists.[111] The JFB's commissions branched out to include: care for endangered girls (*Gefährdetenfürsorge*); follow-up care (*Nachgehendefürsorge*); adoption and foster home placement; tuberculosis care; home economics training; women's suffrage in Jewish communal elections; vacation care for needy women and children (*Erholungsfürsorge*); and the support of Wyk, a convalescent home for children.[112]

The goals of the Frauenbund under a democratic government attest to its moderate nature as a feminist organization. Its stress on social work was a long-term, gradualist effort. It sought to better the conditions of poor Jews without involving itself in labor or socialist causes. Apart from its support of suffrage in the Jewish community and international peace movements, the Frauenbund showed no interest in politics. Thus, reflecting its social composition, the JFB maintained a compromise, middle-of-the-road position between traditional women's charities and more militant feminism.

When the Nazis came to power they forced independent women's associations to disband, but permitted the JFB to continue functioning and even allowed it to grow. One can only speculate as to why this was the case. Nazi leadership may have been too busy in its first year to pay much attention to Jewish organizations.[113] Also, once the Nazis had agreed upon a preliminary policy regarding Jews, the JFB may have appeared useful to them. In the first few years the Nazis promoted Jewish self-awareness to encourage massive emigration. A secret seven-page SS "Situation Report—Jewish Question," written in 1934, stressed the need to support Jewish cultural organizations and all other Jewish movements devoted to creating Jewish self-consciousness.[114] The Nazis also encouraged occupational retraining programs which prepared Jews for resettlement in other countries. The JFB fit both categories: it rewrote its goals to eliminate feminism and internationalism and to espouse an entirely Jewish orientation, and it participated in the retraining of women. After the Nuremberg Laws (1935) which regulated the mixing of Aryan and Jewish races, it also encouraged emigration and suggested the creation of a Jewish school system where special subjects, such as Hebrew and crafts, would be offered to prospective emigrants. Thus, the Nazis may have simply taken advantage of the sincere efforts of the organization. Finally, the Nazis may not have regarded the activities of women particularly seriously, due to their well-known disdain for women. As compared with Jewish men and their associations, Jewish women and women's organizations were treated more mildly by the regime in its first years.

Nazi policy toward the Jews vacillated, and their attitude toward the JFB reflected this.[115] While permitted to carry out its normal activities, the JFB, like all Jewish organizations, was subject to spying and harassment. Leaders were summoned to police headquarters to sign oaths that they were following all the laws, to defend their charges, or to defend themselves against false accusations, and the president of the JFB had to submit the constitution of the organization for Nazi scrutiny. The newsletter was also watched by the government. Self-censorship saved the publication from temporary or permanent confiscation—a fate that befell several Jewish papers—until the JFB was dissolved. The government's inconsistencies encouraged those Jews who hoped to stay in their homeland, allowing them to give positive interpretations to the ambiguities of Nazi law. The fact that their organizations were allowed to function and even to expand probably contributed to the fateful decision of some to remain until it was too late.

The Organization's Structure

The organizational structure of the Frauenbund consisted of grass-roots affiliated societies, JFB locals, regional and provincial associations, and a loose alliance with other major Jewish women's associations. National leaders instigated and coordinated efforts from Berlin, but most activity took place at the local level. In 1905, the JFB counted 72 affiliated societies. The size of the affiliates varied from smaller ones of about 100 members to societies of more than 600 members. By 1913, the JFB had a membership of 32,000 women belonging to approximately 160 affiliates.[116] The real life of the Frauenbund was found in its locals. They were initiated by the national leadership in an attempt to unite and guide affiliated groups in a particular city. The leaders of locals were usually the most progressive members of the organization. They were supposed to remind their followers of the connection between social work and social and political rights. They wrote for the JFB newsletter, served on its board of directors, and were in charge of lectures, seminars, and workshops ranging from feminist topics to discussions of Jewish customs and ceremonies. They appealed to very old charities as well as more modern groups and encouraged individuals to join the JFB directly. Thus, individuals and groups representing different approaches and interests worked side by side within the local, maintaining a degree of autonomy—groups could even retain their separate identity—but promising to "execute the program of the JFB as it applied to local conditions."[117] Locals were thus a grass-roots means by which JFB elites in Berlin and Frankfurt imparted their ideas. At the same time, locals experienced tensions between the more progressive leaders and their more hesitant following. Compromises were most often resolved to the satisfaction of the locals, since there was no way that Berlin could enforce its decisions.

By 1914, an increase in the number of individual members and affiliates brought membership to 35,000. The war years witnessed the continued growth of the Frauenbund, which encompassed 215 affiliates, 10 locals, and 44,000 members by 1917. The organization swelled in the 1920s, doubling its affiliates to 430, inaugurating 24 more locals, and boasting a membership of 50,000 members.[118] Even in 1935 when the JFB needed Gestapo permission to add new members, 2 more locals and 20 more affiliates joined the organization. Membership remained relatively steady because those who emigrated were replaced by new members from disbanded women's organizations. Meetings, however, were reduced in frequency at the end of 1935 by Nazi order.

Because most of the actual social and cultural work of the JFB took place in affiliated and local groups, their treasuries were some-times larger than that of the national organization. They acquired funds from dues, gifts, subsidies, and imaginative fund-raising ideas, and were able to support homes and institutions for women. In Hamburg, for example, the group owned a home for women (which also served as a hostel), a cafeteria for middle-class patrons, and a convalescent center for children. Pappenheim's own group in Frankfurt was supported by very wealthy members: two patrons donated the house and garden at Isenburg and, in 1914, the group received a gift of 30,000 marks from another member. All locals contributed to the JFB's national projects and funded (as well as participated in) its adoption services. Finally, the larger locals were given the honor (and a large share of the financial burden) of holding JFB national assemblies in their cities.

The JFB's regional and provincial associations expanded its effort beyond the major cities, modernizing and coordinating existing women's clubs in rural areas. As Jews continued their migration to large urban centers, those who remained in small towns became increasingly isolated. The regional organization offered Jewish women who stayed behind personal contact with and moral support from other Jewish women. This creation of a sense of community was as important to the JFB leadership as the coordination of social welfare activities and the growth of locals. The regional and provincial associations invited women from small towns to their conventions and spoke of enlivening small communities. During the Hitler years they considered themselves to be "lifelines" to the small Jewish communities.[119]

Associated organizations further extended the Frauenbund's influence. The B'nai B'rith, Centralverein, and Zionists supported women's auxiliaries which coexisted with the JFB. The latter's neutrality made it possible for members of these organizations to join the JFB as individuals in order to pursue its distinctive goals. Both Ottilie Schönewald, a member of the board of directors of the Centralverein, and Rahel Straus, a Zionist, served on the JFB's board of directors. Declaring that it provided a means of communication among all Jewish women, the JFB invited the larger women's auxiliaries to formally associate with it. The B'nai B'rith and Women's Association to Help Palestine associated as early as 1929, and the Centralverein women agreed in 1933. Prior to these arrangements, many local B'nai B'rith and Centralverein groups had joined JFB locals or regionals directly. The organization which represented Orthodox women, the Agudat Yisroel, did not associate, because it considered the demands of Jewish feminists too radical. Yet it, too, worked with the JFB, and many Orthodox women belonged to the Frauenbund as individual members.

The national leadership, which made policy decisions and inspired new directions, consisted of an executive committee and an expanded board of directors. The former, made up of the president, vice-president, secretary, treasurer, and deputy treasurer, was elected (or, as was generally the case with the JFB, reelected) every four years at a national convention and was responsible for the execution of the JFB's policies and the management of its treasury. The expanded board of directors comprised the executive committee, chairpersons of the commissions, and representatives of local, regional, and associated organizations. The board set policies in the years between national conventions and kept channels of communication open to Jewish organizations and to the German women's movement. The national leadership coordinated the work of locals and regionals and its business office in Berlin served as an information bureau for any questions related to the women's movement. This office did not, however, "represent" the JFB in the same way as other Berlin headquarters spoke for their associations. The JFB remained purposely decentralized: most decisions were made at the local level.

All JFB leaders shared a strong emotional bond and a sense of dedication to an important cause. They remained exceptionally loyal to the JFB and to each other, serving the organization until emigration, death, or deportation forced them to give up their posts. Many of them were prominent in Jewish circles prior to their association with the Jewish feminist organization. Sidonie Werner (1860-1932) of Hamburg, Paul Ollendorff (1860-1938) of Breslau, and Henriette May (1862-1928) of Berlin had their feminist consciousness raised while they were active in Jewish organizations. With the notable exception of Ottilie Schönewald (1883-1956), the last president of the JFB, few came to the JFB from the German women's movement, although all supported it. Many of the early leaders were teachers, while the later ones, such as Hannah Karminski (1897-1942), the JFB's executive secretary, were professional social workers. Whereas the first generation was more vocal as feminists, the second generation was more moderate, but no less devoted to the JFB. Although the leaders were better educated and more self-assured than their followers, they were in many ways representative of the large number of nameless women who desired a tolerable existence for both sexes. All gained great personal satisfaction from the friendships they made in the organization and from what they accomplished.

The Frauenbund belonged to the mainstream of the nineteenth- and twentieth-century women's movement, which tried to enlarge woman's sphere by increasing her opportunities and broadening her outlook. Reacting against the restricted role foisted upon women, the JFB attempted to improve the self-image of Jewish women and to elevate their status. It sought to replace the subordination of Jewish women with their independence. Its demands, like those of its model, the German feminist movement, were essentially re-formist, reflecting the limited life options available to women at that time. It eschewed a militant stance in both substance and rhetoric, insisting that the purpose of emancipation was service. During the 1930s the JFB continued to divide its efforts between demanding women's rights and providing social welfare programs. Its feminist spirit declined precipitously, and understandably, as life under the Nazis became more intolerable, and it concentrated on social work.

While the JFB engaged in general social work and provided cultural activities for its members, most of its efforts were directed toward three areas which were tied intimately to its feminist and Jewish concerns: the fight against white slavery, the campaign for suffrage in the Jewish community, and the attempt to provide job training for women. The next three chapters will deal with each of these separately.

Notes

1. *BJFB*, July 1936, p. 8.

2. Amy Hackett, "The Politics of Feminism in Wilhelmine Germany, 1890-1918 (Ph.D. dissertation, Columbia University, 1966), p. 12.

3. Hugh Wiley Puckett, *Germany's Women Go Forward* (New York: Columbia University Press, 1930), pp. 128-30.

4. Agnes Zahn-Harnack, *Die Frauenbewegung: Geschichte, Probleme, Ziele* (Berlin: Deutsch Buch-Gemeinschaft, 1928), p. 163.

5. Hackett, in "Politics," pp. 40-60, discusses the reasons for this "surplus."

6. Katherine Anthony, *Feminism in Germany and Scandinavia* (New York: Henry Holt and Company, 1915), p. 181.

7. Margrit Twellman, *Die Deutsche Frauenbewegung, Ihre Anfänge und erste Entwicklung, 1843-1889* (Meisenheim am Glan: Verlag Anton Hain, 1972), p. 312.

8. Puckett, *Germany's Women*, pp. 10-13.

9. Ibid., p. 143.

10. Johannes Prüfer, *Friedrich Fröbel* (Leipzig: Verlag von B.G. Teubner, 1920), pp. 74-119; Marie Kuntze, *Friedrich Fröbel* (Leipzig: Verlag von Quelle und Meyer, 1930), pp. 119-27.

11. Kuntze, *Fröbel*, p. 121.

12. Morgenstern collection, ALBI, no. 718 (II, 11).

13. Goldschmidt collection, ALBI, no. 501 (IV).

14. Goldschmidt collection, ALBI, no. 501 (IV); Josephine Siebe, *Henriette Goldschmidt: Ihr Leben und ihr Schaffen* (Leipzig: Akademische Verlagsgesellschaft, 1922), p. 152.

15. Goldschmidt collection, ALBI, no. 501 (IV).

16. Henriette Goldschmidt, "Vom Kindergarten zur Hochschule für Frauen," in *Zeitschrift für Pädagogische Psychologie* (1918). See also Siebe, *Henriette Goldschmidt*.

17. Siebe, *Henriette Goldschmidt*, p. 77.

18. Gerda Caspary, *Die Entwicklungsgrundlagen für die Soziale und Psychische Verselbständigung der Bürgerlichen Deutschen Frau um die Jahrhundertwende*, vol. 3 (Heidelberg: Verlag der Weiss'schen Universitätsbuchhandlung, 1933), p. 18.

19. Leonard Krieger, *The German Idea of Freedom* (Boston: Beacon Press, 1957), pp. 4, 14, 460, 469-70. See also: Amy Hackett, "Feminism and Liberalism in Wilhelmine Germany, 1890-1918," in *Liberating Women's History; Theoretical and Critical Essays*, edited by Berenice A. Carroll (Urbana: University of Illinois Press, 1976), pp. 127-36.

20. Krieger, *The German Idea*, pp. 4, 14.

21. Puckett, *Germany's Women*, p. 152.

22. Anthony, *Feminism*, p. 11. See also Mara Mayer, "Fears and Fantasies of the Anti-Suffragists," *Connecticut Review* 7, no. 2 (April 1974), pp. 64-74.

23. Puckett, *Germany's Women*, p. 158; Zahn-Harnack, *Die Frauenbewegung*, p. 273. See also, Evans, *The Feminist Movement in Germany, 1894-1933*.

24. Hackett, "Politics," p. 1044.

25. Zahn-Harnack, *Die Frauenbewegung*, p. 30; Gertrud Bäumer, *Helene Lange* (Berlin: W. Moeser Buchhandlung, 1918), p. 27.

26. Rahel Straus, *Wir Lebten in Deutschland: Erinnerungen einer Deutschen Jüdin, 1880-1933* (Stuttgart: Deutsche Verlags-Anstalt, 1962), p. 221; Hedwig Wachenheim, *Vom Grossbürgertum zur Sozialdemokratie* (Berlin: Colloquium Verlag, 1973), p. 59. This rhetoric occurred in the U.S. as

well. See, Mary Ryan, *Womanhood in America, From Colonial Times to the Present* (New York: Franklin Watts, Inc., 1975), p. 264.

27. Dohm, quoted by Anthony, *Feminism,* pp. 242-43. See also: "Geschichte und Familiengeschichte: Die radikale Feministin Hedwig Dohm und ihre Enkelin Katia Mann," in *Sexismus: Uber die Abtreibung der Fraüenfrage,* Marielouise Janssen-Jurreit (Munich: Carl Hanser Verlag, 1976), pp. 11-27.

28. Evans, *The Feminist Movement,* chap. 2.

29. *Protokoll über die Verhandlungen des Parteitages der Sozialdemokratischen Partei Deutschlands. Abgehalten zu Gotha, 1896,* p. 163. Quoted in Karen Honeycutt, "Clara Zetkin: A Socialist Approach to the Problem of Woman's Oppression," *Feminist Studies* (Spring-Summer 1976), pp. 131-44. For a different interpretation of Zetkin's feminism, see: "Feminismus und Sozialismus: Das hundertj ährige Dilemma," in *Sexismus,* Janssen-Jurreit, pp. 227-42. On the reasons for the split between bourgeois and socialist women, see Ilse Reicke, *Frauenbewegung und Erziehung* (Munich: Rösl und Cie Verlag, 1921), pp. 38-39. The definitive analysis of the causes of the split still must be written.

30. Hackett, "Politics," pp. 146, 674.

31. Paula E. Hyman, "The Other Half: Women in the Jewish Tradition," *Response* 17 (Summer 1973), p. 72.

32. Jacob Segall, "Die jüdischen Frauenvereine in Deutschland," *ZDSJ* (January, February 1914).

33. Schönewald, unpublished memoirs, ALBI.

34. Werner collection, ALBI, no. 3079 (35).

35. Robert Neuman, "The Sexual Question and Social Democracy in Imperial Germany," *Journal of Social History* 7 (1974), p. 272.

36. Abortion—permitted only for medical reasons—carried a penalty of six months to five years imprisonment for the patient and up to ten years for the abortionist. Contraception, while widely practiced, was limited by law. The sale and manufacture of contraceptives dangerous to a woman's health as well as door-to-door and automat sales were prohibited, as was the manufacture of abortifacients. Hackett, "Politics," pp. 941-42.

37. Atina Grossmann, "Abortion and Economic Crisis: The 1931 Campaign against no. 218 in Germany," *New German Critique,* no. 14 (Spring, 1978), pp. 119-137.

38. Zahn-Harnack's opinions appear in her *Die Frauenbewegung,* p. 105. On Zetkin, see Honeycutt, "Zetkin," p. 136.

39. Schönewald collection, ALBI, no. 3896 (II, 7).

40. *BJFB,* September 1930, pp. 1-2.

41. Arthur Ruppin, *The Jews of Today* (London: G. Bell and Sons, Ltd., 1913), p. 71, cited by Ismar Schorsch, *Jewish Reactions to German Anti-Semitism, 1870-1914* (New York: Columbia University Press, 1972), p. 13.

42. The crude birth rates by religion for Prussia, Bavaria, and Hesse at the turn of the century were:

PRUSSIA

	Catholic	*Protestant*	*Jew*
1880-1881	40.5	38.3	30.5
1890-1891	41.1	37.4	24.5
1900-1901	42.3	34.9	19.9

BAVARIA

	Catholic	*Protestant*	*Jew*
1881-1885	40.1	36.0	28.4
1896-1900	39.2	34.6	18.8

HESSE

	Catholic	*Protestant*	*Jew*
1881-1885	36.2	32.4	26.8
1896-1900	37.6	32.7	19.9

John F. Knodel, *The Decline of Fertility in Germany, 1871-1939* (Princeton: Princeton University Press, 1974), pp. 137-38.

Statistics for Frankfurt/Main for 1910 indicate:

General Population	*Jews*
24.4	13.5

Stefan Behr, *Der Bevölkerungsrückgang der deutschen Juden*, (Frankfurt/Main: J. Kauffmann Verlag, 1932), p. 45.

The crude birth rate of Jews in Prussia (where the majority of German Jews lived) declined from 15.7 per 1,000 in 1910 to 11.6 in 1925 and to 5.3 in 1933. Whereas in 1910 and 1925 the crude birth rate was only half that of the total population, by 1933 it had declined to a third. Erich Rosenthal, "Jewish Population in Germany," *Jewish Social Studies* 6 (1944), pp. 263-65.

43. Jewish sociologists estimated that birth control, rather than abortion, was the customary practice among Jews. Although the samples used were

too small to make firm statements (since abortions were illegal except in cases where the mother's life was in danger), it was estimated that in 1909/ 1910, 1.5 Germans and .6 Jews out of 100,000 Germans had had abortions. In 1916, the estimates were 1.8 and .9, respectively. Behr, *Bevölkerungsrückgang*, p. 96.

44. Rosenthal, "Jewish Population," p. 270. The JFB estimated that the average Jewish family had four children in 1875, three in 1900, and one or two in 1925. *BJFB*, August 1926, p. 1. Their estimate for 1900 was probably too high. See also Hackett, "Politics," p. 37.

45. Hackett, "Politics," p. 941.

46. Ibid., pp. 929-31, 939-40; *BJFB*, July 1931.

47. Caspary, *Die Entwicklungsgrundlagen*, pp. 37-38. Also, see Edward Shorter, "Female Emancipation, Birth Control and Fertility in European History," *American Historical Review* (June 1973), pp. 605-40.

48. The widespread eugenics movement of the 1920s, popular among liberals, conservatives, and socialists, no doubt influenced feminist attitudes regarding the need to propagate. See: Loren R. Graham, "Science and Values: The Eugenics Movement in Germany and Russia in the 1920s," *American Historical Review* (December 1977), pp. 1133-64.

49. BJFB, March 1928, pp. 4-5; *BJFB*, December 1928, pp. 1-2; *BJFB*, July 1933, pp. 2-3.

50. Bund Deutscher Frauenvereine, Archives; Signatur A3 bb.

51. Ibid.

52. The acknowledgment of the importance of female sexuality in Judaism was a mixed blessing. While it nurtured a humane attitude toward female sexual pleasure, it gave credence to those in Jewish tradition who viewed women as licentious. David M. Feldman, *Marital Relations, Birth Control and Abortion in Jewish Law* (New York: Schocken Books, 1975); Charlotte Baum, Paula Hyman, Sonya Michel, *The Jewish Woman in America* (New York: Dial Press, 1976), p. 7; Phillip Segal, "Elements of Male Chauvinism in Classical Halakhah," *Judaism* 24 (Spring 1975), pp. 226-44.

53. Hackett, "Politics," p. 936.

54. Rahel Straus, "Ehe und Mutterschaft," in *Vom Jüdischen Geiste: Ein Aufsatzreihe*, edited by Der Jüdische Frauenbund (Berlin: Biko Verlag, 1934), p. 21.

55. The title "mothers of civilization" is used by Ryan in *Womanhood*. In America, too, women were told that they "control[led] the destiny of every community." p. 147.

56. O'Neill, in *Dissent: Explorations in the History of American Radicalism*, edited by Alfred F. Young (De Kalb, Ill.: Northern Illinois University Press, 1968), p. 276.

57. For similarities with "social motherhood" in America, see Ryan, *Womanhood*, pp. 225-26.

58. Schönewald collection, ALBI, no. 3896 (II, 3).

59. Ibid.

60. Ryan describes Jane Addams as a "social housekeeper," a woman who "found . . . good housekeeping . . . required that a woman enter the public sphere . . ." *Womanhood*, p. 229.

61. *BJFB*, August/September 1927, pp. 6-7.

62. Glenda Gates Riley, "The Subtle Subversion: Changes in the Traditionist Image of the American Woman," *The Historian* 32 (February 1970), pp. 210-27.

63. Rudolf Glanz, "Das jüdische Element in der modernen Frauenbewegung," *Ungarländische Jüdische Zeitung* 13 (1912), pp. 197-202.

64. *BJFB*, February 1928, p. 2; *BJFB*, June 1932, pp. 4-6.

65. *Gemeindeblatt* (Frankfurt), July/August 1931.

66. According to Puckett, "emancipation" was a word made popular by St. Simonists and Young Germans. It was also a foreign—that is, a French—word. Thus, it affronted bourgeois Germans on two levels. *Germany's Women*, pp. 8, 14.

67. *BJFB*, September 1926, p. 4.

68. Liegner collection, ALBI, no. 3902 (III).

69. *BJFB*, January 1937, p. 11.

70. Schönewald collection, ALBI, no. 3896 (IV, 4).

71. Schönewald collection, ALBI, no. 3896 (II, 7), (IV, 16).

72. *BJFB*, June 1929, p. 1.

73. *BJFB*, March 1930, pp. 6-8.

74. *BJFB*, July 1929, p. 9.

75. *BJFB*, February 1920, pp. 1-3.

76. *BJFB*, March 1930, pp. 7-8.

77. *BJFB*, August 1930, p. 5.

78. *IF*, November 5, 1908, p. 11; *BJFB*, August 1930, pp. 5-7.

79. For the legend of Lilith see Sally Priesand, *Judaism and the New Woman* (New York: Behrman House, Inc., 1975), pp. 3-6, and Mary Gendler, "The Vindication of Vashti," *Response: A Contemporary Jewish Review* 18 (Summer 1973), p. 157.

80. Mrs. A. Sidgwick, *Home Life in Germany* (New York: Macmillan, 1912), p. 117.

81. *BJFB*, April 1929, p. 6; *BJFB*, January 1937, pp. 4-5.

82. *BJFB*, November 1929, p. 12; *BJFB*, March 1930, pp. 7-8; and Dora Edinger, private interview, February 17, 1975, New York.

83. *BJFB*, December 1928, pp. 1-2; *BJFB*, July 1933, pp. 2-3.

84. *BJFB*, October 1931, pp. 5-6.

85. This solidarity extended to Jewish female convicts as well. The JFB national bureau supported a prison visiting service. JFB members called on inmates in an attempt to bring comfort. They sought help for the prisoner's family and received permission from authorities to hold religious services and bring special foods on important holy days. *AZDJ*, May 1, 1914, p. 3; *IF*, October 18, 1916, p. 10; and Klara Caro, former member of board of directors of JFB local in Cologne, interview, December 9, 1974, Palisades, N.Y.

86. *BJFB*, June 1929, p. 17; and *IF*, November 27, 1930, p. 5.

87. *BJFB*, October 1932, p. 12.

88. *BJFB*, January 1937, p. 5.

89. *BJFB*, January 1931, pp. 8-9.

90. *AZDJ*, September 26, 1913, supplement, p. 3. The war interfered with the publication of this book. *AZDJ*, February 19, 1915, supplement, p. 1.

91. Mehler, *Wir* (Berlin: Jüdischer Buchverlag, 1937).

92. In America, Elizabeth Cady Stanton did edit a "Woman's Bible" in 1895.

93. *BJFB*, December 1930, pp. 5-6.

94. Bund Deutscher Frauenvereine, Archives, 3 Abt. no. 5.

95. *BJFB*, December 1930, pp. 5-6.

96. Hackett, "Politics," pp. 176-87.

97. Ibid., p. 305; Evans, *The Feminist Movement*, p. 200.

98. *AZDJ*, April 4, 1913, p. 5, supplement.

99. Bund Deutscher Frauenvereine, Archives, 3 Abt. no. 5.

100. Hans Müthesius, ed., *Alice Salomon* (Cologne: Carl Heymanns Verlag, K.G., 1958), pp. 82-86.

101. *BJFB*, April 1927, pp. 3-4.

102. For a discussion of the generation gap in the interwar German feminist movement, see Jill Stephenson, *Women in Nazi Society* (New York: Barnes & Noble, 1975), p. 26. In America, a writer for the League of Women Voters, which was also having difficulty recruiting young members, noted that feminism was not popular among the young and that "such rights as the old feministic movement has already won for the females of the species, the young accept as a matter of course." In the 1920s the flappers rejected the feminist thesis that emancipation would allow women more service and would let them compete with men at every level. According to William O'Neill, they decided to enjoy themselves. "Feminism," p. 292.

103. Rosenthal, "Jewish Population," pp. 243-47.

104. Schönewald collection, ALBI, no. 3896 (III, 1); *AZDJ*, April 4, 1913, supplement, p. 6; *AZDJ*, November 12, 1920, supplement, p. 2.

105. *BJFB*, July 1929, pp. 5-6. It existed in name more than in reality. Aside from a few congresses, it never acted and did not even have international offices. Conversation with Dora Edinger, July 1975, New York.

106. Although the military claimed its study was intended to refute charges by anti-Semites that Jews were shirking military duty, the JFB (and other Jewish organizations) rightfully felt that such a survey (done only on Jews) was anti-Semitic in intent. Results, too, could be used against Jews, since Jews participated in similar numbers to urban groups, but relatively less than all Germans combined. *AZDJ*, February 9, 1917, supplement, p. 2. The military never published the results of the census.

107. *BJFB*, January 1928, p. 1.

108. Most Zionist women preferred their own small women's groups and later joined the Women's International Zionist Organization.

109. Caro interview, December 9, 1974.

110. *AZDJ*, November 12, 1920, supplement, p. 2.

111. The *Mittelstandsküche* (middle-class cafeteria) was an alternative to the *Volksküche* ("people's kitchen," a soup kitchen for poor people). Class-conscious German Jews preferred the former, where they paid a few pennies for their meals and felt that they were thus maintaining their status. The JFB could afford only these types of kitchens, because it depended on the small donations.

112. *BJFB*, January 1928, p. 2.

113. For example, the Reichsvertretung der deutschen Juden (Central Association of German Jews), founded in the fall of 1933 to represent the collective interests of German Jewry, simply informed the Ministry of Interior of its formation. In 1935, the Nazis forced the organization to change its name to the Reichsvertretung der Juden in Deutschland. Kurt Jacob Ball-Kaduri, *Das Leben der Juden in Deutschland im Jahre 1933 — Ein Zeitbericht* (Frankfurt/Main: Europäische Verlagsanstalt, 1963), p. 147.

114. Karl A. Schleunes, *The Twisted Road to Auschwitz: Nazi Policy toward German Jews, 1933-1939* (Urbana: University of Illinois Press, 1970), pp. 178-80.

115. Schleunes, in *Twisted Road*, argues that Nazi policies regarding Jews were often uncoordinated and contradictory.

116. Siddy Wronsky, "Zur Soziologie der jüdischen Frauenbewegung in Deutschland," *Jahrbuch für Jüdische Geschichte und Literatur* (1927), p. 91. The number of affiliates increased to 87 in 1907 [Meyer collection, ALBI,

no. 877 (XI, 2)], and 93 by 1908 (*IF*, January 16, 1908, p. 4). See also: *AZDJ*, April 4, 1913, supplement, pp. 4-5.

117. *BJFB*, January 1928, p. 1.

118. Segall, "Frauenvereine," p. 23; *AZDJ*, February 19, 1917, supplement, p. 2; *BJFB*, January 1928, p. 1; Schönewald collection, ALBI, no. 3896 (IV, 16).

119. *BJFB*, June 1929, p. 17. Individuals could join regional associations directly if they lived in a town where no Frauenbund group existed. Schönewald collection, ALBI, no. 3896 (III, 9).

BLÄTTER DES JÜDISCHEN FRAUENBUNDES

FÜR FRAUENARBEIT UND FRAUENBEWEGUNG

OFFIZIELLES ORGAN DES JÜDISCHEN FRAUENBUNDES VON DEUTSCHLAND
(UMFASST 430 VEREINE MIT ÜBER 50000 MITGLIEDERN)

Redaktion: Berlin N 24, Monbijouplatz 10. Alle redaktionellen Anfragen und Einsendungen sind zu richten an die Geschäftsstelle des Jüdischen Frauenbundes, Berlin N 24. Fernspr.: D 2 Weidendamm 7140.

Geschäftsstelle und Anzeigenverwaltung: Biko-Verlag, Berlin SW 19. Kurstr. 34-35. Fernspr.: A 6 Merkur 1182. Postscheck-Konto: "Druckerei Biko", Berlin NW 7, Nr. 21442.

Die „Blätter des Jüdischen Frauenbundes" erscheinen einmal monatlich, in der ersten Woche jedes Monats. Redaktionsschluß am 20. jedes Monats. Bestellungen nimmt jede Postanstalt und der Biko-Verlag, Berlin SW 19, Kurstr. 34-35 entgegen. Bezugspreis: vierteljährlich 90 Pfg., jährlich RM 3.60 einschließlich Bestellgeld. Einzelnummer 50 Pfg. Anzeigenpreise: die 5 gespaltene Nonpareille-Zeile 60 Pfg. Seitenpreise auf Anfrage. Schluß der Anzeigenannahme am 25. jedes Monats.

Nr. 12   BERLIN / DEZEMBER 1930   VI. JAHRGANG

DER WARSCHAUER INTERNATIONALE KONGRESS ZUR BEKÄMPFUNG DES MÄDCHENHANDELS

An den Vorstand des Jüd. Frauenbundes, z. Hd. von Frau Bettina Brenner, Leipzig.

Es scheint mir nicht nur für die im J.F.B. organisierten Frauen, sondern für die jüdische Welt im allgemeinen wichtig, zu erfahren, wie sich der VIII. Internationale Kongreß zur Bekämpfung des Mädchenhandels in Warschau dargeboten hat. Ich berichte deshalb.

Um zuerst von dem Rahmen der Veranstaltung zu sprechen, ist zu erzählen, daß die bekannte polnische Gastlichkeit sich in liebenswürdiger Weise gezeigt hat. Die Gastlichkeit des polnischen Nationalkomitees, die besonders durch die „Dames Chauvinesses" (Stiftsdamen) in dem Stiftungshaus der Gräfin Potocka Formen so feiner, persönlicher Kultur trug, ließ alle begeisterten Worte des Dankes in den drei Kongreßsprachen nur eben das ausdrücken, was alle Teilnehmer empfanden. Auch große Empfänge in prächtigen, kunstgeschmückten Räumen brachte die offizielle Note, die solchen Zusammenkünften eigen ist, ihre äußere Wirkung, wenn auch nicht ihre innere Bedeutung zu unterstreichen.

Vom allgemeinen Standpunkte gesehen, bewegten sich die Verhandlungen in den bekannten, herkömmlichen Geleisen von Frauen- und Kinderschutz: Paßfragen, Repatriierung von Prostituierten, Schutzalter, Auslandsstellungen für Mädchen, besonders als Artistinnen usw.

Neu aufgenommen war der nicht fernliegende Gedanke der Bekämpfung des Zuhälterwesens, der nach den Wegen und Umwegen, die einer Resolution vorgeschrieben sind, noch viel Jahre bedürfen wird, um seine Keimfähigkeit zu beweisen!

Auch die Abolition der Reglementierung, die Aufhebung der Bordelle, diese Grundforderung jeglicher ernst gewollten Bekämpfung des Mädchenhandels, ist nach vieljährigen Kämpfen noch nicht in allen Ländern anerkannt. Es war nur ein winziger Ansatz einer etwas lebhafteren Bewegung in der Versammlung, als Prof. Uhde (Graz) mit dem ihm eigenen Pathos eine Entschließung verlangte, derzufolge der Völkerbundskommission für Frauen- und Kinderschutz kein Antrag empfohlen werden sollte, der nicht mit der abolitionistischen Linie übereinstimmt. Aber auch dieser Wunsch, der im Augenblick, da er ausgesprochen wurde, nur von ideologischer Bedeutung war, konnte sich durch die Stellung der lateinischen Länder (die wie der Osten, der Balkan u. a. nicht ohne Bordelle auskommen zu können glauben) und durch die ängstliche Haltung einiger Nationalkomitees in der Abstimmung nicht einmal zu einer warmen Einstimmigkeit, zu einer Resolution verdichten.

Mit diesen wenigen, uninteressanten Worten wäre der Kongreß im allgemeinen genügend charakterisiert, und indem ich noch beifüge, daß der nächste Kongreß in Berlin stattfinden soll, wäre der Bericht erschöpft, wenn nicht gerade von diesem Kongreß für die jüdische Welt mehr und anderes zu erwarten gewesen wäre.

Wenn ich nun in diesem Zusammenhang den in unserem Frauenkreise zum Kennwort gewordenen Begriff der Sysiphus-Arbeit gebrauche, so wissen Sie, daß ich damit die Stellung der Juden im Mädchenhandel und zu seiner Bekämpfung meine.

Ich setze als bekannt voraus, daß der Internationale Kongreß zur Bekämpfung des Mädchenhandels in Warschau 1930 den Ausgangspunkt hätte werden können, sich jüdischerseits zu unleugbaren Tatsachen zu bekennen und einen sauberen Bekämpferwillen zu dokumentieren, in einem Lande und in einem Kreise, in dem die

---

3. **Front page of the JFB monthly, "Newspaper of the Jüdischer Frauenbund: For Women's Work and the Women's Movement."** This particular issue focuses on the international white slavery conference held in Warsaw. The lead article is by Bertha Pappenheim. *Courtesy Leo Baeck Institute, New York.*

chapter 4

Prostitution, Morality Crusades, and Feminism

The White Slave Traffic and Its Opponents

The fight against white slavery was one of the original reasons for the founding of the Jüdischer Frauenbund. Its earliest leaders, who had been active in reform movements that sought to end the traffic in women, planned their organization to help the Jewish victims of white slavery. Thus, the attempt to eradicate white slavery was one of the first goals of the JFB. By drawing attention to white slavery's human toll, Jewish feminist reformers not only sought to relieve the plight of abused women, they also hoped to win a general improvement in the condition of all women. Moral outrage at the plight of white slaves contributed to the growth of a feminist consciousness.

White slaves were women and girls who were lured, tricked, or forced to go abroad by traffickers who smuggled them across borders and sold them into prostitution. While prostitutes and white slaves had not been unknown in preindustrial Europe, commercialized prostitution grew into a flourishing enterprise in the expanding urban centers of nineteenth-century Europe and America. Young women of the new industrial proletariat, unable to find secure or remunerative employment, often engaged in prostitution to supplement their wages or to support themselves or their families through a recession or a seasonal layoff.[1] Migrations of young lower-class or peasant men to the Americas produced a "surplus" of women in Europe who could no longer look toward marriage as a means of support.[2] Male emigration also produced a demand for prostitutes abroad to satisfy the desires of new immigrants who could not yet support wives.

The new middle classes placed their wives on a pedestal, denying them an economic function and exalting instead women's place in the home. The middle-class home had become the "ultimate bastion" against the rapid cultural and economic changes of the age.[3] The stability of this refuge depended upon the mother's devotion to her offspring and spouse. This devotion seemed to the Victorians to be incompatible with female sexual desire which could lead to promiscuity. Thus, the middle classes affected an excessive gentility, and female passions were directed to love of family and domestic duties rather than to sex. Female sexuality was ignored, denied, and repressed, and the experts concluded that "the majority of women (happily for them) are not troubled with sexual feelings of any kind."[4] Men, however, were supposed to exercise their "natural" passions, and since middle-class marriages took place relatively late and neither contraception nor sexual mores permitted premarital sex, young men made use of prostitutes. Their visits to prostitutes did not end at the time of their marriage. Couples who decided to limit their families usually practiced either sexual restraint or early withdrawal, and husbands occasionally resorted to prostitutes for sexual gratification. Also, many a middle-class husband faced with an "Angel in the Home" who approached sex (as her husband expected) impassively and dutifully looked for a sex object in the brothel who gave the appearance of sharing his pleasure in sex.[5] He despised the prostitute for his own guilty indulgences as he revered his wife for remaining a symbol of his respectability.

The average amount of time that women remained full-time prostitutes was not over five years.[6] Therefore, the cities of Western Europe, Latin America, and the United States were in constant need of a replenished supply. While statistics are unreliable because they exclude clandestine and part-time prostitution and reflect the biases of the compilers, it is clear that prostitution in the later nineteenth century was conspicuous. In the 1870s it was estimated that there were about 15,000 prostitutes in Vienna and approximately 27,000 in Berlin.[7] In London, figures ranged from 8,000 to 80,000 in the late 1850s, with one English newspaper comparing the number of prostitutes to "an army of occupation."[8] In Germany, the total number of prostitutes was estimated at between 100,000 and 200,000 at the turn of the century and at 330,000 by 1914.[9] In

Buenos Aires in 1903, 1,276 women registered as prostitutes upon their arrival from Europe, and in 1909, 800 new prostitutes signed in.[10] This "traffic in flesh" was condoned by large portions of society and most governments. Victorians despised prostitutes, but they used them. The "respectable classes" and their governments dismissed the causes of prostitution in a "vast conspiracy of silence."[11] They preferred only to regulate the spread of venereal disease through the compulsory medical examination of prostitutes, their forced hospitalization if they were found to be infected, and the licensing of "clean" brothels.

This silence was at last broken by Josephine Butler, a dynamic and educated member of the English gentry, whose work among prostitutes in the 1860s had convinced her of the need for reform. In 1864, when Parliament passed the Contagious Diseases Acts to "regulate" prostitution, Butler and her associates began a campaign to have the Acts repealed. Known as abolitionists, they and their counterparts on the Continent attacked regulation as immoral, unhygienic, and unlawful.[12] They argued that governments should deal with the economic and social origins of prostitution. Regulation, they protested, did not stop the spread of venereal disease, because no attempt was made to keep men from spreading infections. It simply made prostitution less of a hazard for its male clients. Thus, regulation accepted and reinforced the "double standard" of morality, which allowed society to punish women for what was considered normal and healthy in men. Abolitionists demanded one moral code for both sexes.[13] To be sure, they did not seek greater permissiveness for women, but demanded premarital virginity and marital fidelity from men. They further insisted on one legal code, arguing that criminalization not only singled out women for punishment, but denied them due process as a result of the manner in which prostitutes were treated by the police and the courts. Finally, reformers maintained that it was impossible to raise standards of morality and rehabilitate prostitutes as long as regulation constituted the quasi-sanctioning of prostitution.

In 1875, English abolitionists founded the International Abolitionist Association with branches on the Continent. Ten years later, a convention of the International Abolitionist Association was alerted to the existence of a widespread traffic in women and girls for purposes of sexual exploitation. The business of dealing in human flesh was well organized and ruthless. A minority of the girls were actually kidnapped. Most were semiwilling victims who answered what appeared to be job announcements. Employment ads for waitresses, cooks, maids, and governesses were commonly used ploys. The ads demanded a picture of the girl. If she was accepted by the alleged employer, she received money for her voyage and was met by the trafficker at the train or boat. Other victims, approached at railroad stations or ports by procurers, were offered free lodgings. Once they found themselves in a brothel, most were entrapped by their own fears and ignorance as well as by the brutality of their keepers, the connivance of the police, and the general apathy of public opinion. A letter from a former Jewish white slave allows a glimpse into the abject conditions which surrounded her:

The woman handed me over to bandits, and when I wanted to run away from them they locked me in a room without windows and beat me savagely. Time passed and I got used to the horrible life. Later I even had an opportunity to escape, because they used to send me out on the streets, but life had become meaningless for me anyway, and nothing mattered anymore. I lived this way for six months, degraded and dejected, until I got sick and they drove me out of that house.[14]

A member of Butler's International Abolitionist Association, William A. Coote, formed a branch organization dedicated entirely to the suppression of the white slave traffic. He began to organize National Committees for the Suppression of the White Slave Traffic in all the European capitals, in Egypt, Canada, the United States, South America, and South Africa.[15] As a result of his activities, a German National Committee was founded in 1899 and an international convention on the white slave problem was held in London that same year. Both the German National Committee and the international organization met frequently in succeeding years.

While abolitionists and those who concentrated on fighting white slavery all hoped to end the sexual abuse of women, they did not agree on the means by which to achieve this goal and they attracted different followings. The anti-white slavery forces, fearful of the hostility of police (who supported regulation[16] and whose cooperation and vigilance were essential), concentrated on apprehending traffickers, preventing young women from falling into the hands of procurers, and rescuing girls who were white slaves. Thus, anti-white slavery organizations focused on the supply side of prostitution while abolitionists opposed regulation and attempted to eradicate the immediate source of demand, the brothel.[17] The White Slavery," and a list of people to contact for help in every Partly, this was because the latter was associated in the popular mind with feminism. More importantly, the need to fight white slavery was more obvious and its appeal more emotional and more conservative.[18] Prostitutes were seen as innocents, literally dragged into a life of degradation, an image which evoked greater sympathy than the abolitionist view of prostitutes as the silent symbols of social injustice.

Yet, the differences between those opposing white slavery and those antagonistic to regulation should not be exaggerated, for they shared similar analyses. Both groups assumed that women were forced into prostitution. The notion that a prostitute might consider herself a working woman whose decision was a "rational choice" was foreign to them.[19] Both groups agreed that social misery was the general cause of sexual vice, and both included socialists who asserted that sexual exploitation was the result of economic exploitation and that wage slavery was conducive to white slavery. All felt betrayed by government leaders who protected and used brothels as well as by respectable husbands who passed venereal disease to innocent wives. Behind the flattery of the gentle sex lay a crass sexual reality brought into focus by the treatment of prostitutes in a male-dominated society. Exposés of prostitution and white slavery revealed how powerless women really were. In fact, Christabel Pankhurst, a leader of the English suffragettes, saw the vote as a means to combat the connected evils of political and sexual powerlessness. She maintained that "the Danger of Votes for Women is . . . a revolt against the evil system under which women are subhuman and the sex slaves of men."[20] Female reformers in both movements felt their own victimization and impotence in society. Josephine Butler declared, "The degradation of these poor unhappy women is not degradation for them alone; it is a blow to the dignity of every virtuous woman too, it is dishonour done to *me*, it is the shaming of every woman in every country in the world."[21] Without resorting to the language of sexual purity, Kate Millet more recently expressed a similar view in her description of prostitution as "paradigmatic, somehow the very core of the female's social condition. It not only declares her subjection right in the open . . . but the very act of prostitution is itself a declaration of our value. . . . It is not sex the prostitute is really made to sell: it is degradation."[22] Women familiar with the situation of white slaves and prostitutes could not help but sense this and perceive their individual vulnerability: only good fortune separated them from their sisters.

EARLY JEWISH REFORM MOVEMENTS AGAINST THE TRAFFIC

England was also the home of the first organized Jewish effort to stem the growth of prostitution and white slavery among Jews. Jewish reformers discovered that many of the girls and traffickers who came from Russia, Rumania, and Galicia were Jews. Europe was primarily a transit point from where they embarked for Latin America (Rio de Janeiro, Montevideo, and, particularly, Buenos Aires), South Africa (Johannesburg, Pretoria, Transvaal), and the Middle East (Alexandria, Cairo, Port Said). The price for girls paid to traffickers by brothel owners varied between 600 and 1,000 marks in 1900.[23] Jewish reformers pointed out that, before 1880, Jewish prostitution had not been a "disturbing factor."[24] They traced its source to the recrudescence of active Russian persecutions of Jews in 1881. The resulting economic hardships and the desire to emigrate were seen as prime causes of white slavery and prostitution.[25] Poverty caused some women to sell themselves knowingly, and traffickers took advantage of others who wanted to emigrate by offering them fine futures abroad. These procurers even posed as philanthropists, promising to alleviate the economic distress of women. In their haste to leave Eastern Europe, women accepted the lures held out to them and were forced into prostitution as soon as they arrived at their destination. Also, the process of emigration—even when legitimate futures awaited them—was fraught with dangers for girls traveling alone. Procurers posing as morals police, clergy, employment agents, or simply "helpful" persons lurked at ports, railroad terminals, and on trains.[26]

In 1885, the same year that the International Abolitionist Association was made aware of the white slave traffic, the Jewish Association for the Protection of Girls, Women and Children was founded in London. Headed by male leaders of the English-Jewish community, the association concentrated on white slavery rather than on abolitionism. This was because of the conspicuous involvement of Eastern European Jews in the international white slave traffic. German Jews were slower to appreciate this problem. In 1897, the B'nai B'rith Lodge of Hamburg agreed to establish a Jewish Committee to Combat White Slavery. It solicited members in England, Austria, and in the port cities of Germany.[27] Almost its entire membership was male, although two women's groups, both of which later became charter members of the JFB, also joined. In 1900, the Jewish Committee edited a book of articles including a translation of the *Lupaner*, a Brazilian police document in which the names and activities of traffickers were exposed.[28] The publication of this book was intended only for members of the committee, and it was labeled "in strictest confidence."[29]

The details of the report are incomplete and impressionistic. They tell more about the concerns of the Jewish reformers than about the actual and comparative involvement of Jews in the traffic. Yet, they indicate that Jews were guilty of many of these crimes. In Buenos Aires, for example, the report recorded at least thirty-five traffickers who were "almost all Polish Jews." It mentioned that between 2,600 and 2,800 prostitutes were crowded into two streets in that city, and that 40 percent were Polish, 15 percent were Russian, and 10 percent were from Austria-Hungary. It assumed that most of the women from these three countries were Jewish (and this was probably correct, since statistics for 1903 and 1909 indicate a high percentage of Jews from these areas). The report estimated that there were between 80 and 100 traffickers in Brazil and that they were mostly Jews, and it added that in Russia the bordellos were run "primarily by Jews."[30] The report also described the lifestyle of Argentinian traffickers:

They dress with ostentatious elegance, wear huge diamonds, go to the theater or opera daily; they have their own clubs and organizations where the "wares" are sorted, auctioned and sold. . . . They have their own secret wireless code, are well-organized, and—heavens, in South America everything is possible!—shortly they may send a delegate to the Argentinian congress.[31]

The Jewish Committee discussed the brutal poverty in Eastern Europe which drove many Jews to these crimes, even forcing some parents to sell their children into prostitution. "Whoever knows the hair-raising poverty and subjugation of the Jews there, will understand that it can happen that a father could sell his own daughter in order to provide the most necessary means of sustenance for his other children and his wife."[32] The report noted with relief that almost no German Jews were involved in the traffic.

The Jewish Committee chose to study the traffic in cautious silence. It wanted to conceal its investigations from traffickers and anti-Semites. Also, it feared offending the Victorian sensibilities of German Jews by publicizing the facts that were discovered. When it finally did submit an article on white slavery to several Jewish newspapers, it prefaced the exposé by acknowledging that:

Some may be shocked . . . and ask, how can something so . . . delicate be discussed openly? This does not belong in papers that we want our wives or children to see. One should not touch such dirty subjects, but in any case, one should keep the family and home free of them.[33]

At the same time as it was discreetly enlightening the German-Jewish public, the Jewish Committee circulated a letter signed by rabbis from German and Austrian cities which asked Galician leaders to warn their communities of the dangers of white slavery.[34] The committee also set up small home industries for unemployed Galician Jewish women. Convinced that international crimes had to be combatted by international organizations, the Jewish Committee contacted and conferred with the Jewish Association for the Protection of Girls and Women in London, the German National Committee, and other non-Jewish societies with similar missions.

In 1902, the B'nai B'rith Jewish Committee sponsored a conference for all Jewish charities interested in solving this problem.[35] This was the first conference on white slavery that Bertha Pappenheim attended. She later described her shock:

I remember the time when—despite the fact that I had been involved in social work for several years—the words "white slavery" rang in my ears for the first time. They were strange to me and I did not know what they meant, could not grasp that there were people who bought and sold . . . girls and children.[36]

One month later she attended the Second International Conference for the Suppression of the Traffic in Women and Children. There she met two other activists, Sidonie Werner and Henriette Fürth, and discussed the possibility of founding a national organization of Jewish women which would fight Jewish involvement in white slavery by establishing wide-ranging social welfare programs.

By the time the JFB was established, a network of organizations against white slavery existed, but the crime proved difficult to expunge. In 1910, for example, the first Jewish International Conference on White Slavery released its own survey. In Germany, 182 traffickers were listed, among whom were 19 Jews. Austria counted 101, including 65 Jews. Of 93 known South American traffickers, 80 were Russian or Polish Jews. In Galicia, 38 of the 39 known traffickers were Jews, while 104 of the 124 Russian traffickers and 68 of the 105 known Hungarian traffickers were also Jews. Of the 127 French traffickers 34 were Jewish. Most lived in the port cities and capitals: for example, 25 lived in Vienna, 22 in Lemberg, 6 in Trieste, 37 in Budapest, 21 in Warsaw, and 24 in Paris.[37] Thirty percent of these traffickers were women who either owned brothels or served as procuresses. Statistics for prostitutes were available only for Buenos Aires. In 1903, that city had 42 known houses of which 39 were owned by Russian Jews.[38] By the end of 1909, these figures had jumped to 199 and 102, respectively. Out of 537 women in 199 houses, 265 were Jewish. Of 800 new prostitutes registering in 1909, 236 were Jewish, of whom 213 were Russian. Jewish women lived mainly, though not entirely, in Jewish houses. The Jewish International Conference also reported on Jewish prostitutes in Transvaal, Johannesburg, Pretoria, Salisbury, the Philippines, Alexandria, Cairo, Port Said, Calcutta, Odessa, Constantinople, and China.[39]

In *Sisyphus Work*, Pappenheim documented the extent of Jewish prostitution she found during her travels in 1911 and 1912. She visited a hospital for venereal diseases in Budapest, where all the patients were prostitutes, and one-third were Jewish.[40] In Palestine she heard that the traffic was increasing and was shocked to find three bordellos in the small town of Jaffa.[41] In Alexandria, Greek and Jewish prostitutes dominated the "market," while in one Rumanian port town four of the seven brothels were owned by Jews.[42] In Salonika the leaders of the Jewish community admitted that there were several thousand Jewish prostitutes in that city, and in Constantinople, Pappenheim recorded that almost all of the traffickers and approximately 90 percent of the prostitutes were Jewish.[43] Perhaps the most poignant part of her book was the description of the Jewish girls she met. From Salonika she wrote: "the most beautiful Jewess that I saw here, perhaps one of the most beautiful I have ever seen, or that exists, I found today—in a brothel."[44] The image of the girl haunted Pappenheim. One of the highlights of the trip was a surprise reunion with someone she had rescued eight years earlier. Pappenheim was thrilled to encounter a healthy young woman who supported herself as a governess.[45]

It is difficult to assess the extent of Jewish involvement from these statistics. Neither the report published by the conference nor Pappenheim's notes discussed the vigilance of the police (considering that most of the traffic came from Russia and almost none from Germany, the number of Russian traffickers—124—is astoundingly low compared to those caught in Germany—182). Nor did they speculate on whether foreign Jews who were not fluent in the languages of Europe were simply more obvious and therefore easier for the police to identify than native traffickers. Furthermore, they did not detail the predominantly non-Jewish traffic that existed in other parts of the world, for example, the link that Butler had exposed between England and Belgium. An article published in a widely circulated German-Jewish newspaper in 1910 implied that Jews were still a minority in the overall traffic. It divided white slave markets into international, national, and local enterprises and noted that Jews were rarely involved in the last two categories "except in some Eastern provinces." Furthermore, it argued that few Jews shared in the business of prostitution in France, Italy, Switzerland, or the Scandinavian lands. Also, Russia's enormous traffic in women was concentrated primarily in provinces in which Jews were not permitted to live.[46]

Despite insufficient statistical evidence, Jews who fought white slavery felt cause for alarm. They believed the real and circumstantial evidence warranted an extensive reform movement. Although the JFB at first cooperated with the Jewish Committee, Jewish feminists were not as reticent as their male colleagues: they soon embarked upon a campaign to educate the Jewish community about prostitution, rejecting the traditional notion that innocence was protected through silence on subjects related to sex. When cautioned by Jewish leaders who feared the Frauenbund was adding to the arsenal of anti-Semites, Pappenheim responded that the Jewish community would be guilty of complicity if it did not act against these crimes.[47] Jewish feminists devoted a major portion of their efforts and energies to the problem of white slavery, and the issue of white slavery was also used as a strategy to advance other feminist goals. The B'nai B'rith Jewish Committee continued to show interest in the issue, but Pappenheim's organization extended and, eventually, inherited the entire crusade.

The Frauenbund's Attitudes Toward the Causes and Cures of White Slavery

The Frauenbund approached the problem of the causes and cure of Jewish prostitution and white slavery on three levels: as secular feminists, as Jews, and as Jewish feminists.

As secular feminists, the JFB fell into the abolitionist camp. It joined protests against the existence of brothels and supported feminists in their campaign for abolition of police regulation. It hoped to raise the status of women and, thereby, end this abuse. Its opposition to regulation was based on the same arguments that Butler used. Like English and German reformers, the Frauenbund saw white slavery and regulation as symbols of the degradation of all women. It blamed a society which condoned a double moral standard as the foremost criminal in the vicious circle of white slavery and saw the prostitute as a needy sister. It opposed regulation as a reification of hypocrisy and demanded that sons as well as daughters be taught the virtue of chastity. Pappenheim was particularly distraught that boys in their early teens were using brothels, foreshadowing a new generation of men precisely as hardened by the double standard as the old. "This is how they, the future lawmakers, get to know the female sex—as it appears despicable to them," she declared in exasperation.[48]

From its very first meeting, the JFB dealt with what it (and most German feminists) euphemistically called "the morality question" (*Sittlichkeitsfrage*). Its emphasis would differ from that of German feminists. Since most white slaves were not German and Germany was used only as a transit point, German organizations concentrated on the abolitionist campaign.[49] Jewish feminists, despite abolitionist sympathies, cooperated most intensively with other Jews in the fight against white slavery. This was a result of the JFB's strong Jewish identification. Also, its members' vulnerability as Jews in Germany obliged it to attempt to destroy a highly exploitable issue for anti-Semites as well as to combat whatever anti-Semitism arose as a result of this type of Jewish crime.

Anti-Semitism created a dilemma for all Jewish reformers. On the one hand, embarrassed by the extent of Jewish participation in white slavery and by charges that the "Jewish press" covered this up, they joined national and international organizations which sought to end prostitution. They believed that their work in these groups checked any anti-Semitism that might have arisen as a result of the number of Jews implicated in white slavery.[50] Pappenheim also hoped to win the cooperation of members of other religions, because she believed that representatives of all three faiths would have more influence with government and police officials than Jewish reformers would on their own. When the "goods" were Jewish, "things were not taken as seriously" by the police.[51] On the other hand, Jewish reformers treated the information available on Jewish complicity in sexual vice carefully, out of the fear that anti-Semites would take unfair advantage of it. And, of course, anti-Semites did capitalize on it. In *Mein Kampf*, Hitler claimed that the cause of white slavery and prostitution in Vienna was "the Jew . . . a cool, shameless, and calculating manager of this shocking vice, the outcome of the scum of the big city."[52] Pappenheim was particularly distressed to see a reprint of her earlier writings on white slavery in the *Stürmer*, a Nazi pornographic news sheet which focused obsessively on "Jewish" sex scandals in order to titillate, horrify, and infuriate its Aryan readership.[53] The *Stürmer's* headlines combined anti-Semitism, violence, and sex as they accused Jews of rape, ritual murder, and white slavery. Sex crimes were magnified by the added insult of "race shame" (*Rassenschande*), intercourse between Aryan and non-Aryan, which "polluted" German blood. These were constant (weekly) themes illustrated with obscene cartoons and cruel photographs.

As Jewish feminists, JFB members pointed out that prostitution was also a result of the low status of women in the Jewish religion and culture. It was not enough, the JFB argued, that women were revered as wives and mothers. Jews had to respect women as individuals, offering them the same opportunities as men. Pappenheim maintained that women were seen as purely physical beings (*Geschlechtswesen*) by the religion and treated as such in Jewish society. Neither the poor nor the wealthy Jewish woman was given an adequate education. Destined to dependency, women were qualified only to marry and to produce children. However, the wealthier woman generally had someone to support her, whereas, Pappenheim warned, the poor one with no technical skills was often forced to sell her body in order to live.[54]

The legal status of women in Judaism was identified by the JFB as another special causal factor in the Jewish white slave problem. In Eastern Europe and the Orient, approximately four million Jewish women lived under rabbinical law. Ritual marriages were often performed by rabbis without civil sanction.[55] Since a man "takes" a wife in Judaism, and only two witnesses are necessary, many young women could be tricked into marrying a man whose intentions were criminal, and false marriages became a typical ruse of Jewish traffickers. Also, it was relatively easy to purchase a counterfeit Jewish marriage contract, which only the husband and two male witnesses (possibly accomplices of the trafficker) had to sign. This certificate, or *Ketubah*, made apprehension of the criminal impossible, because he could "prove" he was the victim's husband. Pappenheim quoted a Catholic official in Constantinople in 1911, who complained that "thousands of Jewish girls are ruined each year," because of the *Ketubah*.[56]

Such "brides" followed their husbands to Europe or Latin America, with their parents' blessings, only to find that their marriage was not legally binding. Alone, destitute, unfamiliar with the language and ways of their new land, they worked for these men or entered brothels. Jewish feminists emphasized that such marriage-related white slavery was a result of the inferior social and legal status of Jewish women whose major goals in life were considered marriage and childbearing. Lack of education, economic necessity, and the weight of tradition, wrote an Eastern European emigrant woman, made spinsterhood "the greatest misfortune that could threaten a girl, and to ward off that calamity the girl and her family . . . would strain every nerve."[57] An American reformer concluded that: "The acute horror among the Jews of the state of being an old maid makes swindling of Jewish women under promise of marriage especially easy."[58]

Even when white slavery was not intended, ritual marriage laws caused further complications. Such marriage, without any civil, hence legal, sanction could result in prostitution, because husbands could easily abandon wives who were unprotected by any civil laws. Jewish law stipulated that once abandoned, a woman could not remarry unless she was granted a religious divorce from her husband or unless his death was established by a Jewish witness. No observant Jew would wed an abandoned wife, an *Agunah*. Since the majority of Eastern Jews conformed to the dictates of their religion, these women were condemned to eke out an existence by any means available or to accept job or marriage offers however suspect. To discourage abandonment, the JFB urged rabbis to counsel couples to have civil as well as religious marriages. In 1927, the problem in Eastern Europe (with the exception of the new Soviet state which insisted on civil marriages) was no closer to a solution, and the JFB asked the League of Nations to recommend civil marriages, fearing that Orthodox rabbis would take very long, if ever, to do so.[59]

Jewish divorce laws caused further complications. Where religious marriages were legal (as in czarist Russia) or where civil marriages were performed, a civil divorce still had to be followed (and still has to be followed) by a Jewish divorce in which the husband gave the wife a *Get*, or ritual release. If she did not receive the *Get*, she was stigmatized as an *Agunah*. The Frauenbund insisted that the sexist bias of Judaism as found in the laws regarding the *Agunah* contributed to the white slave problem. In an age of pogroms, wars, and economic insecurity, Jewish husbands were often forced to leave home, and some never returned. The JFB became particularly concerned with the *Agunah* after World War I. Although not in contact with Jewish women in the Soviet Union, it was aware of the extreme misery of Jews in the new Poland (which included more than 2,500,000 Russian Jews). According to Pappenheim, talmudic law subjected thousands of destitute widows whose husbands had disappeared during the war and the pogroms that followed it to a "mass death sentence."[60] She estimated there were 20,000 *Agunot* in Eastern Europe in 1929.[61] They fell prey to traffickers who offered them rosy futures or phony divorces. The JFB along with English-Jewish feminists demanded a general rabbinical convocation which would modernize marriage, divorce, and inheritance laws. But petitions sent by the Frauenbund on behalf of the *Agunot* were ignored. Pappenheim once remarked that her woman's sense of justice (*Rechtsgefühl als Frau*) was deeply offended by the fact that Jewish leaders never tempered religious laws in this area of burning misery. She added that laws regarding business questions were commonly revised, often with a great deal of casuistry.[62]

The National and International Campaigns Against the Traffic in Women

The JFB attempted to end the traffic in women by cooperating with international, German, and Jewish organizations founded for that purpose. It also promoted its own programs which sought to prevent girls and women from falling into dangerous circumstances and to rescue and rehabilitate those who had willingly or unwillingly become prostitutes.

At its first business meeting in 1907, Pappenheim encouraged the JFB to join the Jewish Committee and the German National Committee. She represented the JFB at most national and all international conferences. At these meetings she enjoyed prominence as an expert on the subject because of her tours of the Near East and Eastern Europe where she had visited hospitals for venereal disease, cabarets, brothels, orphanages, shelters, schools, and Jewish ghettos, and had talked with journalists, police, government officials, and Jewish leaders. These conferences were an important means of publicizing the traffic, of broadening the base of public support, and of attracting some religious support as well. Conferees, including feminists, church and mission societies, the Salvation Army, purity associations, abolitionists, and anti-white slavery groups, exchanged information (such as lists of "trusted persons" who could meet girls in various cities and inquire about job offers that they had received, lists of legitimate employment openings, and blacklists of suspicious persons, establishments, or agencies) and suggested ways of improving each other's strategies. Useful national and international contacts were made for future cooperation. Most agreed on ways to end the traffic. All attempted to identify traffickers, organize groups of people to meet unaccompanied girls at train stations and ports, set up employment agencies, and educate young people about the dangers of white slavery.

At almost every national and international meeting on white slavery, delegates of the Frauenbund heard that a large percentage of Jewish girls and women from Galicia and Poland were victims of the traffic. In 1907, Pappenheim informed her followers that:

. . . a great number of Jewish girls become prostitutes and . . . in all the houses of prostitution throughout the world, Jewish girls can be found. In the white slave trade, merchants as well as merchandise are mostly Jewish . . . the dirt cannot be washed away by the tears of deceived and damaged women. Many of the girls who engage in prostitution know that they have only one value, that of a sex object.[63]

In 1908, the convention of the German National Committee invited lecturers from the three main religions in Germany. Pappenheim spoke for the Jewish participants. She pointed out the problems the Frauenbund faced in trying to convince other Jews of Jewish participation in prostitution. Many Jews responded that their religion and ethics as well as the traditional Jewish emphasis on a wholesome home life, made such a phenomenon impossible. Thus, Pappenheim and the JFB saw their primary task as publicizing the facts of white slavery among Jews. Non-Jews interested in white slavery had to be taught different facts. They knew that Jews were implicated in these crimes, but frequently failed to appreciate the efforts of Jews to stem the traffic and the circumstances which drove Jews from Eastern

Europe into it. Pappenheim described Jewish life in Rumania, where only 10 percent of school admissions were allotted to Jews, and where all Jews were severely restricted from practicing agriculture, crafts, or the liberal professions. She stated that Rumania permitted the existence of Jewish prostitutes and pimps while it refused to tolerate an honest Jewish laborer.[64] In Russia, six million Jews lived in poverty. It was general knowledge that a Russian Jewish woman only received permission to live outside of the areas restricted to Jews by registering as a prostitute. German-Jewish sources estimated that one-third of all Galician Jews were *Luftmenschen*, people who were constantly on the verge of starvation.[65] Since the Russian and Rumanian governments made it difficult for Jewish agencies to do rescue work, most efforts were directed toward Galicia. But, in 1908, the JFB did petition the queen of Rumania to help Jewish women who were driven to prostitution.[66] Pappenheim delivered the petition personally and was given an audience. She was impressed by the queen's concern, but realized that "one stroke of the Queen's pen," which the petition had requested, would not solve the Jewish problem in Rumania. Pappenheim concluded that if the queen and other women had greater influence in politics, which was a preserve of men, the white slave problem would have been easier to eradicate. She was, nonetheless, optimistic, because, at the very least, the JFB had provoked interest among official circles in Rumania.[67]

German reform circles appreciated the JFB's efforts and praised Pappenheim's trip to Rumania.[68] American Jews invited her to lecture on white slavery on her trip to the Canadian International Women's Conference in 1909. She reported to Jewish audiences in Chicago and New York, quoting surveys which indicated that 80 percent of the Jewish prostitutes in those cities had been sold or led astray through no fault of their own.[69] She related the difficulties she had convincing Galician girls who wanted to emigrate to America that New York was not a village. American Jews promised to assist the efforts of the JFB, and Pappenheim returned to Germany pleased with the contacts she had made.

In 1910, two important conferences occurred, both attended by the JFB. The first was a diplomatic conference on the topic of white slavery convened by the French government at the request of the

International Bureau for the Suppression of Traffic in Women and Children. By this date, governments were at least aware of the traffic, and some showed a willingness to stem it. Because traffickers usually took their victims abroad, a single case might comprise acts perpetrated in several countries. Governmental action was thus needed to combat the traffic effectively. In 1904, twelve nations, including Germany, had decided to exchange information "relative to the procuring of women for immoral purposes abroad."[70] Each government had agreed in principle to patrol at railroad stations and ports and to repatriate victims of the traffic. Prussia established a central police office to gather and coordinate information in cooperation with the German National Committee, but other German states ignored the problem.[71] The traffic did not diminish in the following years. An international convention, signed by the representatives of the major powers in Paris on May 4, 1910, provided for the increased exchange of information on traffickers and the punishment of persons procuring or enticing girls under twenty years of age, even though the separate acts of the offense were committed in different countries. Laws to enforce this provision and to provide for the extradition of criminals were to be passed.[72]

The Frauenbund joined German feminists in applauding the convention, but its attention focused on the first Jewish International Conference on White Slavery held in London in 1910. The JFB chose Pappenheim and Sidonie Werner to represent German-Jewish women.[73] The delegates to this conference discussed the extent of Jewish involvement in white slavery. Many felt that statistics on Jewish involvement were probably too low. Pappenheim remarked that most surveys reflected only the "dumb ones who were apprehended."[74] Also, there were those who were upset by any Jewish sexual vice. One member of the Frauenbund who discovered that there wre 23 Jews among 2,030 prostitutes in one German city commented: "Not a large number, do you say? But for us just twenty-three too many."[75] The 1910 conference analyzed the methods of procurers and the conditions in which white slaves lived.[76] They were "truly slaves, beaten cruelly when they failed to make money for their captors. Ill-treated, frightened, their spirit and willpower crushed, they were simply chattels in the hands of their owners."[77] The conference also concentrated on various means by which reformers might end the traffic. Pappenheim was an active participant at the Jewish International Conference. She discussed police complicity in the traffic, adding that government bureaucracies were also frequently uncooperative.[78] She called on wealthy Jews to protect the victims of white slavery and voiced her despair at the lukewarm reception to her pleas among well-to-do Jews. The few responses she received were from women. As an abolitionist, she vigorously disputed a suggestion that the conference concentrate only on white slavery. She believed that the brothel was a prime cause of the traffic and urged participants to deal with the broader questions related to prostitution.[79] She also reminded the conferees to study prostitution in small cities and to scrutinize the traffic on ships that plied inland waters (particularly the Danube) rather than concentrate solely on major cities and ports.[80] Furthermore, she suggested that funds be allotted to hire agents to pursue traffickers where no Jewish committees existed. Her recommendations were accepted by the conference, and she was applauded as "one of the most energetic and courageous comrades-in-arms of the movement."[81]

Pappenheim's tours of the Balkans, Russia, and the Middle East enabled her to enlist the help of some local women's groups. In 1911, she convinced Jewish women in Philippopolis (Bulgaria) to organize a society for the care of needy women. That same year, she initiated the Ottoman League against White Slavery[82] in Constantinople. Commenting on the backwardness of some of the women she met, she noted that in Budapest, one woman consented to bring her to the "lionesses' den," or local feminist headquarters.[83] The women, in general, were far more sympathetic than the men. When Pappenheim suggested to the head of a Jewish charity that a women's committee might do research on more effective ways of spending large sums, he replied, "God help me, as long as I have anything to say, no woman will enter these premises."[84]

Pappenheim reported on her study tours at the German and international white slavery conferences. She also wrote a leaflet on the topic of white slavery for the German National Committee. It was presented in 1913, at the Fifth International Congress for the Suppression of the White Slave Traffic in London. All the familiar issues were reviewed, but here Pappenheim argued that not only brothels, but bars, music halls, cafes, and baths were all guilty of exploiting women by pandering to sexual appetites.[85] Another new note was a realization that numbers of feebleminded girls were also involved in the traffic. Her recognition of this abuse of the weakest of the weak had probably come earlier—at least with the founding of Isenburg—but this was the first time she expressed it. In an article written in 1913, Lenin attacked the delegates to the Fifth International Congress for their lack of social awareness:

Duchesses, countesses, bishops, priests, rabbis, police officials and all sorts of bourgeois philanthropists were well to the fore! . . . What means of struggle were proposed by the elegant bourgeois . . . ? Mainly two methods —religion and police. . . . When the Austrian delegate tried to raise the question of the social causes of prostitution, of the need and poverty experienced by working class families, of the exploitation of child labour, of unbearable housing conditions, etc., he was forced to silence by hostile shouts![86]

It was at precisely this meeting that Pappenheim had spoken on the causes of prostitution. She maintained that misery, lack of skills or a trade, low wages, bad housing, and ignorance as well as lack of religious training and general upbringing caused vice. She was not greeted by hostile shouts. A liberal, she did not blame capitalism per se for prostitution. Yet, she understood prostitution as a form of double exploitation: the result of debilitating social conditions as well as sexism. She fought the latter by attempting to raise women's status in a man's world and approached the former, as did most social reformers, by urging governments to improve the conditions of the poor.

World War I caused a brief lull in the international traffic because almost all avenues for emigration from Eastern Europe were closed and traffic through Germany was impossible.[87] The JFB ceased its work in Poland and concentrated primarily on social work and war relief within Germany. While the white slave traffic slackened, the opposite was true of prostitution. In Germany, military authorities procured and regulated prostitutes. There was forcible incarceration in mobile brothels of any woman suspected of having intercourse with more than one man, even if the woman was not paid.[88] In Eastern Europe, too, bordellos catered to the troops of occupying powers, At least some of the bordellos serving the German army consisted of Jewish women and girls.[89] The Frauenbund did not comment on these situations except to sponsor a pamphlet in 1917 intended to enlighten young women on sexual matters.[90]

After the war the campaign against white slavery was carried out under the auspices of the League of Nations, which, according to Article 23(c) of the Covenant, had been entrusted "with the general supervision over the execution of agreements with regard to the traffic in women and children."[91] The League convened an international conference in 1921 which raised the age of consent to twenty-one and introduced a system for the licensing and supervision of international employment agencies.[92] A permanent advisory committee was entrusted with the prevention of the traffic and the protection of women. The Jewish Association for the Protection of Girls and Women was invited to participate on this committee.

In the 1920s the JFB continued to support the services and institutions it had founded in its campaign against white slavery, but its interest in international conferences waned. A decrease in the traffic was perceptible. This was due to greater international vigilance as well as to the success of the League in its campaign for the abolition of licensed brothels, which it deemed the chief markets for the traffic (thus agreeing with abolitionists).[93] Also, whereas between 1880 and 1914 more than 1.5 million Jews left Congress Poland, Galicia, and the Pale—with approximately 70 percent choosing the United States as their destination—after the war their paths of escape were blocked. The United States had severely limited immigration by Eastern Europeans by 1924, and the Soviet Union had closed its borders to most emigration (while its government pursued a vigorous campaign to end all prostitution).[94] Thus, movement from Russia to the United States declined drastically and the traffic which thrived during previous migrations diminished proportionately. And, while the 1920s witnessed the immigration of approximately 79,000 Eastern European Jews into Argentina as well as an increase in the number of brothels in Buenos Aires (to 497), reformers—with the grudging support of the police—cracked down on that country's Jewish traffic in 1930. That year 108 of the 424 members of the largest organization of traffickers were arrested and the others fled.[95] Furthermore, by the postwar period, certain trends in Europe provided alternatives to prostitution. Contraceptives assured a safe means of sexual gratification for husbands, who could therefore have sexual relations with their wives rather than using prostitutes to prevent the enlargement of families. Marriage ages were lowering and premarital sex was less risky and less unusual. Finally, working-class women could find greater opportunities for remunerative employment. In Germany, for example, the 1925 census indicated that three million more women (11.5 million) were gainfully employed than before the war.[96]

In 1927, Jewish sources affiliated with the League reported "no material increase in immorality" among Jews, adding, however, that unauthorized ritual marriages and wife desertion still existed.[97] That same year, the League published a report on the traffic in which 6,500 people in 28 countries had been interviewed.[98] Statistics on Jewish prostitution as well as examples of letters written in Yiddish among traffickers were presented. No conclusion regarding the percentage of Jews involved in the trade was given, although the report noted that in the white slave traffic emanating from Poland, "Jewish women are particularly exposed to exploitation."[99] The study did point out that most of the women who were taken abroad seemed to have been prostitutes in their own country.[100] Claude Montefiore, of the Jewish Association for the Protection of Girls and Women (London), was surprised that the report was not harsher on Jews, commenting in a letter to Pappenheim:

We know that . . . Jews have played a prominent part in the traffic. . . . We know that in certain places in Europe . . . Jewish victims and Jewish traffickers are numerous. In these circumstances, I hold . . . that Jews have not come off very badly in the Report. . . . The language used might have been much more definite. . . . Part II . . . sometimes speaks of Polish Jews, but very often speaks only of Poles, where, unhappily, I fear that Polish Jews are meant.[101]

The JFB maintained formal contacts with anti-white slavery forces until the beginning of the Third Reich. In 1927, it met with delegates from nineteen countries at the Second Jewish International Conference on White Slavery. In 1928, the Frauenbund invited women from Budapest, Czernowitz, Vienna, Lemberg and Lodz to Germany to report on Jewish prostitution and women's activities on behalf of the protection of girls. Although it did not send its own delegate to the Eighth International Congress for the Suppression of Traffic in Women and Children in Warsaw in 1930, it published Pappenheim's report of the proceedings. Pappenheim had represented the German National Committee and was bitterly disappointed with the results of the congress. She noted: "The only people who can be entirely pleased with this meeting are the traffickers."[102] Sources at the conference knew of 450 traffickers of whom eight-ninths were supposedly Jewish. Pappenheim did not mention that this was an improvement compared to a figure of about 1,400 traffickers in the early 1920s.[103] She was upset by the very high percentage of Jews still involved and was frustrated by the absence of Warsaw's chief rabbi, particularly because Protestant and Catholic leaders were in attendance. The JFB did not participate in or report on any further international conferences.[104] White slavery was not dealt with as an issue from 1933 onward as a result of the Nazi takeover. The partial truths about Jewish vice that the Nazis exploited must have been particularly painful for Jews involved in the anti-white slavery campaigns, but it was useless to discuss the extent of or socioeconomic reasons for the Jewish traffic in an atmosphere of hatred and vilification. Thus, the JFB chose silence.

Institutions and Programs to Prevent White Slavery

Despite their isolation after 1933 from national and international organizations, Jewish feminists maintained the institutions and services that they had founded in order to prevent white slavery and continued to aid Jewish girls' schools in Poland. The major services provided by the JFB in its program to protect young women (*Mädchenschutz*) were girls' clubs, railway missions, home economics schools, a fund for early marriages, and Isenburg, the home for "endangered" (*gefährdete*) girls and unwed mothers and their babies.

PREVENTIVE WORK IN EASTERN EUROPE

To prevent the sexual abuse of Jewish women, the JFB conducted a propaganda campaign in Eastern Europe to warn Jews of white slavery. Like most Western Jews, the Frauenbund assumed that its

Eastern coreligionists were unaware of prostitution and white slavery. Considering the large extent of the problem in the cities of Eastern Europe (where most Jews lived), it seems highly unlikely that Jews were oblivious to prostitution, although they may have been less conscious of white slavery. In fact, it is more likely that while prostitution was generally unacknowledged, it was so prevalent a phenomenon that ghetto people would not have been at all surprised by it. The novelist Isaac Bashevis Singer, who as a Chassidic child lived in the Jewish quarter of prewar Warsaw, described the Jewish prostitutes of his neighborhood. His street:

. . . had many houses of ill repute. . . . Outside on the square that served as the thieves' hangout, the pimps also used to congregate. Even then I already knew that there were whores and that it is forbidden to look at them, for the mere sight of them is defiling.

Singer's community was aware of white slavery, too, but perhaps not the extent of it. He:

. . . heard the servant girls . . . talking about how procurers drove about at night . . . picked up innocent young women. . . . They were forced into a life of sin, and then they were . . . taken to Buenos Aires . . . then a dangerous worm would get into their blood and their flesh would begin to decay.[105]

In the prewar period the Frauenbund sent leaflets to Eastern Europe alerting both parents and children to the perils involved in accepting "job offers" or "marriage proposals" through the mail or press or from strangers. Enlisting the help of local women, it also set up information centers in Lemberg and Czernowitz for girls who planned to travel or who were seeking jobs abroad. Religious leaders refused to get involved. Some rabbis denied that "such things" existed among Jews. Other rabbis were either uninterested or too ignorant or powerless to help. In Budapest, one rabbi told a seething Pappenheim, "the subject doesn't concern me." In Constantinople, a rabbi admitted that there was a synagogue in which prostitutes donated money to have their pimps called to the Torah on holidays. It was referred to as the synagogue of traffickers (*Synagoge der Mädchenhändler*).[106] In Greece, a rabbi confided that if

Jewish prostitutes would not reform he threatened to paint their faces with ink or cut off their braids. He promised them husbands if they behaved for two years! In 1911, Pappenheim wrote a friend that she wished seminaries would teach rabbis about social responsibilities, adding: "I would like to shout in their ears that . . . they are letting the Jewish people rot."[107]

The JFB supported several vocational and educational institutions for girls in Eastern Europe. It was particularly enthusiastic about the Beth Jacob Schools for Girls in Poland. Founded in 1917 by Sara Schenierer, a former dressmaker, these schools taught girls about Judaism and trained them in practical occupations. The older girls, in turn, would go to villages to give other Jewish girls a basic education.[108] The Frauenbund eagerly greeted this network of elementary and high schools, which grew to encompass 250 schools and 38,000 students by 1937. Pappenheim, who traveled to village schools and lived at the Beth Jacob Teachers' Seminary in Cracow for one week, embraced this system as one which would educate Jewish women and, thereby, prevent white slavery. The JFB popularized the schools and sent donations to the organization. Pappenheim attended several of its planning sessions, encouraging its leaders to expand their vocational offerings.

GIRLS' CLUBS AND DORMITORIES

In Germany, the Frauenbund was dependent—as were all feminists—on men of economic means and political power to effect reforms for women. Actually, it was at a double disadvantage, for even when it received the cooperation of some Jewish men in the campaign against white slavery, the latter, in turn, were dependent on their own political leaders as well as those in such distant and diverse lands as Russia, Rumania, Argentina, and the United States. Very early in its campaign, the JFB devised alternative strategies to alleviate the conditions of its sisters independently of the male establishment.

The Frauenbund founded girls' clubs and dormitories, providing entertainment for working girls in an attempt to keep them out of harm's way in their spare time.[109] Pappenheim was particularly concerned about Eastern European Jewish women who came to Germany to find jobs.[110] They frequently lived lonely lives in rented

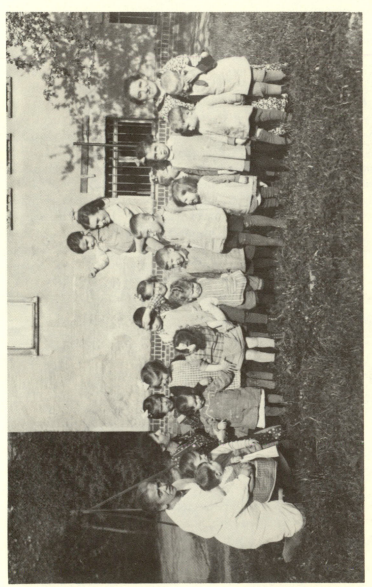

4. Young women attending the JFB's girls' club in Breslau. *Courtesy Leo Baeck Institute, New York.*

The photograph that belongs here is on page 135.

rooms without any pleasant diversions. Away from family influence, confronted by cities and new situations, they were considered by Pappenheim to be easy prey for traffickers. A girls' club would provide Jewish companionship and entertainment after working hours, and, most importantly, would prevent girls from "falling by the wayside." The first such club was established in 1902 by a group which later affiliated with the JFB local in Frankfurt. It offered girls study groups in politics and literature and gave courses in typing, stenography, dancing, gymnastics, and sewing. German and Hebrew were also taught. Considering itself "an organization of women for women," it set aside time to discuss topics of female—and often feminist—interest. Within the next decade, girls' clubs were founded by the JFB in Berlin, Hamburg, Breslau, Leipzig, and Munich, as well as in smaller cities. Jewish organizations and businesses donated the rooms and furnishings. Accommodating fifty to one hundred people, the clubs were frequented almost entirely by working girls from Eastern Europe. Most followed the model of Frankfurt, although some also sponsored libraries, music lessons, guest lectures, handicrafts, bridge, hiking expeditions, and sightseeing tours of neighboring regions. They were usually managed by the JFB local; however, a few had their own boards of directors consisting of the girls themselves. Clubs were open every night of the week, except Friday, and all day on Sunday. Jewish holidays were celebrated at the clubs. In Berlin, for example, participants held *seders* led by JFB members and rabbinical students.

The Frauenbund expanded its protection of girls who lived away from home by providing permanent lodging facilities for them. Four dormitories were established in Berlin, Hamburg, Stettin, and Rheydt. All observed Jewish dietary laws and charged modest rents. The homes had gardens, lounges, small libraries, dining rooms, and music rooms. The Frauenbund intended its homes to be more than dormitories. They were, in fact, supposed to serve as "replacements for the parental home and the family circle."[111] Where the JFB could not afford to build its own homes, it offered housing information and advertised this fact in Jewish newspapers.

HOME ECONOMICS SCHOOLS

Asserting that registered prostitutes were usually girls who had failed as domestic servants because they lacked proper training,[112] the JFB sponsored several home economics schools and urged that all girls learn basic household skills. While its interest in home economics stemmed from other sources as well (see chapter 6), the JFB insisted that careful training could increase a woman's domestic expertise and thus make her career more secure. Yet, the Frauen-bund displayed a peculiar myopia in its insistence that home economics could save girls from prostitution. While proper training could help some, the JFB never alluded to the fact—rather widely known among those involved in campaigns against prostitution—that because of meager wages, hard work, frequent turnover, and seduction by employers, domestic servants occasionally supplemented their income on the streets.[113] This may have been a particularly thorny problem for an organization whose members employed domestics.

AN EARLY MARRIAGE TREASURY

Giving gifts to brides was a holy duty among the ancient Hebrews and medieval Jews, and charities to clothe and dower daughters of the poor had existed in Germany long before the formation of the Frauenbund. Feminists offered different reasons for continuing and expanding these traditions. They hoped that gifts and money would encourage couples to marry at a young age. This, they felt, might reverse the severe population decline affecting Jews, while it limited the potential demand for, and supply of, prostitutes. Abolitionists had traced the increased demand for prostitution, in part, to self-imposed bachelorhood and the resulting increase in the demand for sexual intercourse before marriage. An English journal analyzed this trend in the following terms: "The single man finds quite enough to do to . . . keep up appearances for himself, and dreads the embargo of a wife and family, increasing as they would not only the 'appearances,' but the odium he would suffer if unable to maintain them."[114] German abolitionists noted similar trends among the German bourgeoisie and urged young middle-class couples to give up their "foolish social prejudices" and lower their "pretensions to keep up class appearances."[115] The JFB's members also encouraged simpler lifestyles in order to facilitate earlier marriages, since Jews married even later than Germans. In 1933, for example, two-thirds of the Jews between twenty-five and twenty-nine were single com-

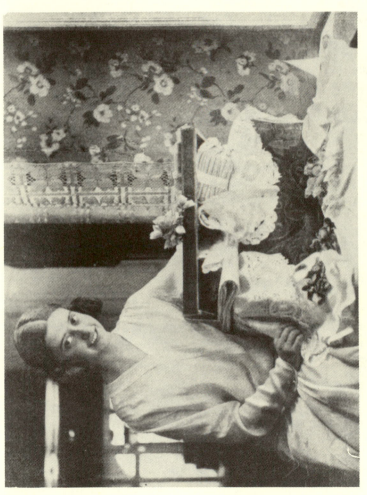

5. A promotional picture for the JFB's program to provide dowries to needy brides. *Courtesy Leo Baeck Institute, New York.*

pared to less than one-half of the German population.[116] The JFB leaders wished that young women would be "more moderate in their demands, and ready to start married life in a simpler way. . . . and all this helps to raise the standard of purity."[117]

Jewish feminists realized that economic considerations could not be ignored when they appealed for early marriages. Their early marriage fund was intended for poor girls, but was also used by middle-class couples, particularly during the inflation and depression years. Frauenbund locals subsidized the furnishing of homes, collected trousseaus, and gave cash gifts to young newlyweds. The JFB national also offered free insurance to couples who married at an early age.[118] Although complete statistics are unavailable, it seems that from the mid-1920s until the mid-1930s most locals supported the marriages of small numbers of young people.[119]

It is doubtful that the JFB's early marriage scheme either limited the demand for prostitutes or caused the supply of prostitutes to diminish (particularly since it probably did not reach "potential" prostitutes in the first place). It probably did not help to increase the fertility of Jews either. Although a woman marrying in youth was likely to have more children than one who married in middle age, it is by no means clear that those couples who married early chose to forego the use of contraceptives. Thus, the JFB in its typically moderate manner attempted to transform a time-honored Jewish custom into a social program, but its goals—the prevention of prostitution and the strengthening of the Jewish population—eluded it.

RAILROAD STATION AID

The Frauenbund established outposts at railroad depots (*Bahnhofshilfe*) and ports (*Schiffsaufsicht*) where volunteers met unaccompanied girls.[120] These volunteers actually vied with traffickers who, as mentioned, frequently procured destitute young women as they disembarked. The Frauenbund offered food, hostels, financial aid, and information to female travelers and acquired contacts who would assure the safety of traveling girls in the port cities of Bremen, Rotterdam, Marseilles, and Trieste. It also furnished these young women with job counseling and placement services. In 1907, the JFB assigned volunteers to ports and to railroad stations in border towns and in large cities.[121] By 1908, the JFB's placard announcing its railroad services hung in third-class coaches next to notices from Catholic and Protestant associations.[122] On the placard was a Star of David with the initials "J.F.," the words "Combat White Slavery," and a list of people to contact for help in every major city and port. Aid posts carried a sign depicting a Star of David with "Jüdischer Frauenbund" printed on it, and volunteers wore yellow armbands with the motto "Help by Women for Women." In 1909, there were twenty railroad volunteer posts. Their number increased to sixty by 1926.[123]

Almost all JFB railroad station work was coordinated with Catholic and Protestant railroad missions which had been founded in the 1890s. Each Christian confession supported approximately 250 such missions.[124] In 1911, the three confessions decided to advertise on one placard which would advise girls in third and fourth-class coaches to seek any railroad mission for aid. Because it did not have all the installations it needed, cooperation with the missions was essential for the JFB. Its volunteers coordinated their schedules with their Christian counterparts and left the names of rabbis and Jewish teachers with the Christian staffs in towns where the JFB could not provide permanent aid.

In the 1920s, the Frauenbund's Railroad Station Aid Commission noted the need for hostels in the larger cities. This was part of a more general housing problem, recognized by German abolitionists as well. In Frankfurt, Berlin, Munich, Cologne, and Breslau, the JFB locals provided rooms for transients. Frequently, the residents of these facilities remained there until the JFB was able to place them in a job. Despite an apparent drop in the traffic in women during these years—a fact never admitted by the JFB—railroad aid remained an important activity. Demand for its services increased during the depression years as economic stress forced middle-class girls, who were formerly accompanied by their families, to travel alone.[125]

The Nazis did not immediately forbid the JFB's presence in railroad depots, but limited its effectiveness by painting across all references to the JFB on coach and waiting-room placards.[126] The JFB sent its lists of "trusted persons" to the Christian missions which at first agreed to assist Jewish female travelers.[127] Those cities that had subsidized Jewish railroad station aid withdrew financial support, and the JFB was forbidden from taking part in the money-raising campaigns it had formerly organized with the Christian missions. At the same time, due to the severe dislocation among Jews who were affected by racial laws and the beginning of Jewish emigration, more Jewish girls than ever were in transit and in need of railroad station assistance.[128] In 1936, the JFB was prohibited from further work in stations. Its volunteers continued to meet girls who notified the JFB in advance of their arrival, but its effective contribution was halted.[129]

ISENBURG: THE HOME FOR ENDANGERED GIRLS

In 1907, Pappenheim founded Isenburg, a home which became the first place on the Continent where "endangered or morally sick" Jewish girls and unmarried mothers and their illegitimate children could find acceptance or care. Pappenheim challenged customary Jewish disdain for unwed mothers and illegitimate children, believing that the young women could reform and that "no child should be lost to the Jewish community."[130] Her attempt to rehabilitate delinquents and prostitutes met with a "storm of indignation" from some Jewish circles: according to an associate, "they fought everything [she said], called all of it exaggerated . . . would have preferred above all to silence her."[131] Although agreeing fully with a moral code which did not condone premarital or extramarital sex or illegitimacy, the members of the Frauenbund disputed those who would have ostracized unmarried mothers. They feared that the prevailing notion that, once "fallen," a woman might as well take to the streets, encouraged girls to do just that while their babies either lived with them in poverty or were given to an orphanage where non-Jews might adopt them. Frauenbund members sympathized with and were supportive of their "erring young sisters" and felt it was incumbent upon them to return these unlucky souls to "an orderly life" after a period of "rest . . . learning . . . and moral strengthening."[132]

Isenburg was split into family units where mothers lived with and learned to care for their babies. The residents were given training in home economics and ran the home themselves, cleaning, planting fruits and vegetables, and cooking according to Jewish

6. Children at the JFB's home in Isenburg. *Courtesy Leo Baeck Institute, New York.*

The photograph that belongs here is on page 128.

dietary laws. Inhabitants and employees ate in a familial setting and celebrated the Sabbath and all religious holidays together. The girls were placed in jobs upon "graduation." By 1937, Isenburg had cared for 1,500 people of German and Eastern European origin. Its housemother, who served without pay for twenty-nine years, was Bertha Pappenheim. On Crystal Night, November 10, 1938, the home was attacked by Nazis who forced the terrified residents to watch as two of the houses were burned down.[133] The next day the children were brought to an orphanage in Frankfurt and the older girls and employees moved into one house. The home was closed permanently in March 1942. Its inhabitants were sent to the concentration camp at Theresienstadt.[134] The houses, once intended by Jewish feminists to protect young women, were turned over to the Hitler Youth.[135]

The Jüdischer Frauenbund pursued what it conceived to be complementary goals, the eradication of immorality—by rescuing prostitutes and closing brothels—and the promotion of a higher social status for women—primarily through education, jobs, and legal reform. There is no doubt that white slavery existed and that there was a considerable traffic before and, to a lesser extent, after the war. The JFB was absolutely sincere in its horror at the abuse of women and in its intention to rectify this. However, the Frauenbund was not simply on a purity crusade: it sought at all times to call attention to the sexual discrimination which lay at the root of sexual vice. As a feminist organization it challenged traditional roles, while remaining sensitive to the conservative nature of its followers. The stress it placed on the white slave issue served to further more far-reaching woman-oriented goals by stirring the consciences and enlisting the support of sympathetic women who had been socialized to be charitable, but who might otherwise have shied away from a feminist movement. The issue was used to achieve practical action toward the construction of new social welfare and recreational institutions for women and to improve the status of women within Judaism. Thus, the JFB concentrated on discrimination suffered by Jewish women which it alleged contributed to the problem of prostitution: the JFB's attack on discriminatory Jewish marriage laws was an example of this. The Frauenbund fought Orthodox interpretations which subjected wives to the will of their husbands. It rejected the Jewish custom in which a woman became a man's possession upon marriage and only he could break the union with her. And, focusing on the plight of the *Agunah*, it asked rabbinical tribunals to change the laws of abandonment in order to save these women from destitution and possible prostitution. The JFB belonged to the London-based Association for the Improvement of the Legal Status of Jewish Women, but emphasized the prevention of prostitution as its reason for joining this Jewish feminist group. Another example of the use of the white slave issue was the Frauenbund's campaign to educate girls. While discussing feminist arguments within the organization, such as the need for the economic or psychological independence of women, to the Jewish community it stressed how jobs could be a "prophylactic against vice." Similarly, rarely mentioning the "right" to vote in the campaign for suffrage in the Jewish community, the JFB based its demands on the premise that the grave injustices perpetrated on Jewish girls could be rectified if Jewish women played a more prominent role in the community. There is no doubt that the Jüdischer Frauenbund would have fought for the improved status of women even if the white slave issue had not existed. However, it might not have attracted as wide or dedicated a following. It was far more effective to attempt to elevate the legal, social, and economic status of women as well as their self-images by using arguments based upon saving the Jewish community from the scourge of prostitution rather than demanding equality for women. Thus, the white slavery issue was a sincere one which also served wider feminist goals.

Notes

1. Ernst Delbanco, "Das Moderne Prostitutionswesen," in *Einführung in das Studium der Prostitutionsfrage*, edited by Anna Pappritz (Leipzig: Verlag von Johann Ambrosius Barth, 1921), pp. 24-27.

2. Richard J. Evans, "Prostitution, State and Society in Imperial Germany," *Past and Present*, no. 70 (February 1976), p. 107.

3. Glen Petrie, *A Singular Iniquity: The Campaigns of Josephine Butler* (New York: Macmillan, 1971), p. 82.

4. Dr. William Acton from his widely read sexual advice book, quoted in Carl N. Degler, "What Ought to Be and What Was: Women's Sexuality in the Nineteenth Century," *American Historical Review* 79 (December 1974), p. 1467. Degler cautions care in using prescriptive literature to determine sexual habits. Surveys he discovered of upper middle class, educated women in the U.S. between 1890 and 1920 indicated that in most cases married sex was agreeable or enjoyable. Yet, Degler also admits that the popularity of prescriptive sex literature (which denied women's sexuality) would have had an effect on the behavior of women.

5. Petrie, *Josephine Butler*, p. 84.

6. George Kibbe Turner, "The Daughters of the Poor," in *The Muckrakers*, edited by Arthur and Lila Weinberg (New York: Capricorn Books, 1964), p. 426. For a history of prostitution, see Vern L. Bullogh, *The History of Prostitution* (New York: University Books, Inc., 1964).

7. For Vienna: William A. Jenks, *Vienna and the Young Hitler* (New York: Columbia University Press, 1960), p. 124; for Berlin: Petrie, *Josephine Butler*, p. 84.

8. Duncan Crow, *The Victorian Woman* (New York: Stein and Day, 1972), pp. 212-13.

9. Evans, "Prostitution," p. 108.

10. Victor A. Mirelman, "The Jews in Argentina (1890-1930): Assimilation and Particularism" (Ph.D. dissertation, Columbia University, 1973), p. 354.

11. Josephine Butler, as quoted in David J. Pivar, *Purity Crusade: Sexual Morality and Social Control, 1868-1900* (Westport, Conn.: Greenwood Press, Inc., 1973), p. 132.

12. Anna Pappritz, "Die Abolitionistische Föderation," in Pappritz, *Einführung in das Studium der Prostitutionsfrage*, p. 222.

13. Ibid.

14. Isaac Metzker, ed., *A Bintel Brief: Sixty Years of Letters from the Lower East Side to the Jewish Daily Forward* (New York: Ballantine Books, 1971), p. 100.

15. For a complete account of Coote's campaigns as well as those of other purity movements in Britain, see: Edward J. Bristow, *Vice and Vigilance: Purity Movements in Britain since 1700* (New Jersey: Rowman and Littlefield, 1978).

16. Pappritz, "Föderation," p. 249. Police approved of regulation from a sanitarian point of view, arguing that the quarantine of sick women protected the home from venereal disease. Further, they worried that immorality would become a public spectacle unless they restricted the movement of prostitutes. Also, they maintained that regulation preserved public

order, because prostitutes were not allowed to infect "the propertyless and work-shy," or the "families of the poorer part of the population of whom many already occupy a low moral position." Evans, "Prostitution," p. 118. Finally, it should be added that there was the obvious potential for payoffs to the police by prostitutes and women who were not prostitutes, all seeking to avoid examination.

17. While the brothel was the major source of demand, the ultimate source of demand was the male population. Thus, although legislation could have eliminated the organized demand emanating from brothels, social and technological changes were necessary before alternatives to prostitution would become available.

18. Anna Pappritz, head of the German Abolitionist Federation, also suggested that in Germany men who hoped to advance in their careers were more dependent on government employment than men in other nations (whose participation in the abolitionist cause was greater). Germans were therefore hesitant to oppose government policies by joining abolitionist causes. "Föderation," pp. 248-49.

19. Judith R. Walkowitz and Daniel J. Walkowitz, "We Are Not Beasts of the Field: Prostitution and the Poor in Plymouth and Southampton under the Contagious Diseases Acts," *Clio's Consciousness Raised,* edited by Mary Hartman and Lois Banner (New York: Harper & Row, 1974), p. 193.

20. David Mitchell, *The Fighting Pankhursts* (New York: Macmillan, 1967), p. 37.

21. Bristow, *Vice and Vigilance,* p. 82.

22. Kate Millet, *The Prostitution Papers* (New York: Ballantine Books, 1973), p. 93.

23. Jewish Association for the Protection of Girls and Women, *Official Report of the Jewish International Conference on the Suppression of the Traffic in Girls and Women, held on April 5, 6, 7, 1910 in London,* pp. 93, 189. These facts were also exposed in Grossloge für Deutschland Unabhängiger Orden Bne Briss, *Die Wirksamkeit des von der Grossloge für Deutschland U.O.B.B. ernannter Comitees zur Bekämpfung des Mädchenhandels,* pp. 8, 29, 56. See also Deutsches Nationalkomitee zur internationaler Bekämpfung des Mädchenhandels, *Der Mädchenhandel und seiner Bekämpfung, Denkschrift,* p. 4; Deutsches Nationalkomitee, *Bericht über die Deutsch-Nationale Konferenz zu Bekämpfung des Madchenhandels, Frankfurt/Main, 1902,* p. 18; Deutsches Nationalkomitee, *Bericht über die 9 Deutsche Nationalkonferenz zu internationaler Bekämpfung des Mädchenhandels zu Stettin, 13-14 November, 1912,* p. 7; The Jewish Association for the Protection of Girls and Women, *Report: 1915,* p. 24; Anna Pappritz, *Der Mädchen-*

handel und seine Bekämpfung (Berlin: F. Herbig, GmbH, 1924), p. 11.

24. Jewish Association, *Report, 1910,* p. 93.

25. UOBB, *Comitee zur Bekämpfung des Mädchenhandels,* p. 14.

26. Tuch collection, ALBI, no. 7025 (11), p. 18.

27. *Bericht über die Deutsch-Nationale Konferenz, 1902,* p. 17.

28. Deutsches National Komitee, *Der Mädchenhandel* (1903), p. 13. "Lupaner" is the Latin word for brothel. It is also used occasionally in German.

29. UOBB, *Comitee zur Bekämpfung des Mädchenhandels,* p. 3.

30. Ibid., pp. 8, 10, 56; and Mirelman, "Argentina," pp. 353-54.

31. UOBB, *Comitee zur Bekämpfung des Mädchenhandels,* p. 7.

32. Ibid., p. 30; see also: Deutsches Nationalkomitee, *Bericht über die 6 Deutsche Nationalkonferenz zu internationaler Bekämpfung des Mädchenhandels zu Breslau am 8-9 Oktober, 1908,* pp. 102-103.

In 1911, a consul in Salonika told Pappenheim: "What do you expect of Jews, they sell their children like chickens!" Bertha Pappenheim, *Sisyphus Arbeit: Reisebriefe aus den Jahren 1911 und 1912* (Leipzig: Verlag Paul E. Linder, 1924), p. 42. Popular literature also dealt with this theme. In *Yama,* a novel about prostitution in Russia by Alexandre Kuprin, one of the prostitutes was a Jewish girl who had been sold to the brothel by her mother. Kuprin also described Jewish traffickers. The novel appeared in three parts, in 1909, 1914, and 1915. (New York: The Modern Library, 1932), pp. 60, 75, 159-87.

33. Tuch collection, ALBI, no. 7025(6).

34. UOBB, *Comitee zur Bekämpfung des Mädchenhandels,* pp. 16-17.

35. Jewish Association, *Report: 1902,* p. 29.

36. Jewish Association, *Report, 1910,* p. 146.

37. Ibid., pp. 41-42.

38. Deutsches National Komitee, *Der Mädchenhandel* (1903), p. 4.

39. Jewish Association, *Report, 1910,* pp. 33-35. For the United States, statistics were given for Philadelphia for 1910. Fifteen percent of the prostitutes in that city were Jewish, and only 8 percent of the population was Jewish. Ibid., p. 255.

40. Pappenheim, *Sisyphus,* p. 15.

41. Ibid., pp. 126-27.

42. Ibid., pp. 130, 224.

43. Ibid., pp. 42, 51.

44. Ibid., p. 40.

45. Ibid., pp. 23-24.

46. *AZDJ,* November 11, 1910, pp. 529-31. In New York, statistics indicated that about 17 percent of arrested prostitutes in Manhattan from 1913 to 1930 were Jewish in a period when about one-third of New Yorkers

were Jewish. Thus, the number of arrested Jewish prostitutes in that city was proportionately less than the Jewish sector of the population. Baum, et al., *The Jewish Woman in America*, p. 174.

47. Meyer collection, ALBI, no. 877 (XI, 2).

48. Deutsch Nationalkomitee, *Bericht über die 8 Deutsche National-konferenz zu internationaler Bekämpfung des Mädchenhandels zu Karlsruhe am 10-11 Oktober, 1911*, p. 170.

49. In the 1880s and 1890s in Germany, Morality Associations, formed by the Evangelical Church, insisted that the state prosecute and persecute prostitutes rather than control or regulate them. These groups preceded but they also paralleled abolitionist organizations. But, it was the abolitionists who convinced the Bund Deutscher Frauenvereine to take up their cause. See Evans, "Prostitution."

50. Jewish Association, *Report, 1910*, p. 75; Baum, *Jewish Woman*, p. 173.

51. Deutsch Nationalkomitee, *6 Deutsche Nationalkonferenz*, p. 10.

52. While there were no more than 25 Jewish traffickers in Vienna at the time Hitler described (out of a total of 101 in all of Austria of whom 64 percent were supposedly Jewish), the partial truth of his statement must have caused considerable agony among Jewish reformers. *Mein Kampf*, translated by John Chamberlain et al. (New York: Reynal and Hitchcock, 1939), p. 78.

53. Dora Edinger, ed., *Bertha Pappenheim: Freud's Anna O* (Highland Park, Ill.: Congregation Solel, 1968), pp. 20-21.

On the use of sex slanders and sex scandals by anti-Semites, see: Louis W. Bondy, *Racketeers of Hatred* (London: Newman Wolsey Limited, 1946); Arnold Paucker, *Das jüdische Abwehrkampf gegen Antisemitismus und Nationalsozialismus in den letzten Jahren der Weimarer Republik* (Hamburg: Leibniz Verlag, 1968), pp. 69, 79, 273; Z.A.B. Zeman, *Nazi Propaganda* (London: Oxford University Press, 1964), pp. 25, 139.

54. Meyer collection, ALBI, no. 877 (XI, 2).

55. The exception was czarist Russia, where religious marriages were considered legal. Lise Leibholz, "Die Weltkonferenz jüdischer Frauen," *Der Morgen* (June 1929), pp. 288-93.

56. Pappenheim, *Sisyphus*, p. 53.

57. Mary Antin, referring to *shtetl* life at the turn of the century, quoted in Baum, *Jewish Woman*, p. 62.

58. Turner, "Daughters of the Poor," p. 420.

59. *BJFB*, July 1927, pp. 5-6. In Poland ritual marriages were illegal but these rules were flagrantly ignored.

60. Schönewald collection, ALBI, no. 3896 (III, 1).

61. *BJFB*, July 1936, p. 21.

62. Edinger, ed., *Bertha Pappenheim: Leben und Schriften* (Frankfurt/ Main: Ner Tamid Verlag, 1963), p. 19.

63. Meyer collection, ALBI, no. 877 (XI, 2).

64. *Bericht über die 6 Deutsche Nationalkonferenz*, 1908, p. 6. According to other sources, the situation was even more intolerable than Pappenheim described. Jews had no civil or political rights. Their movement was restricted. They were forbidden ownership of guest houses, could not sell alcoholic beverages or tobacco, and could not attain academic degrees. Industrial and railroad workers had to be either two-thirds or full-blooded Rumanians (and Jews were considered foreigners). Laws against peddling handicapped thousands of Jews. Between 1900 and 1907, 70,000 Jews fled Rumania; in fact, Jewish migration from Rumania was proportionately heavier than that from Russia before the war. See: *IF*, May 28, 1908, p. 3; *Encyclopedia Judaica*, 1971, Vol. XIV, pp. 389-93; Moses Rischin, *The Promised City* (Cambridge: Harvard University Press, 1962), pp. 32-33.

65. *Bericht über die 6 Deutsche Nationalkonferenz*, 1908, p. 7. See also: Tuch collection, ALBI, no. 7025 (11), p. 7; *Bericht über die 9 Deutsche Nationalkonferenz*, p. 127.

66. *IF*, March 11, 1908, p. 12.

67. *IF*, April 29, 1909, p. 11.

68. Deutsches Nationalkomitee, *Bericht über die 7 Deutsche Nationalkonferenz zu internationaler Bekämpfung des Mädchenhandels zu Leipzig am 15 und 16 November, 1909*, p. 21.

69. *IF*, August 5, 1909, p. 11.

70. This was the International Agreement for the Suppression of the White Slave Traffic. It was signed at Paris on May 18, 1904, and amended by the protocol signed at Lake Success, New York, May 4, 1949. In *International Agreement for the Suppression of the White Slave Traffic*, p. 1.

71. Pappritz, *Der Mädchenhandel* (1924), pp. 23, 25-26.

72. Denys P. Myers, *Handbook of the League of Nations* (Boston: World Peace Foundation, 1935), p. 230. Germany actually had two laws which— had they been enforced—might have cut the traffic to a minimum. The "White Slavery Paragraph," no. 48 of the Imperial Law of 1897, read: "Whoever leads a woman out of the country while secretly knowing that the purpose to be fulfilled is commercial immorality . . . is subject to punishment." See Pappritz, *Der Mädchenhandel* (1924), p. 38.

73. *IF*, January 19, 1911, p. 12.

74. Jewish Association, *Report, 1910*, p. 45.

75. Jewish Association, *Report, 1927*, p. 60.

76. See Pappritz, *Der Mädchenhandel* (1924), pp. 4-9, for examples of the schemes of traffickers.

77. Jewish Association, *Report, 1910*, p. 35.

78. Ibid., p. 148.

79. Ibid., p. 75.

80. Ibid., p. 45.

81. Ibid., p. 154.

82. Pappenheim, *Sisyphus*, p. 71.

83. Ibid., p. 12.

84. Ibid., p. 11.

85. National Vigilance Association, *The Fifth International Congress for the Suppression of the White Slave Traffic: London, June 30-July 4, 1913*, p. 253.

86. Vladimir Lenin, "The Fifth International Congress Against Prostitution," in *The Lenin Anthology*, edited by Robert C. Tucker (New York: W.W. Norton, Inc., 1975), pp. 683-84.

87. League of Nations, *International Conference on Traffic in Women and Children, Provisional Verbatim Report, June 30-July 5, 1921, Geneva*, pp. 11-12; Pappritz, *Der Mädchenhandel* (1924), p. 11.

88. Katharina Scheven, "Die Sozialen und Wirtschaftlichen Grundlagen der Prostitution," in *Einführung*, edited by Anna Pappritz, p. 144; Evans, "Prostitution," pp. 127-28.

89. Stern, unpublished memoirs, ALBI, no. 939, pp. 58-59.

90. *IF*, February 1, 1917, p. 4.

91. F. B. Walters, *A History of the League of Nations* (London: Oxford University Press, 1952), p. 186.

92. Bullogh, *Prostitution*, p. 184.

93. Walters, *History of the League*, p. 187; League of Nations, "Work of the Traffic in Women and Children Committee during its Sixth Session," in *League of Nations Official Journal, 1927* (C221, M.60. 1927, IV), annex 971, p. 903.

94. On emigration from the Soviet Union, see Zvi Gitelman, *Jewish Nationality and Soviet Politics: The Jewish Sections of the C.P.S.U., 1917-30* (New Jersey: Princeton University Press, 1972), pp. 235-37. On Soviet programs to eliminate prostitution, see William Mandel, *Soviet Women* (New York: Anchor Press/Doubleday, 1975), p. 68.

95. Mirelman, "Argentina," pp. 356-61.

96. Renate Bridenthal, "Beyond Kinder, Küche, Kirche: Weimar Woman at Work," *Central European History* 6 (June 1973), p. 150.

97. League of Nations, "Report by Mr. Cohen, Representative of the Jewish Association for the Protection of Women, for the Year 1926, Traffic in Women and Children Committee, Sixth Session, April 30, 1927," in *League of Nations IV Social, 1926-27* (Doc. C.T.F.E. 334), annex 8, pp. 122-28.

98. Myers, *Handbook of the League*, p. 231.

99. League of Nations, "Report of the Special Body of Experts on the Extent of the International Traffic in Women and Children, II," in *League of Nations IV Social: 1926-27* [C52 (2) M52 (1) 1927, IV], pp. 135-36.

100. League of Nations, "Report of the Special Body of Experts on the Extent of the International Traffic in Women and Children, II," in *League of Nations Official Journal* (1927), p. 378.

101. Pappenheim, *Sisyphus-Arbeit II* (Berlin: Druck and Verlag Berthold Levy, 1929), pp. 27-28. Montefiore was referring to pp. 135-36 of the League Report [C52 (2) M52 (1) 1927, IV].

102. *BJFB*, December 1930, pp. 1-2.

103. Ibid., and Pappritz, *Der Mädchenhandel* (1924), p. 10.

104. The ninth conference was held after Hitler had taken power in October 1933 in Geneva. Another conference followed in Paris in 1937 and in New York in 1949.

105. *Dimensions* (Fall 1967), pp. 15-16. The same was probably true of other Jewish ghettos. In the New York ghetto, Irving Howe wrote that "there were things that everyone knew," but "communities struggling for survival seldom rush to announce their failures." *World of Our Fathers* (New York: Harcourt Brace Jovanovich, 1976), pp. 96-99. In Russia, the well-known Yiddish playwright Sholom Ash exposed the lives of Jewish brothel owners in one of his most powerful plays, "The God of Vengeance."' First produced by Max Reinhardt in Berlin in 1910, the play made its way to the chief stages of Europe and was translated into all the major Western and Eastern European languages, Hebrew, and English by 1918.

106. Pappenheim, *Sisyphus*, p. 53. It was not surprising that traffickers would have their own communal organizations (although one wonders how they could practice their religion seriously and sincerely). In at least two other cities, Buenos Aires and New York, traffickers developed elaborate communal and religious institutions. Mirelman, "Argentina," pp. 356-58; Turner, "Daughters," p. 414; Pappritz, *Der Mädchenhandel* (1924), p. 11.

107. *Sisyphus Arbeit*, p. 16.

108. Judith Gronfeld Rosenbaun, "Sara Schenierer," in *Jewish Leaders*, edited by Leo Jung (New York: Block Publishing Co., 1953), pp. 405-32; Deborah Weissman, "Bais Yaakov: A Historical Model for Jewish Feminists," in *The Jewish Woman*, edited by Elizabeth Koltun (New York: Schocken, 1976), pp. 139-48.

109. "Purity reformers" (the term is used by David Pivar) in America also founded working girls' societies during the 1890s.

110. One of Pappenheim's short stories, "A Friday Evening," describes the plight of such a girl. In *Kämpfe: Sechs Erzählungen* (Frankfurt.'Main: J. Kauffmann, 1916), pp. 117-40.

111. *IF*, January 20, 1910, p. 10.

112. *BJFB*, July 1927, p. 1.

113. Scheven, "Grundlagen der Prostitution."

114. *The Lancet*, February 5, 1853, p. 137, as quoted in Sigsworth, "Victorian Prostitution," p. 85.

115. Scheven, "Grundlagen der Prostitution," pp. 170-72.

116. Rosenthal, "Jewish Population," p. 251.

117. Jewish Association, *Report, 1927*, p. 65.

118. *IF*, February 1, 1917, p. 4.

119. In 1927, for example, the Breslau local helped 18 couples. In 1935, it made it possible for 31 brides to complete their trousseaus. *BJFB*, June 1929, pp. 17-18; *BJFB*, February 1935, p. 11.

120. The JFB chose the title *Bahnhofshilfe* instead of the commonly used term *Bahnhofsmission* in order to avoid the Christian connotation of "mission." *BJFB*, February 1926, pp. 1-3.

121. Meyer collection, ALBI, no. 877 (XI, 2) and *AZDJ*, October 18, (1907, p. 50. Berlin and Frankfurt/Main were two of the busiest stations for Jewish travelers. The JFB locals in these cities soon hired professional staffs (rather than depending on volunteers) to work at these posts.

122. The Catholic and Protestant organizations cooperated in a working committee (*Konferenz für kirchliche Bahnhofsmission*) to which the JFB did not belong. However, the Jewish organization did consult with the Christian organizations.

123. *BJFB*, February 1926, pp. 1-3.

124. *BJFB*, February 1926, pp. 1-3.

125. *BJFB*, November 1932, p. 5.

126. *BJFB*, November 1933, pp. 10-11.

127. *BJFB*, July 1934, pp. 10-11.

128. In the first half of 1933, 185 women were cared for at the Frankfurt/Main station. This figure jumped to 619 in the second half of that year. *BJFB*, July 1934, pp. 10-11. Berlin and Frankfurt maintained their railroad posts until November 1935. Frankfurt assisted 644 Jewish girls between January 1, 1935, and September 30, 1935. *BJFB*, November 1935, p. 10.

129. *BJFB*, April 1937, p. 8.

130. Else Rabin, "The Jewish Woman in Social Service in Germany," in *The Jewish Library*, edited by Leo Jung, Series III, p. 301.

131. Straus, *Wir Lebten in Deutschland*, p. 151.

132. *AZDJ*, August 30, 1907, p. 412.

133. Letter by Helene Kramer co-manager of Isenburg until October 1941. Yad-Vashem, Jerusalem, The Central Archives for the Disaster and the Heroism, 0-1/106, German, 6 p.

134. Ibid.

135. Schönewald collection, ALBI, no. 3896 (IV, 5).

chapter 5

The Pursuit of Influence and Equality in Germany's Jewish Community

"And He Shall Rule over Thee": The Opposition to Women's Suffrage

Feminists challenged male domination of the Jewish community. No longer satisfied with honorary titles and volunteer status, they sought influence and equality in the communal power structure. The JFB demanded leadership positions for women, challenging the role of secondary citizen ascribed to their sex. The exclusion of women from communal responsibility as well as from public rituals stemmed from the patriarchal culture of the ancient Hebrews. Women prayed in the synagogues, but did not share the same religious rights and duties as men. Compounding the injustice, these religious strictures were translated into social and political handicaps. Women paid taxes to and worked for their community, but they had no voice in running it. They were confined by tradition to the roles of wife, mother, and helpmate until the Frauenbund challenged this situation. The JFB's battle for political recognition was lengthy and its foes formidable. They continued to deny Jewish women political rights even after 1918, when the vote had been granted to women in Germany and in the Protestant ecclesiastical community. Jewish feminists reminded religious leaders that modernizing women's status would represent a further, desired step in Jewish acculturation to modern German norms. It would also revitalize Judaism by inviting women's genuine participation. These arguments addressed in microcosm a more general dilemma of German Jewry: the desire to be as German as possible, while guarding Jewish distinctiveness.

Jewish feminists' persistence in the face of male intransigence can only be understood in light of the ties they felt to their *Gemeinde*. Because of a defensive cohesiveness that resulted from a frequently anti-Semitic environment, and because of a positive desire to retain and enhance their *Schicksalsgemeinschaft* (community of destiny), they took their stand within their community. Furthermore, the Jewish community was not simply a voluntary association for purely religious purposes. From the mid-nineteenth century, the Prussian government recognized the autonomy of the Jewish community and allowed it to administer its own cultural and religious life, religious education, and social welfare.[1] Membership was compulsory. Nothing Jewish was outside the jurisdiction of the *Gemeinde*.[2]

These communities usually had a representative body elected by the male members, and an executive council elected by the representative body. In 1890, 2,359 Jewish communities existed. As Jews migrated from small towns to neighboring cities, and then to larger cities, the number of Jewish communities decreased. In 1905, there were 2,282 of them; in 1932, only 1,611 remained in Germany.[3] The largest Jewish communities were (in order) those of Berlin, Frankfurt, Breslau, Hamburg, Cologne, Leipzig, and Munich, and it was in these communities that the JFB campaigned most vigorously for the vote. Despite religious differences between Orthodox and Liberal Jews, ethnic and class tensions between German Jews and Eastern European immigrants, and political disputes between Zionists and those who sought integration into German society, most members hoped to preserve the unity of their *Gemeinde*. Even after the Prussian Secession Law of 1876, which allowed Jews to withdraw from their local community on grounds of liberty of conscience, the overwhelming majority remained loyal. While some of the very religious Orthodox did secede, most of the more traditional Jews, who numbered about 15 to 20 percent of all German Jews, agreed to remain within their original *Gemeinde* provided the progessive (Liberal) majorities respected the needs of their more observant coreligionists. Thus, Liberal members of the various Jewish communities adopted a policy of accommodation out of fear of provoking secession and losing revenue. Representatives were careful not to introduce reforms which might lead to the withdrawal of con-

servative members. The Law of Secession was, according to a pro-
ponent of Liberalism, "the club which the Orthodox held over the
congregation to compel a maintenance of the status quo."[4]

Because the Orthodox members refused to allow women a voice
in *Gemeinde* affairs, and Liberals tried not to alienate their fellow
Jews, feminists were frequently balked by a tiny minority of men.
An example of this occurred in 1930 in a Bavarian community in
which women, supported by Liberals, demanded the right to vote.
The Orthodox representatives objected to their petition and threatened to secede. When the vote was called, a number of Liberals had
already left the session—not by coincidence—and the vote went
against women.[5]

LIBERAL AND ORTHODOX ATTITUDES TOWARD
WOMEN'S SUFFRAGE

A sketch of the traditional attitudes toward women's religious
functions may explain why the question of women's political participation caused such dissension within the *Gemeinde*: the restrictions
on women were religious in nature, but profoundly affected their
political and social status. Man's universal predominance and
woman's powerlessness pervaded Jewish religious writings: Eve's
punishment for tasting the forbidden fruit was that she would be
ruled forever by her husband.[6] Women were seen as physical beings.
Their primary duties were those of wife—accommodating to a
husband's physical comforts, sexual needs, and religious obligations—and mother. The "good" wife or mother was self-denying,
submissive, and chaste, while the "evil" one was bold, direct, dis-
obedient, or aggressive. Because the home and family occupied so
much of her time, woman was exempted from the study of the
Torah and from positive, time-bound commandments, such as
joining in prayer quorums or leading worship services.[7] And, while
woman as wife-mother was predominant, the role of temptress and
seducer was also attributed to her. Females were considered lustful
and frivolous,[8] and contact with them was deemed dangerous to
men's studiousness, fidelity, and chastity. Men taught each other
that "a woman desires less material goods and more sex rather than
more revenue and less sex."[9] Lest they have sinful thoughts, men
were told not to talk to a menstruating wife or engage in conversa-

tion with a woman. Those who found themselves in a situation where it was necessary to speak with a woman turned their heads or lowered their eyes. Even when women came to the synagogue to pray, they were segregated from men. Their apartness was also apparent in community affairs, in which, for the most part, they did not participate; when they did, it was in a supportive rather than a leading role.

This tradition was first questioned by rabbinical reformers. The founders of the liberal branch of Judaism argued that the salvation of the faith depended upon its being delivered from the rigidity of formalism. They asserted that Judaism was a living, ever-developing faith which needed to adapt itself to a more modern outlook by dropping some of its Oriental ways. Theirs was a conscious effort to break with the ghetto and create a form of worship sufficiently like the Christian to diminish social antagonisms between the two groups, stem the number of conversions, and minimize their embarrassment at the non-Western customs evident in the treatment of Jewish women.[10] In their pursuit of modernization, they challenged, in theory, some of the more oppressive restrictions on Jewish women. In 1837, Abraham Geiger, one of the leaders of the movement, wrote: "Let there be from now on no distinction between men and women, . . . no assumption of the spiritual minority of woman, . . . no institutions of the public service, either in form or content which shuts the door of the temple in the face of women."[11] This statement marked a significant departure from the talmudic and rabbinical codes. The status of women was briefly reviewed at a rabbinical conference that took place in Breslau in 1846. A commission recommended that woman should be entitled "to the same religious rights and subject to the same religious duties as man." It also argued that the benediction repeated daily by men, "Praised be Thou oh Lord, our God, who has not made me a woman," be abolished.[12] These suggestions were merely read. They were not discussed and no vote was taken. Although women were seen as theoretical equals by some, no practical results occurred except in the tiny Reform congregation of Berlin. Liberals may have thought about change, but they did not quickly translate their theory into action. In the years before the war, the JFB's demands for a vote in the Jewish community were ignored by Orthodox and Liberal leaders alike, just as German women's demands went unheard by German leaders. After women had attained the vote in Germany, the JFB, emboldened by the victory of its German sisters, renewed its demands on Liberals for a political voice.

Orthodox Jews, suspicious of further encroachments on religious tradition, considered even women's purely political participation an affront. The Orthodox establishment clarified its position in 1919, when the Frauenbund stepped up its campaign for the vote. Rabbi David Hoffmann, head of the Orthodox Berlin seminary, published a formal opinion in which he declared that women could not, according to Jewish law, be elected to a communal office.[13] He based his interpretation on Deuteronomy 17:15, in which the Hebrews were told to "set him over thee . . . one from among thy brethren." Hoffmann. He and Bertha Pappenheim had worked together on a fore women were not included. He did not, however, object to women voting for officers of the community. He noted that the Jewish community, not simply its men, had been commanded by God to elect judges. Thus, women had a duty to vote. Although some Orthodox rabbis disagreed strongly with this intrepretation,[14] Hoffmann concluded that women could participate in the selection of leaders—if a majority of their community agreed to allow them to vote. The JFB used the favorable aspects of Hoffmann's opinion in its propaganda. However, until his decision, the JFB had assumed that "women's suffrage" meant the right to vote as well as the right to hold office. Hoffmann's judgment forced the JFB to fight for both "active suffrage" (*das aktive Wahlrecht*) and "passive suffrage" (*das passive Wahlrecht*). The former meant the right to cast a ballot and the latter indicated eligibility to stand for office. Although the Frauenbund demanded that these rights be granted simultaneously, it usually had to continue to fight for passive suffrage long after active suffrage had been achieved. This was the case, for example, in Hamburg, where the vote was granted in 1919, but where women were not permitted to be candidates for office until ten years later.[15] By 1929, active and passive suffrage had been accepted by twenty-three communities, and eight allowed only the vote.[16]

The JFB's Campaign for Women's Rights

While Jewish feminists appeared conservative in comparison with some secular feminists of their day (in particular, with the radical feminists), in a religious context their demands were radical. Theirs was the only Jewish women's association in Europe or the United States to promote women's rights, challenging Jewish tradition and the monopoly of men in interpreting Jewish law. Except for the London-based Association for the Improvement of the Legal Status of Jewish Women, a small group, no other Jewish women's organization explicitly identified with feminism. Also, the JFB was the only religious women's organization in Germany to promote feminism in its goals and to belong to the German women's movement. Catholic women, who organized in 1903, never joined the Bund Deutscher Frauenvereine and took no stand on suffrage. The Protestant Federation of Women, begun in 1899, supported ecclesiastical suffrage, but did not approve of women's suffrage in the nation and withdrew from the BDF shortly after joining it. The JFB was, therefore, the only religious organization in Germany to demand religious as well as secular suffrage.

Jewish feminists presented their own arsenal of religious arguments in favor of (both types of) suffrage. Their most useful weapon was the opinion of Rabbi Nehemiah A. Nobel of Frankfurt, a well-known and respected religious conservative and a student of Rabbi Hoffmann. He and Bertha Pappenheim had worked together on a commission which was authorized to prepare a new constitution for the Frankfurt *Gemeinde* in 1919. Pappenheim pressed for the complete political equality of women. On December 4, 1919, Nobel wrote her a note in which he stated: "I have decided in favor of active and passive suffrage for women. At your request, I can affirm that, in my opinion, religious considerations which deny . . . the vote can not be supported."[17] Pappenheim was exceptionally grateful to the rabbi, and considered his decision a milestone on the road to suffrage.[18] He had given women an "ethical gift" which Pappenheim compared to Rabbi Gershom's decision against polygamy nine hundred years earlier. The Frauenbund used Nobel's opinion in all of its propaganda. It maintained that he had shown women "new paths of responsibilities . . . meant to improve the well-being of the community." Jewish feminists regarded him as "their teacher and guide."[19]

The Frauenbund maintained that its position was confirmed by the Talmud, *Shabbath* 62a, which stated that on the Sabbath, "a woman may not go out with a . . . ring bearing a signet." The Talmud explained that signet rings were worn by women who occupied positions of responsibility in the community. This particular reference was to a woman who was treasurer of charity funds. She impressed the seal of her ring on orders for the disbursement of alms. The JFB insisted that this passage was a clear indication that women had held high offices in talmudic times and, thus, should hold them in the present.[20] Feminists considered the Talmud's description of women's more compassionate nature as another proof of their worthiness to attain leadership positions. They pointed to the story of Rabbi Hilkia and his wife. During a drought the people asked him to pray for rain. He and his wife stood in separate places beseeching God for mercy. The first sign of rain appeared closer to the woman. The rabbi considered this an indication that women's prayers were more effective than men's, because women were more sensitive to the needs of the poor.[21]

The JFB enlisted the help of the World Conference of Jewish Women in its attempt to justify the vote for women. This organization respected the views of Orthodox rabbis, but argued that rabbis' interpretations frequently differed and, therefore, it rejected what it considered to be arbitrary rules.[22] Because some Orthodox rabbis accepted women's participation, the conference claimed the right to both active and passive suffrage. Like the Frauenbund, it contended that women's participation was indispensable to the preservation of Judaism in the modern age.[23] Despite the Frauenbund's respectful persistence, the Orthodox minority refused to be convinced of the theological legitimacy of feminists' demands.

THE PREWAR STRUGGLE FOR MEANINGFUL POSTS
IN JEWISH COMMUNAL ORGANIZATIONS

The history of the Frauenbund's efforts on behalf of women's rights began at its first delegate assembly in 1905, but the fight for suffrage remained subdued because of its extreme unpopularity until after World War I.[24] Instead, the JFB called for equal status for women in all aspects of communal responsibilities, claiming that it fought for a place in a man's state, much as Jews fought for one in Germany. It demanded the appointment of women to community administrative offices (such as education or welfare commissions) which were usually monopolized by men and the participation of women on the boards of directors of all national Jewish welfare organizations. Pappenheim summarized Jewish feminists' requests by insisting that "Jewish women should feel at home in and necessary to Jewish society."[25] Her colleague, Sidonie Werner, appealed to Jewish leaders to accept the talents that women could offer, but declared self-consciously that she was not "seeking a victory" for women. Poverty, she explained, was within women's domestic sphere because it was closely connected to the home. Their maternal instinct would help women to work in Jewish welfare organizations with greater intensity and patience, thus winning the trust of their charges.[26] The Frauenbund began its campaign to involve women in Jewish welfare organizations in 1906 by offering its assistance to the Hilfsverein, a social service organization through which German Jews aided their Eastern coreligionists. The Hilfsverein accepted and asked the JFB to collect used clothing for Jewish pogrom victims. The women did not object to menial work, as long as they would also be asked to share in decision-making. In 1907, the Frauenbund made this clear to representatives of the Hilfsverein and another Jewish organization, the Alliance Israélite Universelle.[27] In that year, the Second Delegate Assembly of the JFB debated a resolution which demanded that the Jewish Committee to Combat White Slavery amend its constitution to include women on its board of directors. The resolution was presented by the JFB's Frankfurt affiliate, Care by Women, whose president, Bertha Pappenheim, had obviously inspired it. She and Henriette Fürth, another ardent feminist, insisted on this resolution despite the Jewish Committee's invitation to Pappenheim and two other JFB leaders to serve as informal delegates. Some Frauenbund members considered the demand too drastic, and the resolution that was finally accepted stated that the Frauenbund understood the invitation of its delegation to represent "the statutory fact that women would be elected to the board of directors of the Jewish Committee."[28] This particular incident may have been more of a victory in consciousness raising than in substance, but Pappenheim was correct to insist upon it. The principle of women's equality was of utmost importance to her. Jewish organizations had always had their contingent of "honorary ladies" (*Ehrendamen*) who offered their support but were expected to withhold their opinions.[29] She demanded a reform in the overall position of women: "Women do not have the rights of thirteen year old boys—they are seen as sexual beings [*Geschlechtswesen*] rather than as individuals."[30]

In 1908, the Frauenbund proudly reported that the Alliance Israélite had accepted women on its executive committee, and the JFB urged its members to join the alliance. The Hilfsverein had not yet responded to the JFB. In these years the JFB concentrated on its own social welfare programs. Its self-confidence grew and it began to argue that social work was preparing women for participation in public policy-making. By 1911, the JFB's apprenticeship in good citizenship was over. Pappenheim declared that women should no longer allow themselves to be elected to amusement commissions (*Vergnügungsausschüsse*).[31] They should insist that the Jewish community stop ignoring them and should demand a serious role on welfare—particularly child welfare—commissions. A year later (and five years after the Bund Deutscher Frauenvereine had officially embraced the cause of votes for women), the JFB decided to publish a brochure on women's suffrage.

By the outbreak of World War I, Jewish women were still essentially voiceless and powerless in their community, despite modest and halting steps toward their recognition. Protestant women were more successful than their Jewish counterparts in achieving a say in their ecclesiastical community. The Protestant Federation of Women wanted women to elect parish officers and to participate in the selection of pastors as well. Ecclesiastical suffrage was, according to women, "a logical result of the serious active membership which most women still—thank God—have in the church community, a just complement to the duties they gladly assume."[32] Protestant women, like Jewish feminists, faced the hostility of males who approved of their "help" in the church community, but considered demands for equality part of the "children's diseases" (*Kinderkrankheiten*) of the women's movement.[33] Theological arguments were used by both sides: for example, while women pointed to Paul who had written that male and female were "all one in Christ,'" their male opponents quoted the same apostle demanding women's silence in the community.[34] Like Jewish feminists, Protestant women first appealed to local communities for an expanded role for women, but unlike the Frauenbund, they petitioned for suffrage from the beginning. By 1912, they had achieved a limited vote in seven church communities. Their task was easier than that of Jewish women, because the Protestant church—unlike the Jewish communities— was centralized, and Protestant women could therefore also direct their demands to a national office. Immediately after the war, the Protestant church, following the example set by the Weimar Republic, granted women active and passive suffrage.[35] Thus, in postwar Germany, Protestant women already had the rights that Jewish women had only begun to demand.

THE POSTWAR CAMPAIGN FOR COMMUNAL RIGHTS AND RESPONSIBILITIES

In the postwar period, the Frauenbund continued to insist upon greater female representation on the boards of directors of private Jewish welfare organizations. In 1917, two JFB members (Pappenheim and May) were elected to leading positions in the newly founded Zentralwohlfahrtsstelle der deutschen Juden, the largest Jewish welfare organization in Germany. The Frauenbund's association with the Zentralwohlfahrtsstelle was frequently a stormy one, based, in part, on the fact that Pappenheim felt that "women's work was never properly appreciated" by the larger organization.[36] She pressed for a greater voice for women and for appreciation of women's attitudes and opinions. The men with whom she worked either had difficulty understanding her concerns or simply preferred maintaining a predominantly male leadership. The former head of the Zentralwohlfahrtsstelle described her as "a very interesting, but also difficult personality . . . she did not like to work together or get directions from men . . . Miss Pappenheim believed that women were not strongly enough represented and did not play a strong enough role in every organization where she worked."[37] Considering the overwhelming preponderance of men in positions of responsibility in all of the major German-Jewish organizations, Pappenheim was certainly right. Until its dissolution, the JFB insisted that large Jewish organizations accept more women in positions of power. It warned that representation did not always mean real equality and that women had to be wary of being used as tokens rather than acting as effective participants. Still, it urged women to

continue seeking appointments to positions of communal responsibility and sought its own recognition as the representative of all
Jewish women on the boards of directors of all major Jewish organizations.[38] In 1936, the JFB was in the midst of a four-year struggle
for a voice in the Reichsvertretung der Juden in Deutschland, the collective voice of German Jewry under the Nazis. Its demands were met
in a paternalistic fashion while other Jewish organizations (the
Centralverein, Zionist Union, regional *Gemeinde* associations, and
the League of Jewish War Veterans) were represented. At a
meeting of the extended board of directors of the JFB, Leo Baeck,
the president of the Reichsvertretung, explained his organization's
reluctance to allow the women's association into its political leadership. He maintained that women and men were different and had
different functions: "While men possessed perspicacity and fore-
sight, women had the gift of being good listeners . . . of being able
to recognize the needs of mankind . . . and of shaping an evening
with warmth, dignity and substance."[39] The JFB was less than satisfied with this dichotomy. Ottilie Schönewald, president of the JFB,
penciled an angry exclamation mark next to these remarks on the
minutes of the meeting. She firmly rejected "the special position
that we are gallantly accorded. From time immemorial we have
learned that the higher we are placed on a pedestal, the further we
are pushed from the grounds upon which the real . . . decisions
take place."[40] Yet, this was in fact the position the JFB perceived
itself to be in throughout its existence.

The JFB conducted a two-front war for the vote, launching an
attack on the passivity and lack of political awareness of women,
and aiming a steady barrage of petitions, propaganda, and legal
actions at the male establishment. Throughout the 1920s the JFB
attempted to familiarize women with the affairs of the secular and
Jewish communities. It maintained that the average woman was as
capable of holding office as the average man, but that she had to
be educated to the needs of the public. This was a theme that the
JFB adopted from the leaders of the Bund Deutscher Frauenvereine
whose (prewar) qualms about how their sex would vote if enfranchised had always led them to emphasize the need for political
education as a first step to the ballot. These German feminists
stressed community activity and employment as "schooling for

further duties and rights."[41] In this spirit, JFB locals offered courses on the problems, finances, and politics of the German polity and the Jewish communities, and encouraged women to learn how to lead meetings, draft constitutions, and speak in public. The national leadership of the JFB encouraged local and regional groups to observe city council meetings, visit regional welfare facilities, and learn about city and state government. Some groups attended open synagogue council meetings and Jewish community assemblies, returned to the Frauenbund local to discuss and vote on the issues that had been presented to the men, and gave their (unsolicited) decisions to community leaders. The Berlin local urged its members to help candidates for Jewish communal elections who were in favor of women's suffrage. Women toured Jewish community institutions such as schools, hospitals, and old age homes in order to study their administration and problems. The Frauenbund also used its national delegate assembly as a forum for the discussion of problems relevant to German Jewry and passed resolutions which it then brought to the attention of Jewish leaders. The JFB was particularly eager for its members to become educated voters in the Jewish communities in which women finally achieved suffrage. Before elections in such communities, the JFB sponsored meetings to which candidates from contesting parties were invited. The Frauenbund carefully maintained its neutrality by hosting representatives of all parties, even those which opposed women's suffrage! The JFB also established a national commission on community participation (*Kommission für Gemeindearbeit*) headed by Schönewald. This bureau kept a tally of Jewish communities which had granted suffrage to women and noted these successes in the JFB's newsletter. As women began to serve in elected posts, the commission reported on their careers and published letters written by community leaders praising the contributions of women. This office also published accounts of Jewish women's rights in other countries, such as England, where Jews were also split over the issue of women's suffrage in the 1920s.[42]

Although JFB members always stressed their readiness to vote and their duty to participate in the affairs of the Jewish community, only in the 1920s, when Jewish women found themselves voting for delegates to the Reichstag but not to their own communal boards, did the JFB remind the *Gemeinde* that women had a "right" to vote.

A speaker at the Sixth Delegate Assembly of the JFB (1920) spoke of women striving for their "duties and rights."[43] By the mid-1920s, the more progressive communities in Germany had granted at least active suffrage and feminists spoke unabashedly of "demanding their rights."

The Frauenbund expected Jewish men to follow the example set by the Weimar government in respect to women's rights. However, its optimism quickly faded and it girded itself to fight the recalcitrant Jewish communities. In 1919, the Berlin local of the JFB petitioned the Berlin community—containing more than 30 percent of all German Jews—to observe the new German federal law which stated that all public corporate bodies had to allow equal suffrage to women after November 1918. The local also demanded that women participate on all the commissions of the Jewish community. Five years later, with Berlin women no closer to their goal, the JFB organized a national "suffrage week." It held propaganda meetings in communities which had not granted women equality and issued a proclamation which was printed in the Jewish press, stating:

The Jewish community needs our collaboration more than ever . . . we are unanimous in our fight . . . for our rights! Not because we are power hungry. Not because we are suffragettes, but because we are convinced that women's work is necessary for the cultural development of the Jewish community and that we can accomplish good . . . in official communal posts precisely because we are women.[44]

The Berlin JFB held a public meeting to which it invited Bertha Pappenheim, Rabbi Leo Baeck, Ismar Freund, a legal historian and cofounder of the Prussian Association of Jewish Communities (*Preussischer Landesverband Jüdischer Gemeinden*), and representatives of the Berlin community and the Association for Liberal Jewry.[45] More than 150 people—mostly women—attended this session, which brought only words of goodwill from the men who were present. Jewish communities were split over the issue and Orthodox members had to be conciliated. The Frauenbund continued to voice its demand for suffrage in Jewish newspapers, to petition synagogue councils, and to send speakers to the conventions of the large regional associations of Jewish communities.

By the late 1920s the Frauenbund decided to concentrate its efforts in Prussia, where an umbrella organization, the Prussian Association of Jewish Communities, encompassed 650 Jewish communities. In 1927, the JFB participated on a commission of the Prussian Association which had been authorized to recommend to these communities new statutes for their regulation. If the new laws included women's suffrage, all 650 communities would automatically have been obliged to grant women political equality. The proposal regarding the vote stipulated that any adult except those who were insane or who did not possess civil rights could cast a ballot and be elected to office. When the Prussian Association met to ratify the new statutes, women's suffrage was rejected by conservatives. The JFB insisted on a no-compromise stance on women's suffrage—and lost.[46] The final plan allowed each separate community to decide on the suffrage issue. This was a considerable defeat for the Frauenbund, which preferred the imposition of women's suffrage by the Prussian Association to the slow and tedious job of convincing each community to accept women's equality. The latter procedure was complicated by legal intricacies. The Prussian government insisted on its historical right to ratify constitutional changes within Jewish communities that had been under its jurisdiction in 1847. During the Weimar years, the Prussian Minister of Education (*Preussischer Minister für Wissenschaft, Kunst, und Volksbildung*) declared that he would agree only to those changes which did not evoke *any* opposition from within the community. Thus, even if the majority of members agreed to women's suffrage, the state would not permit it if there were an objection from any member of the community. This actually happened in at least three separate cases.[47] The Frauenbund considered this administrative decision to be undemocratic. It maintained that the Prussian ruling had been superseded by Article 137 of the Weimar constitution which stated that every religious community could regulate its own affairs within the bounds of the laws pertaining to the general population. The JFB argued that communities were autonomous and needed no state approval to change their statutes and alluded to two higher court decisions (*Reichsgerichtsentscheidungen*) which were in accord with the JFB's viewpoint. The Frauenbund also noted that the Ministry of Education had submitted the issue for an opinion to the Prussian Interior Ministry which also agreed with the JFB's stance.

A petition to the Interior Ministry to accept the majority decisions of communities regarding women's suffrage met with bureaucratic procrastination.[48] In 1929, the JFB presented a formal inquiry to the Prussian Minister of Education in which it asked his opinion on the legality of individual communities agreeing to women's suffrage by majority vote. He admitted that the Weimar Constitution sanctioned political equality and added that Prussia would approve of such equality "if there were no further questions." The JFB interpreted his answer as an unequivocal endorsement of the vote for women. Its newsletter published his response concluding that "herewith every legal obstacle to the introduction of women's suffrage is removed."[49] This decision was a "relief" to the JFB, because it believed—or said that it believed—that many communities had hestitated to grant women full citizenship rights due to the disapproval of the previous Minister of Education and to the imprecise nature of the laws. It urged communities to take advantage of this decision. Needless to say, the opponents of women's suffrage also interpreted the Minister's statement to their advantage, and the battle for suffrage continued even through the Nazi years.

The 1920s witnessed the enfranchisement of a majority of women in the German-Jewish community. In these years half of German Jewry lived in the seven major cities of Germany, and women could vote in all of these except Cologne. Women's suffrage was also permitted in: (Prussia) Bielefeld, Erfurt, Halle, Königsberg, Magdeburg, Stettin; (Bavaria) Fürth, Nuremberg, Regensburg, Bamberg; (Baden) Karlsruhe, Heidelberg; and (Anhalt) Dessau.[50] The JFB's efforts on behalf of full citizenship for women were responsible for this achievement. Yet, Frauenbund leaders were dissatisfied with the small numbers of women who were elected or appointed to positions of power and disappointed with the failure to achieve political equality for all women.

The Weimar Republic was not the era of emancipation that it was expected to be. German and Jewish women soon discovered that the vote did not confer instant equality. Men were still comfortably ensconced in their traditional leadership positions, while women still suffered the second-class status foisted upon them by the Civil Code of 1895, an old ordinance which remained in force in flagrant violation of the principle of equality espoused in the Weimar Constitution.[51] While popular prejudices against women who aspired to enter a man's world persisted, parties courted women as candidates for elections, but did not place them high enough on the lists to have them elected. Women remained in the lower-paying jobs, and the prestigious fields were dominated by men. Even in the Reichstag, where female representation made up over 9 percent of the total membership in 1919, female representatives were generally confined to the "feminine areas."[52] Like their German sisters, Jewish feminists could point to apparent successes as they strove for a political voice. But men continued to run the Jewish community, and the JFB was forced to appeal to them.

THE QUESTION OF RELIGIOUS EQUALITY

The JFB concentrated mostly on political reforms within the Jewish community, although it did entertain thoughts of some religious reforms as well. It was relatively moderate in its demands that women be allowed to perform certain religious rituals. This was neither the first nor the last attempt by Jewish women to achieve a role in male-dominated ceremonies. Medieval writings record instances in Western Europe when women agitated for the removal of injunctions against the performance of religious commandments. They claimed the right to recline at Passover, to fast with men, and to perform ceremonies. Some women practiced religious commandments from which they were exempt, and others wore prayer shawls.[53] Today again, women in the United States have raised the question of religious equality, demanding that they be counted in the prayer quorum (*minyan*), be bound to execute all religious commandments equally with men, be recognized as witnesses under Jewish law, be allowed to initiate divorce, be admitted to rabbinical and cantorial schools, and be welcomed to full leadership roles in the synagogue.[54]

The JFB suggested that women who brought their children to synagogue had a "duty, not a right" to a say in religious matters.[55] It did not advocate complete equality for women in religious functions and did not make the principle of religious equality part of its official program. It did, however, urge women to help "shape" synagogue ceremonies, by introducing youth services, choral singing, and festive decorations for the holidays. Rarely challenging Orthodox religious rules openly, the Frauenbund favored the innovations of reformers. In 1914, the Elberfeld local announced its support of girls' confirmations, because it believed girls should be given religious preparation equal to that of boys.[56] Members of the JFB also joined choirs when they were newly introduced into synagogue services. In 1930, the JFB national organization came to the defense of one of its locals which had demanded that women be permitted full participation in funeral services. This was the first time that this issue had arisen in Germany, offending Liberal as well as Orthodox rabbis.[57] Liberals argued that they supported women's right to vote because religious writings on that topic were debatable. The duties of women at funerals were very clear, however. They could prepare female corpses, but could not lead funerals. Liberals accused the JFB of a radical departure. The Frauenbund retorted—quite uncharacteristically—that women were fighting "for a right, not a privilege," and promised to continue its campaign for greater equality.

The first woman to preach in any German-Jewish house of worship delivered a sermon from the pulpit of the Reform Synagogue in Berlin in 1928. She was Lily Montagu, a member of the executive committee of the Jewish Religious Union of England, who was attending a meeting of the World Union of Progressive Judaism. She later wrote: "The German women must come down from the galleries and take part literally and in a real sense."[58] Jewish feminists noted her appearance, but did not use the opportunity to demand that women become religious leaders.[59] Several years later, however, the topic "Can Jewish Women Become Rabbis?" was thoroughly discussed in Frauenbund circles. Feminists argued that the Talmud's recommendation that women should not read the Torah, because someone might think that men could not read, was clearly anachronistic.[60] Thus, women should be included in this ritual. Feminists pointed to Beruriah, the wife of Rabbi Meir, as talmudic proof that women could be scholarly. She had participated in legal discussions and some of her opinions were later written into law. The Frauenbund also argued that since women could perform the blessings at the beginning (*Kiddush*) and end (*Havdala*) of the Sabbath if men were indisposed, they were already theoretically capable of these functions. Finally, it pointed out that in the United States, women could preach in some synagogues. Thus, although the JFB did not campaign for women's religious equality, some of its locals did believe that women could become rabbis.

Although its suggestions for religious innovations met with

stormy responses or cold indifference, the JFB did make an impression on the organized rabbinate. In 1928, the Association of German Rabbis (*Allgemeiner Deutscher Rabbinerverband*) allowed women to attend its annual convention for the first time. It limited its invitations to wives of rabbis and delegates of the Frauenbund.[61] Although this was not a religious ceremony—the JFB spoke on the population decline among German Jews—feminists were pleased by the rabbis' recognition of their organization. This was a small, but significant step, they felt, toward some acceptance by the religious establishment.

The struggle for political suffrage and meaningful positions in Jewish organizations seems to have been the JFB's key strategy to enhance the power of women in the community. Women's power would increase as women were allowed access to male political privilege: "To have some link with male power has been the closest that most of us could come to sharing in power directly," Adrienne Rich noted recently.[62] However, upon closer examination, it is apparent that an important *alternative* to such "power over others," as Rich called it, was provided, perhaps unconsciously, by the Frauenbund itself. The feminists' separate organization, "of women, for women," enabled them to derive a sense of solidarity and strength, to achieve self-expression, self-help, and self-respect. It was through this association that women were able to influence each other and, independently from men, to transform aspects of their own lives. Such "transforming power," according to Rich, is significant and essential. The JFB's autonomous woman-oriented activities may have provided the reality of women's power, whereas even a victorious suffrage campaign provided only its illusion. For, procedural democracy did not (and does not) miraculously end discrimination or give women control over their own lives. But, the Frauenbund's organizational and financial resources did allow Jewish women to take initiatives in influencing their own history. This is what Bertha Pappenheim had in mind when she turned exclusively to women to form a national organization to further their own interests. Thus, the Frauenbund provided a separatist alternative for women, focusing on its own crusades and institutions.

The Frauenbund's successes and failures derived in large part from the contradictions inherent in this separatist strategy. Such an alternative to male power erected a "ghetto within a ghetto" and probably caused confusion as to the exact goals of the JFB: were women to build their own organization as an end in itself—women's ability to help each other—or as a means to an end—women's power in the world of men? Sheltered safely within a women's world, JFB members often concentrated on more immediate social welfare concerns, draining personnel and enthusiasm from the political front. Yet, the JFB's "transforming power" allowed members to achieve in areas ignored by the male establishment. It enabled women to make their collective presence felt and gave them a forum from which to resist authority and tradition. Their campaign for procedural democracy (as witnessed in their traditional, liberal strategies to share male power) did not produce entirely satisfactory results. Yet, since they had embarked at the same time on an alternative road, they were able to improve important aspects of Jewish women's lives themselves. Thus, both strategies and alternatives to power were employed with limited, but nonetheless impressive, results by Jewish feminists within the political framework of their chosen community.

Notes

1. In large communities, expenditures for welfare amounted to as much as 30 percent of the total budget.

2. For a complete explanation of the relationship of the Jewish community to the modern state, see Kurt Wilhelm, "The Jewish Community in the Post-Emancipation Period," *LBIYB* (1957), pp. 47-75.

3. This drop in numbers was also a result of the Treaty of Versailles, which caused a loss of 627 communities.

4. David Philipson, *The Reform Movement in Judaism* (New York: Ktav Publishing House, Inc., 1967), p. 383.

5. *Bayrisches Israelitisches Gemeindeblatt*, July 15, 1930, p. 221. The JFB reported in 1928 that Jewish women in England were facing similar problems.

6. Genesis 3:16. These restrictions can be found in the earliest writings of Judaism. See Leonard Swidler, *Women in Judaism: The Status of Women in Formative Judaism* (Metuchen, N. J.: Scarecrow Press, Inc., 1976).

7. Judith Hauptman, "Images of Women in the Talmud," *Religion and*

Sexism: Images of Women in the Jewish and Christian Traditions, edited by Rosemary Radford Ruether (New York: Simon and Schuster, 1974), p. 191. When a woman performed an act from which she was exempt (for example, being present at the sounding of the ram's horn on the New Year's holiday), it had a lesser value than the same act performed by a man. Swidler, *Women*, pp. 83-87.

8. For examples of rabbinical writings on women's lustful natures, see Swidler, *Women*, pp. 123-30. Christian women suffered from the same biblical prejudices. See: Simone de Beauvoir, *The Second Sex* (New York: Modern Library, 1968), p. 167; Maria Henning, "Canon Law and the Battle of the Sexes," in Rosemary Radford Ruether, *Religion and Sexism*, pp. 267-91.

9. Phillip Segal, "Elements of Male Chauvinism in Classical Halakhah," *Judaism* 24 (Spring 1975), pp. 226-44. This quote comes from *Sotah* 21b.

10. Marvin Lowenthal, *The Jews of Germany: A Story of Sixteen Centuries* (New York: Longmans, Green & Co., 1936), p. 243. Charlotte Baum, Paula Hyman, Sonya Michel, *The Jewish Woman in America* (New York: Dial Press, 1976), p. 23.

11. Philipson, *Reform*, p. 473.

12. Ibid., pp. 218-19.

13. Hoffmann, "Ein Gutachten," *Jeshurun* 6 (May/June 1919), pp. 262-66; *Jeshurun* 6 (November/December 1919), pp. 515-19.

14. The leading Orthodox rabbis in Holland and Palestine were opposed to Hoffmann's decision, whereas in Vilna, Warsaw, Bialystok, and Kovno, women had the vote. Hoffmann, "Gutachten," pp. 515-16.

15. Helga Krohn, *Die Juden in Hamburg* (Hamburg: Hans Christians, 1974), p. 200.

16. *IF*, January 20, 1931, n.p., in Dora Edinger collection, ALBI.

17. *BJFB*, February 1928, pp. 2-3.

18. In protocol of the Eighth Delegate Assembly of the JFB. Schönewald collection, ALBI, no. 3896 (III, 1). Pappenheim probably had less of an effect on Nobel's decision than she or her followers ever realized. Nobel admitted to a friend that he had made his judgment based on the needs of Palestine: "Frankfurt could have waited, but Israel can wait no longer. We cannot build the land without giving our girls and women equality. I did it for the land." In Ernst Simon, "N.A. Nobel als Prediger," in *Gesammelte Aufsätze* (Heidelberg: Verlag Lambert Schneider, 1965), p. 380.

19. Schönewald collection, ALBI, no. 3896 (III, 1); *BJFB*, February 1928, p. 3.

20. *BJFB*, February 1928, p. 2.

21. *IF*, January 20, 1931, n.p., in Edinger collection, ALBI.

22. *BJFB*, July 1929, p. 4.

23. *BJFB*, August 1929, p. 11.

24. *IF*, November 5, 1908, p. 11; *BJFB*, December 1930, pp. 5-6.

25. *IF*, January 5, 1908, p. 5.

26. *AZDJ*, January 19, 1906, p. 30.

27. The Alliance was founded in 1860 in Paris. It demanded political and social equality for Jews in several European countries. The JFB belonged to its German branch. In Meyer collection, ALBI, no. 377 (XI, 2).

28. Meyer collection, ALBI, no. 877 (XI, 2).

29. *IF*, January 19, 1911, p. 12.

30. Meyer collection, ALBI, no. 877 (XI, 2).

31. *IF*, January 19, 1911, p. 12.

32. Amy Hackett, "The Politics of Feminism in Wilhelmine Germany, 1890-1918" (Ph.D. dissertation, Columbia University, 1976), pp. 568-69.

33. D. Ed. Freiherr von der Goltz, *Der Dienst der Frau in der Christlichen Kirche* (Potsdam: Stiftungsverlag, 1914), p. 194.

34. Agnes Zahn-Harnack, *Die Frauenbewegung: Geschichte, Probleme, Ziele* (Berlin: Deutsche Buch-Gemeinschaft, 1928), pp. 343-59.

35. Protestant women did not have the right to be elected as pastors at that time, but neither the Protestant Federation of Women nor the Association of Protestant Female Theologians wanted this. The latter, in 1925, suggested that the church devise a position between social worker and pastor for women. In May 1927, the Prussian General Synod admitted women to the position of vicar and assured them a theological education equal to that of men. Zahn-Harnack, pp. 354-58.

36. Schönewald collection, ALBI, no. 3896 (III, 1). In a speech to the Eighth Delegate Assembly of the JFB in 1923, Pappenheim took the Centralverein and the Hilfsverein to task for the same reason.

Another reason for the JFB's frequent disagreements with the Zentralwohlfahrtsstelle was the former's preference for volunteer social workers. The Zentralwohlfahrtsstelle favored professional social workers in its attempt to modernize Jewish welfare organizations.

37. Letter to this author from Dr. Max Kreutzberger, Locarno, Switzerland, August 18, 1975.

38. Schönewald collection, ALBI, no. 3896 (II, 5), pp. 18-19, and (III, 11), p. 24; *BJFB*, March 1934, p. 6; *BJFB*, April 1938, p. 5.

39. Schönewald collection, ALBI, no. 3896 (III, 11), p. 5.

40. Ibid., p. 1.

41. Helene Lange as quoted in Hackett, "Politics," p. 461.

42. *BJFB*, August 1927, pp. 6-7; *BJFB*, February 1928, pp. 1-2; *BJFB*, September 1928, p. 4.

43. *AZDJ*, November 12, 1920, supplement, p. 2.

44. *IF*, March 20, 1924, pp. 2-3.

45. *IF*, April 3, 1924, p. 2; Berlin women received the active vote in 1925. *IF*, October 15, 1925, p. 3.

46. *BJFB*, April 1927, p. 4.

47. Suffrage was delayed for this reason in Cologne, Aachen, and Düsseldorf. *BJFB*, February 1928, pp. 1-2.

48. *BJFB*, November 1927, p. 4; *BJFB*, February 1928, p. 1.

49. *BJFB*, February 1930, pp. 8-9.

50. *BJFB*, February 1928, p. 1. In Bavaria and Baden, women received the vote in some communities as early as 1919, in Frankfurt/Main they were permitted to vote by 1921, Württemberg granted this right in 1924, and the Stettin community enfranchised females in 1926. Berlin women received the active vote in 1925 and the passive one in 1928.

51. The Civil Code raised woman's status above that of a minor. In fact, it gave single women equal rights with men and dropped the husband's guardianship and disciplinary rights over his wife. However, husbands were awarded final authority "in all matters pertaining to common marital life." Thus a husband could restrict his wife's right to engage in legal transactions, employment, or business if detrimental to the marriage and retained authority over his children unless he deserted the family, was declared incompetent, was convicted of a serious criminal act, or died. While the code allowed the wife the right to her earnings, the property or wealth she brought into the marriage was to be administered by her husband. Although feminists fought the code in hopes of improving women's status, they met with little success. Hackett, "Politics," pp. 462-68.

52. Ibid., pp. 1051-52.

53. I. Epstein, "The Jewish Woman in the Responsa," in *The Jewish Library*, edited by Leo Jung, Series III, p. 127.

54. Susan Dworkin, "A Song for Women in Five Questions," *Moment* (May/June 1975), p. 44; Sally Priesand, *Judaism and the New Woman* (New York: Behrman House, Inc., 1975).

55. *BJFB*, November 1936, p. 1.

56. *AZDJ*, January 30, 1914, supplement, p. 4.

57. *IF*, January 16, 1930, p. 2; *IF*, February 6, 1930, p. 3.

58. Philipson, *Reform*, p. 400.

59. *IF*, September 6, 1928, p. 15.

60. *IF*, November 5, 1931, n.p., in Dora Edinger collection, ALBI.

61. *BJFB*, August 1928, p. 5.

62. Adrienne Rich, *Of Woman Born* (New York: W.W. Norton, 1976), pp. 43-45.

chapter 6

Housework as Lifework

Marrying for a Living: Choices Available to Middle-Class Women before World War I

Although Jewish women have rarely been given credit for doing "useful" work, that is, for earning an income, they did, in fact, contribute to the support of their families until the latter part of the nineteenth century. They often cared for the livestock that their husbands bought and sold or ran small shops (sometimes in their living quarters) while their men peddled wares in distant towns. Occasionally, they participated as equal partners in their spouses' undertakings and, in some cases, they took over businesses and ran them successfully.

The commercial success of German Jewry in the late nineteenth century relegated most women to an entirely domestic role. Much like their German counterparts, Jewish men, whether they were wealthy or still struggling to support their families, considered it a disgrace, a sign of financial failure, if their wives or daughters worked. Those women who insisted on vocations—and there were some who did—often precipitated family crises. Fanny Lewald, who grew up in a bourgeois Jewish home, discovered that her independent income humiliated her father: "Even to my own sisters my father made a secret of the fact that I was supporting myself, because it seemed unfitting to him that one of his daughters was self-supporting."[1] German and Jewish middle-class parents considered public employment unladylike and improper for their daughters and often accused the young women of selfishness or the pursuit of luxury if they insisted on earning their own living. One Jewish woman who fought her parents in order to become a literature teacher wrote: "Mother cried . . . Father told me, 'I won't stand in your way, but you are swimming against the tide.'" This young woman rejected marriage in pursuit of her goal, but felt guilty that she had set such a bad example for her younger sisters.[2]

For the Wilhelmine bourgeoisie, as for its American or English counterparts, women's enforced leisure served a social function. Women were expected to assume leisure and consumption patterns which reflected the wealth and enhanced the prestige of their husbands and fathers.[3] Such ladies, refined, well-dressed, unburdened by domestic chores, were themselves luxury items. Also, men placed women beyond the competitive, aggressive, crush of the outside world in order to preserve an island of serenity and beauty to which men could escape. Women were to be chaste, delicate, loving, and pure in order to soothe their work-worn husbands. One German educator (1886) described what he expected from his wife:

I know her soft hands will stroke my forehead and her friendly words will fall like fresh dew drops on the cares of the day. . . . I know that I will hear about other things here . . . than in the outside world, and if the strong tired husband and his success become the pride of the house, I must say, that the friendly wife is its ornament.[4]

This ideal supported—not coincidentally—the widespread image of women as self-sacrificing, dutiful, and nurturing. All of this, and the home itself, would be destroyed forever if women were permitted to leave the private sphere which had been entrusted to them.

Although most Jewish women in prewar Germany remained at home because of their affluence[5] and cultural conditioning, particular problems resulting from anti-Semitism confronted those who ventured out. Whereas growing numbers of German middle-class women entered the world of work in the late nineteenth century, anti-Semitism closed the doors of many "women's careers" (teaching, nursing, post and telegraph operators) to Jews.[6] The few who did struggle through the hostile environment of a university often found their opportunities severely limited by a mixture of anti-Semitism and antifeminism.[7] As late as 1919, Jewish women were warned of pronounced anti-Semitism in teaching, while antifemale attitudes prevailed in most professions.[8]

By 1882, when the first comprehensive employment statistics were published, 11 percent of all Jewish women in Prussia were employed, compared with 21 percent of all Prussian women.[9] By 1895, a German census indicated that 33,129 Jewish women were working in major occupations. Twelve years later this figure showed a 47.8 percent increase, or 48,976 working Jewish women.[10] Until 1907, surveys generally underestimated female labor, excluding women who worked in small family businesses or on family farms. The 1907 census included a new category entitled "family assistants," family members who aided the main entrepreneur, usually the husband or father. One-fourth of all working Jewish women belonged to this group, which may explain the rapid increase in their overall numbers.[11] Still, only 18 percent of Jewish women compared to 30.7 percent of German women earned their living.[12]

The Frauenbund noted the results of the census at its convention of 1907. It took up the "career question" as a central concern at this meeting and at innumerable future gatherings, and considered "furthering the employment opportunities of women" among its primary goals.[13] Frauenbund leaders were careful to advocate careers that they viewed as compatible with economic conditions and cultural values: housework and its logical extension, social housework. The implementation of this solution revealed the many contradictions of middle-class feminism.

The Frauenbund did not demand careers for all women, only for those who needed or desired them. Pappenheim always considered job training to be a means to psychological and emotional independence, and she regarded women with careers as useful to their community. She hoped that as the numbers of women involved in careers grew, their collective importance would be recognized by men. Of particular concern to her was the fate of poor Eastern immigrant girls who, she feared, for lack of work skills often resorted to prostitution.[14] This particular issue was used by the JFB to urge Jewish communities to take job training seriously. Thus, Jewish feminists first appealed to the charitable nature of German Jews and their sensitivity to scandal. Later, they appealed to middle-class parents as well, urging them to consider the necessity and rewards of careers for their daughters and condemning parental resistance and Jewish contempt for working girls.[15] Pappenheim implored parents to give at least as much consideration to their daughters' careers as to those of their sons, so that well-trained women could aspire to remunerative and responsible positions; she decried the fact that sons often received expensive higher educations away from home while daughters were "needed" at home and encouraged to take speed courses in stenography or sales. While boys learned to consider their jobs as important additions to their lives, girls were socialized to think that jobs were merely a way to earn a living or to pass time until they married. Thus, women entered careers with fewer skills than men, furthering the prejudices of employers that women were unskilled or inept, and resulting in the lower pay and status of working women as compared to men.[16]

In the prewar years the Frauenbund frequently discussed careers which women should consider and, as early as 1907, it began to organize employment services for women. It was particularly solicitous of religious applicants who observed the Sabbath. Pappenheim provided a model for the JFB in the employment service founded by her Frankfurt affiliate, Care by Women. Volunteers who met with job seekers followed strict guidelines which included: (1) handling each applicant according to her personal interests and in a friendly fashion; (2) charging no fees; (3) advising women of safe lodgings; and (4) checking all foreign positions for fraud or white slave traffickers before recommending them.[17] In 1908, a job "counseling center" was established as the main priority of the JFB's first local in Breslau. Gradually, more affiliates founded employment agencies. Where this was impossible, individual JFB members or the "trusted persons" (Vertrauenspersonen) also relied upon in the fight against white slavery volunteered to provide job information, recommendations, or warnings regarding their own towns. The list of trusted persons included several hundred names both within and outside of Germany, and it was circulated among all JFB locals. While the leadership formulated plans for a national employment service and set up a Commission for Employment Services, a primitive network of approximately fifty agencies and hundreds of volunteers developed.[18] After laying the groundwork, the JFB began to cooperate with other Jewish employment services, thereby augmenting its files of available jobs. In 1913, it founded the Cartel of Women's Employment Services (*Kartell der weiblichen Arbeitsnachweise*) in cooperation with the B'nai B'rith, and it represented the interests of women in the first major Jewish employment service, the Center for the Vocational Guidance of Jews (*Hauptstelle für Berufsberatung der Juden*) founded in 1916.[19] The latter organization, supported by the Centralverein, included representatives of the JFB, B'nai B'rith, the Association of Jewish Youth Clubs in Germany, and the Association of Independent Craftsmen of the Jewish Faith. It maintained Jewish employment agencies in all of the major German cities.

Home Economics: The Attempt to Professionalize Homemaking

The war and subsequent demographic and economic dislocations forced many Jewish women to become self-supporting. Reflecting this change of circumstances, the Frauenbund began a vigorous effort to make middle-class women aware of opportunities in "social housekeeping" careers, such as social work, kindergarten teaching, nursing, or the management of orphanages, nurseries, and similar institutions. It justified such careers by emphasizing (and exploiting) the notion of the benevolence and selflessness of the feminine character and underlining women's predisposition toward things having to do with the household and children. These careers were either in traditional female areas, or—as was the case with social work in which even in the 1920s four-fifths of the workers were women—in relatively new fields which had not yet been monopolized by men. The JFB leaders believed that these professions would allow women to move beyond their traditional, private boundaries by expanding their motherly role of nurturance without directly challenging the male-dominated sectors of the economy.

Its most strenuous efforts in the area of careers for women before, but most intensively after, the war were devoted to encouraging girls to enter domestic service. Pappenheim lamented the aversion Jewish girls and women had toward domestic labor. They clearly preferred careers in commerce. In 1907, for example, 51.8 percent of Jewish working women were employed in commerce, 27.7 percent in industry, 5.6 percent in the free professions, 4 percent in agriculture, and 8.8 percent in domestic service.[20] The JFB decried the precipitous decline in the number of Jewish domestics, particularly because of the overall increase in Jewish working women. In 1895 there had been 6,298 Jewish domestics, or 15.9 percent of all Jewish working women. In 1907 the number had fallen by 24 percent to 4,771.[21] This was due to several factors. Sixty-four percent of Jewish working males were engaged in commerce, and Jewish commercial success, particularly the expansion of family businesses, provided jobs for female relatives. Fully 30 percent of Jewish women engaged in commercial enterprises were "family assistants." Also, the majority of Jews lived in cities where industry or trade offered young women larger salaries and more freedom, and did not confront them as starkly with an inferior social and political status as did domestic service.[22] Although a greater percentage of Germans than Jews worked as domestics, their numbers fell as well. Whereas there were more than one million German domestics in 1907, their ranks had decreased by 50 percent since 1895.[23] Thus, middle-class Jewish women, many of whom belonged to the JFB and employed domestics, were acutely conscious of the dearth of domestic labor— probably not an insignificant factor in understanding their particular emphasis on training women for this field. But, Jewish feminists were not alone in advancing homemaking careers, particularly after World War I. German feminists also promoted the field of home economics as a reaction to postwar economic dislocations and war deaths which left 2,500,000 more women than men in Germany. Few women retained the option of not preparing for some vocation. Furthermore, as part of a more general "professionalization" of service jobs, German feminists demanded that domestic responsibilities be given the status of a career.[24] In Germany, the profession of social work began in the early twentieth century as did the professionalization of jobs such as salesgirl, bank clerk, and eventually domestic servant.[25] These new careers were pursued through formal courses of study leading to certificates. Home economics schools began to multiply, championed by German and Jewish women's movements.

In their support of home economics training, Jewish feminists were motivated by specifically Jewish concerns as well. Household management could be taught relatively quickly and inexpensively.

This appealed to a Frauenbund faced with numbers of jobless Eastern European Jewish immigrant women. Also, the home economics training that was a prerequisite for domestic service could assist immigrant women who were unprepared for the difficulties of maintaining their own households in their new environment. Furthermore, such training may have been a means by which German Jews hoped to facilitate the acculturation of their Eastern coreligionists whose foreign habits called unfriendly attention to them and caused self-conscious German Jews some disquietude.[26]

Most importantly, the JFB was concerned with the vocational retraining (*Berufsumschichtung*) of Jews. Although the JFB noted that, compared to Jewish men, the job distribution profile of Jewish women more nearly approximated that of their German counterparts, it agreed with those Jews who feared the political consequences of an "unhealthy job distribution."[27] Such notions had plagued Jewish leaders as far back as the era of the German Enlightenment, when both German and Jewish thinkers had argued that it was only natural that people seeking to normalize their civil rights should attempt to achieve a job distribution similar to that of Germans. Jews had to prove they were contributing to the fatherland rather than exploiting it as unproductive middlemen. In the nineteenth century, this meant a movement from trade into agriculture and crafts, and Jewish societies were formed to further these fields. However, the same edicts that accorded Jews civil rights also lifted commercial and trade restrictions on them. Many Jews preferred to utilize the new opportunities in their traditional occupations and took the occasion to move to cities which had formerly banned or limited them.[28] Thus, they adjusted to modern socioeconomic trends rather than heed those leaders who would have made them into farmers. In the process, however, they were often reviled by the victims and critics of capitalism, and anti-Semites accused them of being parasites on the German people. In the face of extreme anti-Semitism in the war and postwar years, large Jewish organizations, including the JFB, committed themselves to an official policy of vocational retraining. The chief reason for retraining was again political: integration could proceed more easily if Jews were not as heavily engaged in commerce. Thus, Jewish social service agencies encouraged Jews to adopt vocations more typical of the general population: men were urged to turn to industry, crafts, and agriculture and women to agriculture and, more importantly, to domestic service and related fields.

The Frauenbund's enthusiastic support of vocational retraining was due also to its concern with the demographic and economic chaos ensuing after the war. War deaths resulted in an estimated 20,000 to 30,000 more Jewish women than men, and inflation and depression impoverished many formerly middle-class Jews. Large numbers of Jewish spinsters could be predicted and many families needed the income of a wife or daughter. Finally, the JFB was alarmed by the social consequences of urban life on German Jewry, that is, by the effects of later marriages, intermarriages, declining fertility, and increasing rates of nervous disorders and suicides.[29] Although opinions differed on the direct causes of nervous disorders and suicides—the JFB related the high rate of male breakdowns to late marriages, whereas other observers blamed city life as well as business and professional pressures—Jewish leaders recognized serious implications. They agreed that problems induced by urban life could not be easily solved and some believed the only cure to be a "return to nature," the resettlement of Jews in agricultural communes.[30] The Frauenbund supported this idea, promoting women's agricultural careers as viable alternatives to urban jobs. In the 1920s it joined various Jewish "settlement commissions" which were intended to train and resettle Jews in agricultural communities in the hope of encouraging earlier marriages, revitalizing the Jewish population, and providing Jewish youth with jobs. Thus, for reasons having to do with the political and social conditions of German Jewry, discussions of women's careers were invariably related to the need to direct girls into certain "acceptable" fields.[31] Despite the attention devoted to agriculture, the most important of these was clearly home economics.

In its endeavor to make "household management" more desirable to young women from all classes, the Frauenbund proposed replacing the term "servant" (*Dienstbote*) with "household helper" (*Hausgehilfin*).[32] Also, it repeatedly asked women to be kinder to their helpers, and it tried to persuade Jews—who, it argued, were particularly snobbish in this regard—to revise their low opinion of domestic work. The JFB suggested improved hours, wages, and working conditions for domestics and supported the organization of domestic workers. Furthermore, it offered model contracts to employers. The Frauenbund recommended home economics training before, after, or in place of women's higher education, idealizing it as "reconstruction work for the community." It added, perhaps to mollify middle-class girls and women or because it ultimately aspired to more prestigious jobs for them, that domestic service might be only a temporary solution and that such training would also count toward "higher professions." In fact, the JFB and other feminist groups lobbied for a law requiring that one year of domestic science become a prerequisite for careers in social work and administrative appointments in hospitals, sanatoria, hotels, and orphanages. Finally, the Frauenbund elevated the "career" of homemaker—in most cases a middle-class luxury—in order to raise the standards and, consequently, the schooling and status of housewives and domestics. Like bourgeois and socialist feminists of its day, the JFB argued that housekeeping was a profession like any other, but that it had been devalued by male society.[33] It encouraged all women to participate in professional training so that they would be better at what was their "natural role" and so that society would respect them.

The JFB's home economics schools and courses (established where funds did not permit extensive building) were its major institutional contribution to the career training of young women. As early as 1913, the JFB had agreed in principle to found its own schools, although it did not build them until the 1920s. Then it appealed, with frequent success, to local Jewish communities and even local governments for financial support of its educational endeavors. The schools were serious occupational institutes, rather than the finishing schools to which the upper middle classes had formerly sent their daughters to learn how to manage servants. The schools offered two curricula which were often intermingled, one for basic training and one that prepared women to manage Jewish welfare institutions.[34] All schools celebrated Jewish holidays and observed traditional customs and dietary laws. One headmistress wrote that her school was "an oasis of genuine Jewish life," and added that this would have justified its existence if it had been the school's only accomplishment.[35]

The first JFB school, the Home Economics Women's School in the Country, was situated in the foothills of the Bavarian Alps near Wolfratshausen. Founded by the Munich local of the JFB in

1926 and supported, in part, by the Jewish community of Munich, this school combined home economics training with a "return to nature." One of its students wrote that activity in the field of agriculture allowed Jews, whose forebears had been estranged from nature for hundreds of years, to fully experience the outdoors for their own physical and emotional health.[36] After finishing at least seven years in a girls' high school (*Mittelschulbildung*), students enrolled in this school. They took courses in such practical subjects as cooking, housework, sewing, washing, ironing, horticulture, poultry farming, dairy farming, and "domestic accounting," as well as in more theoretical subjects including nutrition, health education, infant care, religion, civics, economics, and education. Licensed teachers taught the one-year curriculum and gave final exams. Girls had to pass three days of rigorous testing and exhibit samples of their practical work. Before an audience of teachers, government inspectors, and guests, the girls were examined on their ability to wash and iron different fabrics, clean the chicken coops, plant flower beds, clean floors and windows, and dust and polish furniture. They presented samples of their sewing and mending as well as their menu planning and cooking.[37] Graduates could either enter domestic service or continue their education. Those who sought higher status or pay in household management, social work, or agricultural careers had fulfilled their prerequisite, one year of home economics. A licensed household manager (*geprüfte Hausbeamtin*), who could run orphanages or large households and institutions, had to finish one more year of household management, a half-year practicum, and pass a state licensing exam. Those who preferred careers in gardening faced longer courses of study. After Wolfratshausen they chose a field of specialization such as landscaping or floriculture, served an apprenticeship of three years, and took a state exam. Social service careers demanded two more years of study beyond the home economics preparatory year and a one-year practicum.

The JFB's Paula Ollendorff Home Economics School, founded in 1930 in Breslau, was sponsored jointly by the JFB local, the city, and Jewish private and communal funds. The school was attached to an old-age home for Jewish women. It was hoped that the two institutions would develop a symbiotic relationship; the students could stimulate the older residents who, in turn, could impart some of their practical household know-how to the young women. The students made meals for the home and participated in its domestic management, thereby gathering useful experience and helping the school to pay its own way. This institution prepared domestics, vocational and nursery school teachers, and household helpers. The latter position, requiring one year of home economics, a one-year practicum, and a state exam, involved slightly more responsibilities than that of an ordinary domestic. However, the jobs differed more in theory than in practice. The JFB also added small home economics institutes to its rest home in Lehnitz (near Berlin) and its children's sanatorium in Bad Segeberg (Holstein). Students combined home economics with care of the elderly and with child care, respectively. Religious training was stressed and, in the Segeberg school, those who wished to receive their diploma had to pass an oral exam given by a rabbi.

The Frauenbund attempted to keep tuition costs down by making the schools pay for themselves as much as possible. In Wolfratshausen much of the food used at the school was grown by the students, and in Breslau, Segeberg, and Lehnitz the students saved the JFB part of the costs of hired help in the attached institutions. The Frauenbund also provided scholarships for needy applicants. Proposals for a one-year national women's service (*weibliches Dienstjahr*), in which the government would sponsor women's basic home economics training in return for a year of service, were frequently discussed and supported by Jewish (as well as German) feminists. Many JFB members approved of such a plan as a means to insure a free and compulsory home economics education for all girls, but these ideas never engendered widespread support and the German government did not act upon them.[38]

The JFB's job placement services reached a wide audience as a result of its own counseling centers, its liaison with other Jewish organizations, and its monthly newsletters. The latter, begun in 1924, provided a forum for advertising the needs of job seekers as well as potential employers. The JFB was particularly concerned with the placement of apprentices who had finished their home economics schooling, but were required to fulfill one-half to one year of practical training before receiving their state certificates. Since employers preferred fully experienced help, the Frauenbund had difficulties finding positions for graduates and devised an alternative solution. Families that needed help could exchange their daughters who had graduated from home economics schools and the latter could, thus, fulfill their formal apprenticeships. Since parents were trading offspring, it was assumed that they would treat their *Haustochter*, or "household daughter" as one of their own children. While the JFB emphasized this advantage, it should be noted that the apprentice's wages were to be replaced by "family closeness." In reality this system of unpaid "daughters" provided cheap household labor while it served as an inducement to (formerly) middle-class women who did not want to be treated as servants.[39]

The JFB also tried to obtain apprenticeships for dietitians, cooks, and domestic managers in private industry, businesses, hospitals or orphanages, particularly those owned or managed by Jews. Pappenheim worried that Jewish employers were prejudiced against women of their own religion who needed free Saturdays. Arguing that giving jobs was better than giving alms, she entreated employers to hire Orthodox workers and to respect their Sabbath. The Frauenbund also had to urge Jewish women, including its own members, to hire Jewish domestics. Fears that Jewish domestics might resist hard work, that their parents might interfere, or that they would expect to be treated as part of the family, prevented housewives from hiring them. The Frauenbund tried to counter such notions, while urging housewives to be considerate of their helpers.

The JFB's "retraining" effort was futile. It ran counter to the historical development of Jewish employment and to the basic tendencies of advanced, capitalist economies in which commerce and industry, rather than agriculture, crafts, or domestic service, offered opportunities for profitable employment. And, although the major reason for the JFB's failure to convince Jewish women to switch fields was due to socioeconomic patterns beyond its control, the ambivalent feelings of Jewish feminists toward domestic service and their objective position as employers of domestics did not enhance the JFB's credibility among those it sought to persuade. Originally, home economics training, while intended to prepare all women for later life, was considered vocational training for the poor. Middle-class women could use their home economics preparation as a prerequisite for, or complement to, what the JFB itself referred to as "higher" professions. Only slowly and hesitatingly, under the duress of the 1920s and 1930s, did the Frauenbund begin to suggest domestic service as a career for middle-class women. Even then it hedged, hoping aloud that most would advance to related fields once the crises had abated.

The JFB took no note of the contradictions in its home economics campaigns. Even as the upgrading of housekeeping to a profession was intended to improve women's status and offer greater job satisfaction, it was also, at least implicitly, an acknowledgment of the lack of choices available to them. Home economics schooling "was a bid to elevate the status of women within the context of a social order divided into a public realm of male endeavor and a private world of female existence."[40] Those feminists who supported home economics education often did so as a means of challenging patriarchal authority in the home (as a result of women's greater technical and managerial expertise) and thereby enhancing women's highly restricted position. Furthermore, the JFB's middle-class perspective made it insensitive to the negative features of home economics training. Although it promoted social work and woman-related fields such as kindergarten teaching or nursing, the JFB devoted by far the largest share of its considerable efforts to the "domestic service profession," whose members were more commonly known as maids. By helping poor Jewish girls to become maids, the Frauenbund was, not entirely by coincidence, providing a secure source of well-trained, dependable, dependent, and cheap labor for middle-class households. While admitting some of the disadvantages of household employment, even when compared to the most unskilled factory work, the JFB never viewed it as a form of class privilege and exploitation. The Frauenbund did not recognize that paid housework was humiliating because of the subordinate social relationship it involved, rather than because of the work done. Instead, housewives congratulated themselves for providing jobs to needy women. And, it was clear from the frequency of exhortations in the JFB newsletter, which called on Jews to treat their domestics better, that—rhetoric of household "careers" aside—JFB members treated servants as servants. The Frauenbund was caught between the ideals of providing careers for women, status for housewives, and a more "German" job profile for Jews and the realities of the selfish class interests of many German-Jewish women. While it theoretically regarded all jobs as equal, in reality some were more equal than others, a fact not lost on the scores of immigrant and German-Jewish women who shunned domestic service.[41] Despite years of JFB propaganda in favor of training women for domestic careers, in the midst of the Weimar era only 9.3 percent of Jewish women—up from 8.8 percent in 1907—were employed as domestic help, and 53 percent were engaged in commerce, compared to 51.8 percent in 1907.[42] The depression and the Nazis finally forced Jewish women into new fields. When, in 1935, the secretary of the JFB stated that "vocational retraining is taken seriously by all JFB members," it was not due to the Frauenbund's programs but to the increasing proletarianization of Jews in Germany.[43]

Housekeeping for Survival: Depression and the Third Reich

The depression presented new difficulties for Jewish—and all other—feminists. Hostility toward the *Doppelverdiener*, the second earner in a family (usually the married woman engaged in paid employment), already apparent during the postwar demobilization, reached a peak of intensity as a result of increased unemployment. Married women in the civil service or the professions came under public attack.[44] While men's organizations called for their dismissal, Catholics decried the harm done to the family by the working wife. Even some women's associations, concerned with the numbers of unemployed single women, were less than supportive of the *Doppelverdiener*. In May 1932, the German government issued a law which allowed governments, public corporations, banks, and railway companies to dismiss married women whose economic circumstances "seemed constantly secure."[45] Even more distressing was the use of the *Doppelverdiener* issue to begin a general attack on all working women. The slogan "women belong at home," a war-horse of nineteenth-century antifeminists, was mustered into service once more to meet the new crisis.[46] Even the "feminine" fields of social work and related areas were no longer safe refuges. Men's groups called for the restriction of women to their "characteristic occupation," and some even echoed the tired argument that women were not intellectually equal to men and therefore should not be accorded positions of responsibility. The most strident voices were those of the Nazis who railed against the "Jewish-intellectual" concept of the highly educated woman and demanded "jobs first for the fathers of families."[47]

The women's movement was placed on the defensive. It attempted to retain the gains in the areas of education and employment which it prided itself on having achieved.[48] The JFB maintained that work was a means toward self-preservation and self-fulfillment for many women. It insisted on their right to work and reminded the skeptical that many single and married women supported their families. It combatted not only German antagonists of working women, but Jewish opponents as well. The JFB warned the League of Jewish War Veterans—which it suspected of attempts to expand the already generous prerogatives that veterans enjoyed in the job market— that it would strongly oppose any move to exclude more women from the economy. It repeated this position in writing to other major Jewish organizations and received notes of "total agreement" from all, including the veterans.[49] As the number of jobless women grew, the Frauenbund became more convinced of the correctness of recommending domestic service careers for women, since home economics majors had relatively better chances of employment than those in commercial courses. The chronic depression led to an increase in the absolute and relative number of women interested in domestic careers.

This trend continued during the Nazi years. Upon coming to office, the Nazis' "April Laws" purged political undesirables and Jews from the professions, government, and civil service (including teaching) positions. Furthermore, the "Law Against the Overcrowding of German Schools" limited the enrollment of Jewish students in high schools and universities. Only Jews who were war veterans, or whose fathers or sons had served, were exempt from these decrees. Also, Jews who had been active in their professions before the Weimar era and were not politically suspect could not be fired automatically, although "reasons" for their dismissal were often invented. These exclusionary laws did not eliminate all Jews from the professions, because the Nazis—accepting their own slogans about "Jewish cowardice" in the war and the Jewish "takeover" of the Weimar Republic—were unaware that so many Jews had fought in the German army or had practiced their professions before 1918. About 30 percent of Jewish lawyers and 25 percent of Jewish doctors were barred. Jewish women, however, fared proportionately worse than Jewish men. Women were only exempt insofar as their fathers or sons had fought. Also, since most Jewish female professionals had attained their positions after the war, fewer could escape these decrees on the basis of prior service. Finally, the Nazis also used these laws to eliminate women from the professions. Gertrud Bäumer, former president of the Bund Deutscher Frauenvereine and an official in the Ministry of the Interior, believed that her firing as well as that of other women on "political grounds" was a deliberate act of discrimination against women.[50] In fact, women did lose more. In 1933 in Prussia, for example, 1 percent of male teachers and 4.5 percent of female teachers were discharged (at least two-thirds of the women were "non-Aryan" and almost all of the women practice-teachers who were fired were also "non-Aryan"). These dismissals provided a convenient method by which the government found teaching assignments for 60 percent of 1,320 job applicants in 1933.[51] In June 1933, the Nazis decreed that married women whose husbands were employed by Reich, provincial (Land), or local governments were to be dismissed.[52] No woman under thirty-five could be given a permanent appointment in a public service position. Also, women would be paid less than men. Finally, all other qualifications being equal, a male candidate for a government position would be given preference over a female. The meager ranks of Jewish women not already thrown out of work were thinned still further by this decree. For example, Jewish women whose fathers or sons had served in the war but whose husbands were government employees now lost their jobs.

The Frauenbund viewed home economics careers as one of the few remaining means of economic survival for Jewish women. From early 1933, the Nazis began to deny Jews an economic existence in Germany by narrowing their field of activity, boycotting their businesses, and urging employers to fire them. As the position of Jews became steadily more insecure, Jewish women generally found jobs more easily than men.[53] This was partly because women were paid lower salaries than men. Also, women adapted to retraining programs better than men. The number of women who successfully underwent retraining in these years was almost evenly distributed between the ages of twenty and fifty, whereas men most frequently could be retrained between the ages of twenty and thirty, and stopped by forty. Furthermore, there were many vacancies in domestic service, particularly after the Nuremberg Laws of September 1935, which forbade the employment of Aryan housemaids under the age of forty-five in Jewish homes. And, as many young people emigrated, the Jewish community needed social workers and nurses to replace those it lost. Finally, domestic service skills were marketable outside of Germany. Many formerly middle-class women began their new lives abroad in domestic service or in professions related to home economics. They frequently supported husbands or fathers whose commercial experiences were ill suited to economies still in the throes of the depression.

Whereas, in the 1920s, the JFB had encouraged young women to consider home economics careers, in the 1930s it argued that these jobs had "practically become the law" and exhorted women with higher aspirations as well as professional women to, respectively, train and retrain for careers in domestic service, household management, cooking, gardening, tailoring, hairdressing, and similar fields. The Frauenbund recognized that women were being pushed out of all but these "feminine" areas. Faced with overwhelmingly hostile forces, the JFB did not fight to reinstate women; it resigned itself instead to alerting them and helping them adjust to what it considered the inevitable economic trends. Skirting the fact that women were being asked to return to a premodern role, which had no prestige and which limited their personal freedom, the JFB worked to alter attitudes. Its leaders maintained that manual work should be respected as highly as intellectual work, quickly adding (lest they be misunderstood) that home economics and cooking were challenging fields which required intelligence. They regarded the home economy (*Hauswirtschaft*) as a vital part of the national economy (*Volkswirtschaft*). Like other Jewish social welfare agencies which redirected people whose vocational aspirations and social expectations had been high, the Frauenbund emphasized the dignity, security, and satisfaction that were to be gained from a job well done, no matter how menial it seemed.[54]

After 1933, the Frauenbund joined the Reichsvertretung in coordinating vocational programs for women. This included providing schooling and supervising final exams in all schools, finding apprenticeships, and placing qualified personnel. Despite an increasing number of home economics graduates,[55] the JFB's employment services could never fill all of the job offers for fully trained domestics, because young women who finished their apprenticeships left the country as soon as they could. To slow this loss of qualified labor, the Frauenbund considered demanding one year of domestic service from those it had supported and trained. However, by 1935, the JFB understood the extreme necessity of emigration and made no attempt to detain its graduates. In 1936, the Nazi regime closed down all private employment agencies. The Jewish services were allowed to conclude their business by early 1937. Thereafter, schooling continued, but placement effectively ended.

Although the Frauenbund devoted most of its attention to the training of domestics, it also recognized the need for the agricultural education of women as a means to facilitate their emigration. Agriculture lagged behind other career choices of women: of the 3,600 residents of Jewish farm-training centers in Germany in 1936, only one-third were women.[56] This was partly because women who chose farming had to decide to emigrate immediately, as Jews could neither own nor cultivate German soil (except with special government permission). Since most female agricultural trainees went to Palestine, those who did not choose the Middle East as their destination avoided farm schools. The fact that almost no women planned to emigrate to agricultural settlements other than those in Palestine caused consternation among JFB leaders. They worried that men who went to Argentina or South Africa would be forced to marry non-Jews. Thus, to prevent intermarriages, the Frauenbund urged young women to join settlements in all parts of the world.[57] The JFB recognized that another reason for the lack of enthusiasm with which women turned to farming was the extremely difficult life of female settlers. Women not only helped men in the fields, but were responsible for the household and children as well. They had to manage the dietary and hygienic problems of primitive environments, while raising animals, vegetables, and fruits for their families. The Frauenbund cautioned women to prepare themselves thoroughly for the rigorous demands of this existence. In the Nazi years, its offerings at Wolfratshausen fulfilled the prerequisites for certificates of entrance to Palestine. Whereas enrollment there had been around twenty girls per semester in the 1920s, after 1933 the number jumped to fifty and then eighty students.[58] The school was allowed to function until Crystal Night when Nazis hurled rocks into the bedrooms of the sleeping students and damaged the building and grounds. In 1939, all retraining programs that had not already been destroyed were restricted to preparing for emigration and, then, prohibited entirely. While vocational training and retraining was proceeding, the JFB was also moderately successful in influencing boys and girls to consider new careers. Among boys, agriculture and metal-work increased in popularity and commercial fields decreased. The results of a poll of the career aspirations of high school-aged girls in 1936 revealed that they were also changing their occupational expectations. The JFB reported that 24 percent of the girls preferred manual professions, such as seamstress (19 percent), fashion designer, hairdresser, photographer, painter, bookbinder, or potter. Seventeen percent decided on jobs as domestic servants, one-third of these opting for the benefits of an extra year at a home economics school. While only 1 percent considered the severely restricted teaching profession, 11 percent hoped to become social workers, particularly in the child-care fields. Others chose agriculture (6 percent), further education (10 percent), and immediate emigration (2 percent); and 13 percent were uncertain of what they wanted to be.[59] Clearly, girls were no longer opting for the formerly dominant commercial fields, and the most noticeable increases were in the crafts and the home economics areas. In fact, by 1937 the JFB began to relax its propaganda in favor of the housekeeping professions, relieved that more women than had been expected had entered domestic service and that housewives had begun to rely on themselves.

The Frauenbund's attitude toward jobs for women reveals the complexities and contradictions inherent in middle-class German-Jewish feminism. Unlike the nineteenth-century German feminist movement which made the right to work a central feature of its program, Jewish feminists almost never demanded for themselves the right to work outside the home. Reflecting the middle-class comfort of their generation of German Jews, few Frauenbund members desired or earned an outside income.[60] They were anxious, however, about the economic survival of the next generation of women. They urged families to educate all young women, but their immediate target of concern in the prewar period was the Jewish immigrant girl from Eastern Europe. Domestic education was necessary, they asserted, to prevent white slavery, help immigrants adjust to German norms, and revise the occupational profile of Jews. Thus, the original impetus to educate women for careers came from the Frauenbund's commitment to social work within the Jewish community rather than from feminism. In later years, too, its emphasis on domestic and social service must be seen, in part, as an effort by a social work agency to accommodate women to what it perceived as economic and political necessities.

The Frauenbund's demand for a career education for every woman was in the progressive feminist tradition. Believing that careers provided personal enrichment for women, it challenged an attitude, still widespread in Jewish circles in the early twentieth century, that a woman's place was only in the home. Yet, its emphasis on woman-related fields had contradictory implications. On the one hand, it was a maneuver by which women could enter the occupational world without challenging men directly. Women simply stepped from their role as housewife and mother to that of social housewife (household manager, administrator of rest homes, social worker) and social mother (kindergarten teacher, nursery school director). This rather limited sphere of action was regarded by the JFB as a significant first step toward career equality. Leaders reminded members that selflessness and service would bring women respect and power, and that once women had established themselves in one area it would be easier for them to insinuate themselves into male-dominated fields. On the other hand, because the Frauenbund—like its German counterpart—upheld the notion that housework was woman's work, it failed to educate and influence public opinion to envision a greater role and variety for women in the job market.[61] Also, an acceptance of responsibility for the private sphere meant that the woman who responded to the lure of an outside career faced a double burden, one the JFB was loath to acknowledge. Perhaps its members secretly assumed, as do many middle-class feminists in our own day, that maids would harmonize the contradictions in the dual role of housewife and career woman. Most likely, they also were implicitly conceding the impossibility of reconciling German males, upon whom they were economically, legally, and socially dependent, to a less housewifely and more career-oriented woman.

The Frauenbund's insistence that housework be treated with the same regard as other employment was also a progressive feature of its program, despite its failure. Like socialist and bourgeois feminists in Germany and domestic feminists in the United States, it argued that homemakers ought to enjoy greater respect and recognition. By making home economics a subject of study and endowing it with methods which were as "scientific" and thus as worthy of respect as men's, the JFB tried to upgrade the position of women in the home and raise the standard of the housekeeping profession. Yet, while successfully expanding training in home economics and alerting the Jewish public to the possibilities of such careers, the JFB offered nothing but the symbolic rewards of status to the jobs of servant and housewife, both of which involved hard labor, with no recognition, at exploitative or no wages.[62] In both cases the "professionalization" of housework was an ideology which served patriarchal privilege, and in the case of the domestic it also served class privilege. Nor could the JFB modify the belief that housework was menial or convince others to consider a woman's achievements as a homemaker in the same way that the work of a carpenter, farmer, or professor was judged. And, although it would be anachronistic to condemn German-Jewish women for not asking men to share housework, the Frauenbund's exaltation of homemaking was excessive. While most members were housewives, many had maids to do the more arduous work. Also, those members who had careers or devoted much of their time to the JFB clearly did not suffer from their lack of exposure to housework. Finally, the cry from the rank and file for domestic help belied the "joys" of cooking and cleaning. Thus, despite untiring efforts, the JFB was confronted time and again with the contradictions and difficulties involved in its attempt to "further the employment opportunities of women."

Notes

1. Fanny Lewald, *Für und Wider die Frauen* (Berlin: Verlag von Otto Janke, 1875), as quoted by Hugh Puckett, *Germany's Women Go Forward* (New York: Columbia University Press, 1930; AMS reprint, 1967), p. 149.

2. Ettlinger, unpublished memoirs, *Archives of the Leo Baeck Institute*, no. 93, pp. 79-84. See also, Maas-Friedmann, unpublished memoirs, ALBI, p. 7.

3. Thorstein Veblen, *The Theory of the Leisure Class* (New York: New American Library, Mentor Edition, 1953).

4. Jürgen Zinnecker, *Sozialgeschichte der Mädchenbildung: Zur Kritik der Schulerziehung von Mädchen in bürgerlichen Patriarchalismus* (Weinheim and Basel: Beltz Verlag, 1973), pp. 116-17.

5. For an indication of the extent of Jewish prosperity at the beginning of the twentieth century, see: Schorsch, *Jewish Reactions to German Anti-Semitism, 1870-1914* (New York: Columbia University Press, 1972), pp. 15-16. For the period between 1910 and 1939, see Erich Rosenthal, "Jewish Population in Germany, 1910-1939," *Jewish Social Studies* 6 (1944), pp. 233-73. In this period only 9 percent of Jews who worked were found in the category of manual laborers, while half were self-employed and one-third were classified as clerks.

6. Siddy Wronsky, "Zur Soziologie der jüdischen Frauenbewegung in Deutschland," *Jahrbuch für jüdische Geschichte und Literatur* (1927), p. 88.

7. On the difficulties women had to face in their struggle for a university degree, see Puckett, *Germany's Women*, pp. 187-89, 200-202.

8. Henriette Fürth, "Erwerbstätigkeit und Berufswahl der Jüdischen Frau," *Zeitschrift für Demographie und Statistik der Juden* 15 (January-March 1919), p. 4; Agnes Zahn-Harnack, *Die Frauenbewegung, Geschichte, Probleme, Ziele* (Berlin: Deutsche Buch-Gemeinschaft, 1928), pp. 153-58. Also, see Helene Lange, *Lebenserinnerungen* (Berlin: F. A. Herbig, 1921), pp. 145-58; Katherine Anthony, *Feminism in Germany and Scandinavia* (New York: Henry Holt and Company, 1915), p. 46.

9. *ZDSJ*, VII, no. 5 (May 1911), pp. 79-80. In the 1890s, Prussia's Jewish working women made up 68 percent of all German-Jewish working women and can therefore be used as a sample of German-Jewish women. *ZDSJ*, I, no. 4 (April 1905), p. 105.

10. *ZDSJ*, VII, no. 5 (May 1911), pp. 79-80; *ZDSJ*, VII, nos. 7/8 (July/August 1911), p. 105.

11. Three-fourths of all family assistants were women.

12. *ZDSJ*, XV, nos. 1/3 (January/March 1939), pp. 3-4. It is fair to as-

sume that many of these Jewish working women were immigrants of proletarian, Eastern European origin, thus making the percentage of working German-Jewish women even smaller. See: *ZDSJ*, nos. 1/6 (January/June 1920), pp. 2-24; *ZDSJ*, nos. 1/4 (January/April 1923), pp. 10-20.

13. Schönewald collection, ALBI, no. 3896 (III, 1).

14. *AZDJ*, October 18, 1907; *BJFB*, November 1928, pp. 1-2; *BJFB*, March 1929, p. 2.

15. It seems Jewish salesgirls bore the brunt of such disdain. Meyer collection, ALBI, no. 877 (XI, 2). It has been suggested that an integral part of the salesgirl's job was to sell a product by (symbolic) seduction, through the use of feminine wiles. Employers looked for attractive women who could tempt the public with their products. Most clerks and salesgirls became obsolete by thirty. Renate Bridenthal, "Beyond *Kinder, Küche, Kirche*: Weimar Women at Work," *Central European History* 6 (June 1973), pp. 161-62.

16. Women were found in subordinate positions in all fields of enterprise. For example, in 1907, in the field of commerce, in which most Jews were engaged, 58 percent of Jewish males were independent owners compared to only 32 percent of women. Considering that this category included independent seamstresses as well as industrialists who ran large enterprises, women's status was actually appreciably lower than these statistics indicate. Although salary scales are unavailable, in commerce, particularly in family businesses, many husbands depended on the unpaid labor of their wives. This was because frequently neither spouse considered the woman's work as employment or accorded her the wages or esteem that accompanied the man's occupation. In other work, for example, agriculture, where females outnumbered males, only 15 percent of the women were independent proprietors compared to 43 percent of the men. In the industrial sector, women were found in a similarly subordinate position: whereas 44.6 percent of men were owners or managers, only 27.1 percent of women belonged to this privileged group. Finally, one finds that in the least remunerative and/or respected types of jobs, household employment, day labor (*Lohnarbeit wechselnder Art*), and agriculture, respectively 99.4, 73.5, and 57.2 percent of the Jews in these categories were women. *ZDSJ*, XV, nos. 1/3 (January/March 1919), pp. 2-4.

17. *IF*, January 19, 1911, p. 12.

18. *AZDJ*, January 24, 1908, supplement, p. 12, and December 23, 1910, supplement, p. 2; *IF*, January 19, 1911, p. 12. The commission was founded in 1912. *AZDJ*, January 24, 1913, supplement, p. 1. The majority of these fifty agencies was sponsored by the JFB. The Frauenbund also successfully appealed to the B'nai B'rith and the Association of Friends of the Sabbath

to support agencies which remained part of the JFB network. *AZDJ*, January 24, 1913, supplement, p. 1.

19. *AZDJ*, November 12, 1920, supplement, p. 2; *IF*, September 17, 1925, p. 11; *IF*, February 1, 1917, pp. 3-4.

20. In cities with more than 100,000 inhabitants the statistics for Jewish working women were even more skewed toward commerce. The 1907 census showed approximately 57 percent of Jewish women engaged in commerce and 32 percent in industry compared to the reverse for German women. *Statistik des Deutschen Reichs*, vol. 207 (Berlin: Verlag von Puttkammer und Mühlbrecht, 1910), pp. 581-82.

21. *ZDSJ*, VII, nos. 7/8 (July/August 1911), p. 106; *ZDSJ*, XV, nos. 1/3 (January/March 1919), p. 2.

22. *ZDSJ*, I, no. 4 (April 1905), p. 2. In these years the servant was subject to a special law, the *Gesinde Ordnung*, which deprived her (99 percent of all domestics were women) of all rights toward her employer. Women's and labor groups demanded the repeal of this law, but in the meantime domestics flocked from their jobs to enter industry. Anthony, *Feminism*, p. 187.

23. Anthony, *Feminism*, p. 187.

24. The movement to professionalize the job of housewife can be traced to the German feminist Hedwig Heyl. She also supported the idea of a professional organization of housewives, which was formed in 1915 as the Association of German Housewives' Societies. Ilse Reicke, *Frauenbewegung und Erziehung* (Munich: Rösl und Cie Verlag, 1921), pp. 45-46. In America, feminists led by Catharine Beecher supported the domestic science movement in the 1910s and 1920s. See Kathryn Kish Sklar, *Catharine Beecher: A Study in American Domesticity* (New Haven: Yale University Press, 1973).

25. By 1917, social workers had formed their own professional organizations. In larger cities it was not unusual to find salesgirls' schools (*Verkäuferinnen Schulen*) attached to vocational schools. There girls could study the "technical and psychological" side of this profession. They were expected not only to represent their employer and product, but to "educate and form" the consumers' tastes. *Die Frau und Ihr Haus* (Cologne), XII, no. 8 (August 1931), p. 196.

26. At the turn of the century in the United States, German-Jewish women also suggested domestic service careers to women who had recently arrived from Eastern Europe. Rudolf Glanz, *The Jewish Woman in America: The Eastern European Jewish Woman* (New York: Ktav Publishing House, Inc., 1976), pp. 18-19. Home economics courses were used to "Americanize" all nationalities of immigrants in the early twentieth century.

Public schools, settlement houses, and charity organizations offered courses in domestic science. The habits and techniques of household management were transmitted along with doses of patriotism and middle-class notions of privacy, orderliness, manners, and thrift. Barbara Ehrenreich and Deirdre English, "The Manufacture of Housework," *Socialist Revolution* 26 (October/December 1975), pp. 29-31.

27. Schönewald collection, ALBI, no. 3896 (III, 3). See also: S. Adler-Rudel, "Zehn Jahre jüdische Berufsberatung," *Jüdische Wolfahrtspflege und Sozialpolitik* 3 (March 1932), pp. 49-59; E. Baron, "Berufsumschichtungbestrebungen innerhalb der jüdischen Bevölkerung Deutchlands," *ZDSJ*, no. 4 (April 1927), pp. 16-26; Rudolph Stahl, "Vocational Retraining of Jews in Nazi Germany, 1933-1938," *Jewish Social Studies* 2 (1939), pp. 169-94; Sucher B. Weinryb, *Der Kampf um die Berufsumschichtung: Ein Ausschnitt aus der Geschichte der Juden in Deutschland*, Jüdische Lesehefte, no. 13 (Berlin: Schocken, 1936).

28. An increasing proportion of Jews moved to the expanding urban centers. In Berlin, in 1881, Jews represented 4.8 percent of the population of the city, whereas they represented slightly over 1 percent of the total population of Germany. By 1910, 54.5 percent of Prussian Jewry lived in cities of 100,000 or more and 71 percent lived in cities of over 20,000. These figures were nearly double those of the Prussian population. Schorsch, *Jewish Reactions*, p. 14.

29. Various Jewish sources voiced alarm at these trends. See, for example, *ZDSJ*, V, no. 6 (June 1909), p. 93, which indicated that Jews suffered the highest suicide rate compared to all other religions. *BJFB*, October 1927, pp. 4-5, gave a similar report for 1925. The decline in birth rates can be found in *BJFB*, August 1926, p. 1; *BJFB*, October 1927, pp. 4-5; and *BJFB*, August 1929, p. 6. On intermarriage, see *ZDSJ* (January/February 1924), p. 25; *ZDSJ*, III, nos. 4/6 (April/June 1926), p. 129; *ZDSJ*, V, no. 1 (July 1930), p. 14.

30. These ideas were also popular with the Zionist movement, which considered the occupational development of the Jews in the diaspora abnormal, and with the Jewish youth movement, which sought to alter what it regarded as an unhealthy occupational distribution and to rejuvenate "citified" Jews through a return to nature.

31. Although its primary efforts in the Weimar period were directed toward practical vocational training, the JFB did encourage qualified women to seek university educations. Between 1911 and 1923, the number of Jewish women enrolled in Prussian universities increased by 105 percent, a significant jump although the actual numbers were low. In 1911, 266 Jewish women matriculated; in 1928, their number increased to 838; and in

1932, 1,408 were studying at Prussian universities. By 1929, the JFB reported that Jewish women made up 7 percent of all women in German universities. Since about 1 percent of the German population was Jewish, the large representation of Jewish women was noteworthy. Also, Jewish women constituted one-quarter of all German-Jewish students, a considerably higher proportion than that of German women among German students. In 1931, for example, 28 percent of all Jews attending the university were females, whereas only 17.9 percent of German students were female. See: *ZDSJ*, II, no. 2 (February 1925), p. 33; *BJFB*, August 1931, p. 4; *BJFB*, September 1933, pp. 10-11; *IF*, January 24, 1929, p. 15.

32. Meyer collection, ALBI, no. 877 (XI, 2). By the late 1920s this was actually a new occupation, which was one step above that of *Hausangestellte* (house employee). *BJFB*, October 1929, pp. 5-6; *BJFB*, March 1933, p. 6.

33. Even leaders like Clara Zetkin, whose feminism was often too strong for her male socialist colleagues, did not challenge the traditional sexual division of labor within the family, criticizing only the unequal social and economic value attached to housework. Karen Honeycutt, "Clara Zetkin: A Socialist Approach to the Problem of Woman's Oppression," *Feminist Studies* (Spring-Summer 1976), p. 135.

34. *AZDJ*, April 4, 1913, supplement, p. 5.

35. Lotte Pick, "Die Jüdische Haushaltschule zu Wolfratshausen," in *Von Juden in München: Ein Gedenkbuch*, edited by Hans Lamm (Munich: Ner Tamid Verlag, 1958), pp. 87-88.

36. *BJFB*, February 1930, p. 7.

37. *BJFB*, June 1929, pp. 14-15.

38. Later, the Nazis introduced a "Year of Duty" for a variety of their own reasons. This year was supposed to be spent either in agriculture or in domestic service before young women started certain types of regular industrial or office work. The scheme, begun in 1938, does not seem to have been enforced thoroughly and engendered criticism by industrialists who feared a decline in their labor supply. Tim Mason, "Women in Germany, 1925-1940: Family, Welfare and Work. Part II," *History Workshop*, issue 2 (Autumn 1976), p. 15. See also Leila J. Rupp, *Mobilizing Women for War: German and American Propaganda, 1939-1945* (New Jersey: Princeton University Press, 1978), pp. 81-82; Claudia Koonz, "Mothers in the Fatherland: Women in Nazi Germany," in *Becoming Visible: Women in European History*, edited by Renate Bridenthal and Claudia Koonz (Boston: Houghton Mifflin Company, 1977), pp. 461-62.

39. *BJFB*, October 1932, p. 3. The contract for a household daughter included free (kosher) food and a room in place of a cash reimbursement to

the helper. Housewives had to provide a heated bedroom with a locked closet as well as a bath. The workday extended from 6:30 A.M. until 8:30 P.M., and the "daughter" was allowed one free afternoon a week and one free Sunday afternoon every other week. She could have an extra evening off a week if she enrolled in any courses. The housewife was obligated to teach her helper cooking, ironing, washing, window cleaning, home decorating, rug beating, mending, child care, and simple bookkeeping. The former could not overwork her "daughter" (although there was no way of checking this) and could not ask her to do heavy work on the Sabbath. As surrogate mothers, the housewives were supposed to watch that their helpers kept themselves and their belongings neat and clean. Also, "daughters" had to tell the housewife where they spent their free time and had to return home by ten or eleven o'clock. It is not difficult to imagine how obnoxious some of these rules must have been to adolescents and young women. Liegner collection, ALBI, no. 3902 (IV, 14).

40. Barbara Ehrenreich and Deirdre English, "The Manufacture of Housework," p. 24.

41. *ZDSJ*, nos. 1/4 (January/April 1923), pp. 10-20.

42. *ZDSJ*, VII, no. 5 (May 1911), pp. 79-80; *ZDSJ*, XV, nos. 1/3 (January/March 1919), p. 2;   *BJFB*, January 1934, pp. 7-8.

43. *BJFB*, March 1935, p. 4.

44. Ursula von Gersdorf, *Frauen im Kriegsdienst, 1914-45* (Stuttgart: Deutsche Verlags-Antstalt, 1969), p. 35. Frieda Wunderlich, "Deutsch-mann über Alles," *The American Scholar* 7 (1938), pp. 94-105.

45. Jill McIntyre, "Women and the Professions in Germany, 1930-1940," in *German Democracy and the Triumph of Hitler*, edited by Anthony J. Nicolls and Erick Matthias (London: Allen and Unwin, 1971), pp. 181-82, 186.

46. Schönewald collection, ALBI, no. 3896 (II, 7). For similarities in the American situation, see Mary Ryan, *Womanhood in America*, p. 315.

47. McIntyre, "Women and the Professions," pp. 182, 189.

48. Whether these gains were, in fact, real is discussed by Bridenthal in *"Kinder, Küche, Kirche."* She concludes that the number of employed women did not increase as much as it shifted into different sectors and that as a whole, women lost status in the work sector during the Weimar years.

49. *BJFB*, March 1934, p. 3.

50. Jill Stephenson, *Women in Nazi Society* (New York: Barnes & Noble, 1975), p. 155.

51. Ibid., pp. 155-56.

52. McIntyre, "Women and the Professions," p. 192.

53. The Berlin Employment Department of the Jewish Community placed

39 percent of female commercial applicants compared to 13 percent of male applicants in 1933; 46 percent of females and 13 percent of males in 1934; 51 percent of women and 12 percent of men in 1935; and 52 percent of the women who applied compared to 22 percent of the men in 1936. In the case of industrial workers, 49 percent of female applicants were placed in 1933 and almost 100 percent in 1936. A. Szanto, "Economic Aid in the Nazi Era: The Work of the Berlin Wirtschaftshilfe," *Leo Baeck Institute Yearbook* (1959), p. 213.

54. It remains unclear as to how successful the JFB's propaganda was in changing attitudes, considering the psychological and social importance German Jews attached to their careers. Rudolph Stahl maintains that German Jews had a more difficult time changing careers than did Eastern European Jews, because the former had adopted the Protestant belief that a job was a "calling" and were thus far less amenable to giving up their lifework. "Vocational Retraining," p. 189.

55. There were thirty home economics schools in 1937. Stahl, "Vocational Retraining," p. 182. All came under the jurisdiction of the Reichsvertretung and, although the JFB was not directly involved in most, it participated in the exam procedures. *Frankfurt Israelitisches Gemeindeblatt*, May 1936, p. 311.

56. *BJFB*, June 1936, pp. 1-4. Also, the results of seven years (1933-1940) of retraining programs in Berlin indicated that whereas about 60 percent of the men who retrained chose agriculture, the majority of women picked woman-related fields, crafts, and occupations related to textiles (millinery, fashion design, etc.). Only a few women turned to agriculture, and some took up carpentry and bricklaying. Szanto, "Economic Aid," p. 215. By 1937, there were thirty farm schools scattered throughout Germany. Most were under Zionist direction. Stahl, "Vocational Retraining," pp. 180-81.

57. However, another problem remained. The JFB found it difficult to tell parents to let their fifteen to eighteen-year-old daughters emigrate to distant lands and found colonies with groups of bachelors. The solution was to send young married couples to the agricultural training farms so that they would form the nucleus of new settlements. Then girls could be sent to overseas colonies with their "safety" assured. Schönewald collection, ALBI, no. 3896 (III, 7), p. 8. It is doubtful whether this plan ever had time to work, because these discussions took place in June 1936, and the agricultural training courses took two years to complete.

58. *BJFB*, June 1929, p. 15; Stein-Pick, unpublished memoirs, ALBI.

59. *BJFB*, February 1937, p. 3. This poll of career *aspirations* differed somewhat from the statistics gathered by the Reichsvertretung's employment service, which, as of December 1935, had *placed* 1,032 girls in apprenticeships in: agriculture and gardening, 17.5 percent; handicrafts, 23.9

percent; home economics, 26 percent; sales, 18.1 percent; other, 14.5 percent. S. Adler-Rudel, *Jüdische Selbsthilfe unter dem Naziregime: 1933-1939* (Tübingen: J.C.B. Mohr, 1974), p. 50.

60. It is fair to assume this, since almost all of the JFB's members were housewives, and a 1925 survey indicated that 82.9 percent of Jewish housewives did not work outside the home. Heinrich Silbergleit, *Die Bevölkerungs und Berufsverhältnisse der Juden im Deutschen Reich* (Berlin: Akademie Verlag, 1930), p. 120.

61. Like the JFB, American feminists argued that there were instinctual differences between men and women which made certain work, that is, housework, more suitable to the former and other work better for the latter. The problem was to make the two kinds of work equal. See Carol Lopate, "The Irony of the Home Economics Movement," *Edcentric: A Journal of Educational Change* 31-32 (November 1974), pp. 40-42, 56-57.

62. The JFB never made a distinction between jobs for which women were paid and those for which they were not. It seems that in a system based on financial rewards and profits, free labor would always be accorded lower status than paid work. The JFB either avoided or did not recognize this issue.

chapter 7

Conclusion

Between 1933 and 1938 the Jüdischer Frauenbund joined other Jewish organizations in a struggle for survival. This endeavor took several forms: fighting anti-Semitism; preventing the disintegration of communal organizations; insuring the continuation of Jewish practices; helping needy Jews; and preparing people for emigration.[1] During the Hitler years, the feminism of the JFB became less pronounced, because it concentrated on social work and because of the misogynist nature of the Third Reich. In June 1933, the Bund Deutscher Frauenvereine disbanded itself rather than face *Gleichschaltung*—the process by which all leaders were replaced by Nazi supporters and the organization was forced to participate in Nazi activities. The JFB had resigned from the German feminist organization a few days earlier, and the BDF had accepted the Frauenbund's withdrawal with "deepest regret."[2] While the JFB continued to demand equality for women within the Jewish community, maintained its services and institutions for women, and represented the needs and views of women to the newly established Jewish central organization, the Reichsvertretung der deutschen Juden, the needs of German Jews took precedence over purely feminist goals.

From the time of its founding, the JFB had been aware of anti-Semitism, and many of its programs reflected the insecurities of German Jews. In the 1920s, the Frauenbund included the fight against anti-Semitism in its goals. Yet, its efforts in this area were limited before 1933 and nullified by the Nazis thereafter. During the Weimar years, the Frauenbund, like German Jewry in general, was divided over the tactics to employ against anti-Semitism. While the Central-verein and others who desired integration into German life argued for "enlightenment work" (*Aufklärungsarbeit*) among Germans, Zionists refused to engage in such "apologetics" and concentrated on reviving a sense of Jewish community. The division was not merely over tactics. The Centralverein argued that Jews belonged to the German state and *Volk*, whereas Zionists considered Jews to belong to their own *Volk* while residing in the German nation as its citizens.[3]

The JFB insisted that Jewish women had to show "Jewish solidarity" as Zionists demanded and to "prove our worth" as those desiring German acceptance advocated. It denounced an "either-or" strategy which pursued only one of these paths as superficial and phony.[4] In November 1930, two years before Zionists and assimilationists buried their differences to fight anti-Semitism, the Frauenbund brought its members together in a nonpartisan enlightenment campaign.[5] It invited non-Jewish women's and youth organizations to Frauenbund lectures, social evenings, and tours of synagogues.[6] Agnes von Zahn-Harnack, leader of the BDF, led one of these "enlightenment" meetings. Representatives of the Catholic women's organization, women theologians, and feminist leaders attended. Zahn-Harnack asked the JFB to invite Christian women to holiday festivals, synagogue services, and discussions, noting "the fight against anti-Semitism must originate with Christian women."[7] The Frauenbund prepared and distributed literature which explained Jewish history, ethics, and customs to its Gentile guests.[8] These writings expressed both the desire to belong to Germany and the wish to maintain a Jewish identity. The JFB often compared the emancipation of Jews with that of women, asserting that while each group hoped to fit into the dominant society, each had acquired a consciousness of its unique qualities which it deserved to retain. The JFB also argued that German and Jewish women should fight anti-Semitism because Jews and feminists shared the same struggle for emancipation and the same ideal of an open, liberal, pluralistic society.[9] It appealed to the women's movement—which it described as one which strove for humanistic ideals in a spirit of social service and sympathy with the weak—to fight anti-Semitism, "not *for us*, but for the idea of a German spirit in which we all believed."[10] Since those who heard JFB pleas for a liberal, pluralistic society were generally not the same people who promoted racial hatred, it would be more accurate to apply the term "enlightenment" to the bridging of differences among various factions of Jewish women than to the stemming of bigotry.

The Frauenbund's "self-discipline" (*Selbstzucht*) campaign was probably even less successful than its enlightenment efforts in fighting anti-Semitism. Begun in 1915 and continued throughout the 1930s, this attempt to encourage "simplicity in the appearance of women and girls" was the JFB's second answer to the rise of anti-Semitism. It reflected the defensive posture of those who saw self-discipline as a key to acceptance and self-defense: for example, the executive director of the Centralverein insisted that "stepchildren must be doubly good."[11] It also mirrored a century-old reflex of Jews who had learned to be inconspicuous for fear of reprisals from their enemies. If only they could "lie low," then "this storm, too, would blow over."[12] All Jews, particularly women, were cautioned to avoid the envy and resentment of anti-Semites by maintaining a simple standard of living. Jewish newspapers and organizations urged Jewish women to avoid any dress or action that could lead to embarrassment and warned "women who drape themselves in glittering jewelry" that they were abetting the enemy.[13] The JFB's fears of anti-Semitism obfuscated its normally keen feminist analysis. Its leaders urged women to be "less loud and ostentatious," and warned that "one person's weaknesses are generalized and hurt all Jews."[14] Insecure and confused, the JFB appropriated and propagated the negative images of Jewish women which were shared by Jewish men and anti-Semites alike. In doing so, it helped to convey two false impressions: an exaggeration of the number of Jewish women bending under the weight of gold and diamonds, as well as an exaggeration of the extent to which modesty could mitigate anti-Semitism. If the Jews bore any responsibility for the virulent anti-Semitism of this era, it had preciously little to do with women's dress. These self-conscious, demeaning, and futile attempts to mollify anti-Semites were the consequences of the illusion that anti-Semitism could be affected by Jewish behavior and of Jewish women's "double jeopardy." Members of the Frauenbund, both as Jews and as women, demonstrated the self-hatred characteristic of oppressed minorities, blaming themselves for their victimization.

The Frauenbund was more successful in helping to sustain the

Jewish community. During the Nazi years, it cooperated with the Reichsvertretung as well as with that organization's social welfare bureau, the Zentralausschuss für Hilfe und Aufbau (Central Board for Help and Reconstruction).[15] The JFB provided volunteers for some of the social welfare offices of Hilfe und Aufbau and shared responsibility for the divisions in charge of Jewish schools and institutions.[16] It also added its own new locals, attracted new members, and initiated closer ties with the Women's International Zionist Organization, the B'nai B'rith sisterhoods, and the Jewish youth movement. Its newsletter and cultural activities concentrated on teaching Jewish customs, history, and religion. Holiday celebrations had always been sponsored by the Frauenbund, but they took on new meaning under Nazism. Passover, Purim, and Hanukkah were observed in the context of persecutions as hideous as the ancient ones they commemorated. The Frauenbund also joined the Bureau for Jewish Adult Education set up by Martin Buber in 1934. The JFB's delegates attended study groups conducted by the Bureau and returned to their locals to lead workshops on Judaism. The JFB arranged a summer school course in which women had the unusual opportunity of attending lectures on talmudic literature by Buber and Franz Rosenzweig.[17] Locals sent speakers, lending libraries, gifts, and social invitations to Jews in small towns who could not afford Jewish cultural and religious institutions of their own.

The JFB had always promoted Jewishness, but its efforts took on a new, psychological dimension in these years. In Nazi Germany, Jews were depicted as evil and inferior. Cultural and religious activities gave a sense of perspective and an élan vital to a group facing rejection and hopelessness. They provided occasions for people to feel secure among their own, and they also functioned as "collective therapy" intended to help Jews retain self-respect.[18]

The Frauenbund was as conscious of the need to provide material assistance to people whose social and economic conditions were deteriorating as it was of the need for psychological encouragement. When the Nuremberg Laws of 1935 excluded Jews from Germany's Winter Welfare (Winterhilfe) program, their own social agencies were allowed to organize relief.[19] The Frauenbund aided in the collection of money, clothing, and fuel. In Berlin, Frauenbund volunteers scoured the city to ask for donations. Every month, their eighteen collection posts in that city gave approximately 30,000 care packages, arranged according to special dietary requirements, to needy families.[20] As Jews continued to lose their livelihoods, the JFB was active in helping Jewish middle-class women—and through them, their families—adjust to a lower standard of living. After the Nuremberg Laws forbade the hiring of Aryan domestics under forty-five in Jewish households, the JFB increased its housewife assistance program. Its locals set up cooking, darning, sewing, nursing, and home repair courses. The last were intended to teach women (who could not count on their husbands, because "Jewish husbands are not as handy as Aryan husbands") to fix minor household malfunctions, because it was becoming increasingly difficult to find German repairmen who would enter a Jewish home.[21]

The JFB also wrote its own cookbook for Jews who had difficulty buying kosher meat after Hitler forbade ritual slaughtering. It went through four editions in its first year (1935). Mutual aid was encouraged: women were urged to "specialize" in one particular area of housework in order to teach others their expertise. In various cities, the Frauenbund organized communal kitchens for those who could not cook for themselves; children's "play circles," a form of day-care for mothers who needed time to do chores; communal maid services which provided domestics for a half day's work; and dialogue afternoons, where women could discuss their problems and receive advice as well as moral support. True to form, the JFB never suggested that men should help out in the home. Even when men were unemployed, the JFB considered the household "woman's sphere." It was the *Frankfurter Israelitisches Gemeindeblatt* rather than the Frauenbund's newsletter which ran an article entitled "Men Learn to Cook." The author, a male, suggested that Jewish husbands who were unemployed help out in the home. The article insisted that the time was over when men who helped in the home were laughed at. Men had to learn how to prepare simple meals in case women got sick or had to be away from home for a few days. The main emphasis of the article was that men should be active in order to avoid despair and resignation. The article explained that the "heavy" housework could wait "a few days" (presumably until the wife recovered or returned). This article was still more progressive than the JFB's stance. Again, the JFB was demanding "super-

women" who would accomplish all household chores and, if necessary, take on an extra job to support the family if the husband lost
his job.[22]

The JFB pleaded with housewives to save their energy by return-
ing to "Spartan simplicity" in their households and involving their
children in housework.[23] It recognized the danger that women might
bury themselves in housework to escape from reality. The Frauenbund assumed that women maintained the equilibrium of the home
and, in the midst of confusion and despair, it called on women to
provide consolation, support, and comfort to their families and
community. Its newsletter repeatedly emphasized the pivotal role
of women in providing pleasant home environments for their har-
ried families. In turn, it attempted to offer women practical, intellectual, and spiritual support.

The final major area of JFB concern was the preparation of women
for emigration. When the Nazis first came to power, their policies
were relatively restrained and often contradictory.[24] This led Jews
to miscalculate tragically the security of their position in Germany.
Most hoped to be able to outlast the Nazi regime. The Frauenbund
did not encourage emigration at first and, in 1934, actually condemned the transfer of children without their parents.[25] But it was
finally convinced by the Nuremberg Laws that emigration was
necessary. Then, the Frauenbund increased its efforts to retrain girls
for domestic service, agriculture, and handicrafts—vocations that
were suited for Palestine and other places of refuge. The JFB newsletter devoted entire issues to the process of emigration. Its leaders
described practical problems, cultural differences, and women's
legal status in areas as diverse as Paraguay, Shanghai, and New
York City.[26] JFB members also accompanied children to safety in
foreign lands and returned to Germany to continue their work. As
more women emigrated, the JFB established useful contacts in
many parts of the world.

As November 1938 approached, the JFB was involved in planning
its "Winter Work" schedule. Its program, which included Winter
Welfare, cultural activities, holiday parties for children, and the
promotion of women's emigration, was discussed in the last issue of
the newsletter. After Crystal Night, the Jüdischer Frauenbund was
ordered dissolved. Its treasury and institutions were absorbed by

the Reichsvertretung, and those national leaders who were left in Germany joined the staff of that organization.[27] Although these women had many opportunities to emigrate, they continued to work for the Jewish community with pride and courage. Their work became more and more depressing to them. In July 1942, Hannah Karminski, former executive secretary of the JFB, wrote a friend: "This work can no longer give any satisfaction. It hardly has anything to do with what we understood 'social work' to mean. . . . but, because one continues to work with people, once in a while there are moments in which being here (*das Noch-Hier-Sein*) seems to make sense."[28]

Those women who were not in national leadership positions continued to perform social work along with other Jews from their community. In Berlin, a provisioning group (*Verpflegungsgruppe*), led by Bertha Falkenberg, the former head of the JFB in Berlin, provided food and aid to deportees at the Berlin railroad station. The Gestapo permitted about forty women to pack one day's worth of food for the deportees. It took days to prepare the thousands of rations that were necessary for each transport. By the end of 1942, food was scarce, and the transports were very frequent. The number of women who performed these services shrank to eight as they were deported. At that date the Gestapo forbade all further provisioning.[29]

Most of the JFB leaders were deported in 1942 and became victims of Hitler's "final solution to the Jewish problem." Hannah Karminski wrote a friend of her last visit with Cora Berliner (the former vice-president of the JFB) on the day of the latter's deportation:

C. and our other friends took books along. They agreed on the selection. To my knowledge C. took *Faust I* and an anthology. When I went to visit them on the last day, shortly before their departure, they were sitting in the sun in the garden reading Goethe.[30]

Notes

1. These categories were suggested by A. Margaliot, "German Jewry's Struggle for Survival," *Jewish Resistance during the Holocaust. Proceedings of the Conference on Manifestations of Jewish Resistance* (Jerusalem: Yad Vashem, 1971), pp. 101-102.

2. *BJFB*; June 1933, pp. 11-12.

3. Arnold Paucker, *Das jüdische Abwehrkampf gegen Antisemitismus und Nationalsozialismus in den letzten Jahren der Weimarer Republik* (Hamburg: Leibniz Verlag, 1968), pp. 39-49.

4. *BJFB*, December 1930, pp. 5-6.

5. Paucker, *Abwehrkampf*, p. 44; *BJFB*, December 1930, pp. 5-6.

6. *BJFB*, November 1931, pp. 10-11; *BJFB*, December 1931, p. 8; *BJFB*, October 1932, p. 11; *IF*, November 5, 1931, n.p.

7. *BJFB*, December 1931, p. 7.

8. While coordinating its efforts with the Centralverein, the JFB was sensitive to the feelings of its Zionist members. On the JFB's cooperation with the CV, see *BJFB*, December 1931, p. 8. The Frauenbund wrote its own "enlightenment" literature because its Zionist members objected to the apologetic tone of CV materials. *BJFB*, December 1930, p. 7.

9. *BJFB*, December 1930, pp. 5-7; *BJFB*, September 1932, pp. 4-5.

10. *BJFB*, September 1932, pp. 4-5.

11. Ludwig Holländer quoted by Peter Gay in "Encounter with Modernism: German Jews in German Culture, 1888-1914," *Midstream* (February 1975), p. 60.

12. Mass, unpublished memoirs, ALBI, II, 7.

13. *IF*, February 7, 1918, p. 10; *AZDJ*, September 16, 1921, supplement, p. 2. In 1922, a self-discipline organization (*Selbstzuchtorganisation*) with ties to the CV was formed in Berlin by Adolf Asch, a Jewish attorney. It sought to keep Jews from receiving unfavorable public attention. For that reason, it asked Jews to be inconspicuous and suggested that Jewish women "avoid all showy luxury in clothing and jewelry." Asch, unpublished memoirs, ALBI, p. 3.

14. Edinger collection, ALBI. "Aus der Welt der Frau," April 19, 1934, p. 12; *BJFB*, September 1934, pp. 4-5; *BJFB*, May 1936, p. 14. The JFB may have hoped to avoid splitting the Jewish community by sex (as it was already split by party), and therefore remained silent in the face of the crass exaggeration of men. More likely, however, was the JFB's acceptance of a widespread belief that women were frivolous and conspicuous.

More insight was displayed by Thorstein Veblen who recognized feminine clothing and lifestyles to be symbols that reflected the wealth and differentiated the status of males. In German society there appears to have been a general tendency to blame ostentation and derivative evils exclusively on women, without regard for these broader functions served by female display. This became apparent during World War I. Also, Adolf Hitler, who absorbed all prevailing misogynist beliefs and may have consciously appealed to them as well, railed against women in his last days in the bunker.

He accused them of losing the war due to their moral decadence and ordered the wives of Nazi officials to dress modestly. See: Veblen's, *The Theory of the Leisure Class* (New York: New American Library, Mentor Edition, 1953); Claudia Koonz, "Crisis and Role Change: German Women in War and Depression" (paper presented at the Berkshire Conference on the History of Women, Bryn Mawr, Pa., June 11, 1976); Amy Hackett, "The Politics of Feminism in Wilhelmine Germany, 1890-1918" (Ph.D. dissertation, Columbia University), pp. 909, 933.

15. *BJFB*, March 1934, p. 12. Hilfe und Aufbau joined the Reichsvertretung in 1934. For a complete explanation of these social service organizations, see: *Jüdische Wolfahrtspflege und Sozialpolitik* (Berlin), 1936, p. 91; Giora Lotan, "The Zentralwohlfahrtsstelle," *LBIYB* (1974); S. Adler-Rudel, *Jüdische Selbsthilfe unter dem Naziregime, 1933-1939* (Tübingen: J.C.B. Mohr, 1974); Kurt Jacob Ball-Kaduri, *Das Leben der Juden in Deutschland im Jahre 1933—Ein Zeitbericht* (Frankfurt/Main: Europäische Verlagsanstalt, 1963), pp. 118-25.

16. Schönewald collection, ALBI, no. 3896 (II, 11).

17. In her autobiography, Frieda Sichel, former president of the B'nai B'rith Sisterhoods in Germany, related her experience at the JFB's summer school in Nauheim (1935): "A large number of women grasped this outstanding opportunity to sit at the feet of one of the most erudite philosophers and thinkers of our time. . . . But even this . . . was no longer safe. In the middle of a lecture a burst of stones shattered the windows, but Buber continued as if nothing had happened. . . . the violent interruption was completely ignored." *Challenges of the Past* (Johannesburg: Pacific Press, 1975), p. 76.

18. Rabbis noticed increased attendance at synagogue services. Joachim Prinz, a rabbi in Berlin, called his sermon on the night before the boycott of April 1, 1933, an "attempt at collective therapy." "A Rabbi under the Hitler Regime," in *Gegenwart im Rückblick*, edited by Kurt Grossmann and Herbert Strauss (Heidelberg: Lothar Stiehm Verlag, 1970), pp. 232-38; Max Nussbaum, "Ministry under Stress, A Rabbi's Recollection of Nazi Berlin, 1935-40," in Grossmann, *Gegenwart*.

19. Adler-Rudel, *Selbsthilfe*, p. 162, and Lotan, "Zentralwohlfahrtsstelle," pp. 205-207.

20. *BJFB*, November 1935, p. 1; *BJFB*, January 1936, pp. 6-7.

21. *BJFB*, December 1935, p. 8.

22. *Frankfurter Israelitisches Gemeindeblatt*, January 1936, p. 137.

23. *BJFB*, June 1935, pp. 9-10.

24. Karl A. Schleunes, *Twisted Road to Auschwitz: Nazi Policy toward German Jews, 1933-1939* (Urbana: University of Illinois Press, 1970).

25. Schönewald collection, ALBI; no. 3896 (III, 2); *Jüdischer Rundschau*, January 19, 1934, p. 4.

26. *BJFB*, December 1936, June 1938, entire issues. On women's legal status, see Schönewald collection, ALBI, no. 3896 (II, 7), (III, 4).

27. Schönewald collection, ALBI, no. 3896 (IV, 4). In February 1939, the JFB's institutions were taken over by the Reichsvereinigung der Juden in Deutschland which succeeded the Reichsvertretung.

28. "Letters from Berlin," *LBIYB*, vol. I (1957), p. 312.

29. Hermann Pineas, unpublished memoirs, ALBI, pp. 10-13. These pages were written by his wife who served in this group and went underground soon thereafter, thus saving her life.

30. "Letters from Berlin," p. 312.

Selected Bibliography

Abbreviations

ALBI   Archives of the Leo Baeck Institute, New York
AZDJ   *Allgemeine Zeitung des Judentums* (Berlin)
BJFB   *Blätter des Jüdischen Frauenbundes: Für Frauenarbeit und Frauen-
        bewegung* (Berlin)
IF   *Israelitisches Familienblatt* (Hamburg)
LBIYB   *Leo Baeck Institute Yearbook* (London)
ZDSJ   *Zeitschrift für Demographie und Statistik der Juden* (Berlin)
ZSBB   *Die Zeitschrift des Schwesternverbandes der Bne Briss* (Frankfurt/
        Main)

Archives

Bund Deutscher Frauenvereine, Archives, Deutsches Zentralinstitut für
    soziale Fragen, Berlin-Dahlem 3. Abt. Der Bund und die ihm ange-
    schlossenen Organisationen
        5. Jüdischer Frauenbund
Leo Baeck Institute Archives, New York
    Collections:
        Berent, Margarete
        Berliner, Cora
        Bloch familie
        Edinger, Dora
        Eschelbacher, Ernestine
        Goldschmidt, Henriette
        Jacoby, Margaret
        Karminski, Hannah
        Krämer, Clementine

Liegner, Lilli
Meyer, Johanna
Morgenstern, Lina
Ollendorff, Paula
Pappenheim, Bertha
Schönewald, Ottilie
Tuch, Ernst
Werner, Ella
Werner, Sidonie
Memoirs:
   Asch, Adolf
   Badt-Strauss, Bertha
   Bauer [no name]
   Bergmann, Else
   Ettlinger, Anna
   Gova, Sabina
   Herzfeld, Ernst
   Karminski, Hannah
   Livneh, Emmy
   Maas-Friedmann, Lucy
   Pineas, Hermann
   Schönewald, Ottilie
   Stein-Pick, Charlotte
   Stern, Arthur
Yad Vashem Archives, The Central Archives for the Disaster and the Heroism
0-1/106 German.

Periodicals and Newspapers

Allgemeine Zeitung des Judentums. Berlin. 1900-1925.
Blätter des Jüdischen Frauenbunds: Für Frauenarbeit und Frauenbewegung.
   Edited by Hannah Karminski. Berlin. 1924-1938.
Israelitisches Familienblatt. Hamburg. 1904-1930.
Jeshurun: Monatsschrift für Lehre und Leben im Judentum. Edited by Dr.
   J. Wohlgemüth. Berlin. 1919-1920.
Jüdische Wohlfahrtspflege und Sozialpolitik: Zeitschrift des Zentralwohl-
   fahrtsstelle der deutschen Juden und der Hauptstelle für jüdische
   Wanderfürsorge und Arbeitsnachweise. Berlin. 1929-1935.
Menorah. Vienna and Berlin. 1929-1931.
Newsletter. National Council of Jewish Women. New York. 1933-1936.

Zeitschrift des Schwesternverbandes der Bne Briss. Edited by Dora Edinger. Frankfurt. 1928-1933.

Zeitschrift für Demographie und Statistik der Juden. Berlin-Halensee. 1900-1925.

Reports and Yearbooks

Altmann-Gottheiner, Elizabeth, ed. *Jahrbuch des Bund Deutscher Frauenvereine.* Leipzig: Verlag B.G. Teubner, 1920.

Deutsch Nationalkomitee. *Bericht über die Deutsch-Nationale Konferenz zu Bekämpfung des Mädchenhandels.* Berlin: Bernhard Paul, 1903.

_____. *Bericht über die III Deutsche Nationalkonferenz zu Bekämpfung des Madchenhandels.* Berlin: Bernhard Paul, 1905.

_____. *Bericht über die IV Deutsche Nationalkonferenz zu internationaler Bekämpfung des Mädchenhandels zu Bremen.* Berlin: Bernhard Paul, 1906.

_____. *Bericht über die 6 Deutsche Nationalkonferenz zu internationaler Bekämpfung des Mädchenhandels zü Breslau, am 8-9 Okt. 1908.* Berlin: Bernhard Paul, 1908.

_____. *Bericht über die 7 Deutsche Nationalkonferenz zu internationaler Bekämpfung des Mädchenhandels zu Leipzig, am 15-16 Nov. 1909.* Berlin: Thormann & Goetsch, 1909.

_____. *Bericht über die 8 Deutsche Nationalkonferenz zu internationaler Bekämpfung des Madchenhandels zu Karlsruhe, am 10-11 Okt. 1911.* Berlin: Bernhard Paul, 1911.

_____. *Bericht über die 9 Deutsche Nationalkonferenz zu internationaler Bekämpfung des Mädchenhandels zu Breslau, am 8-9 Okt. 1908.* Berlin: Bernhard Paul, 1912.

The Fifth International Congress for the Suppression of the White Slave Traffic. London. June 30-July 4, 1913. London: National Vigilance Association, 1913.

International Agreement for the Suppression of the White Slave Traffic, signed at Paris on 18 May 1904. United Nations Publication, 1950.

International Conference on Jewish Social Work: in Conjunction with the Third International Conference on Social Work. London. July 8-10, 1936. Synopsis of the Reports.

Jahrbuch für die jüdische Gemeinden Schleswig Holsteins und der Hansestädte (der Landesgemeinde Oldenburg und des Regierungsbezirks Stade). Hamburg: Verlag Ackerman & Wulff, 1929-1937.

Jewish Association for the Protection of Girls and Women. *Official Report of the Jewish International Conference on the Suppression of the Traffic in Girls and Women.* London. April 5-7, 1910. London: Wertheimer, Lea & Co., 1910.

————. *Official Report of the Jewish International Conference on the Suppression of the Traffic in Girls and Women and the Preventive, Protective, and Educational Work of the Jewish Association for the Protection of Girls and Women.* London: Women's Printing Society, Ltd., 1927.

————. *Report:* for year ending December 31, 1902. London: Burt & Sons, Printers, 1903.

————. *Report:* for year ending December 31, 1914. London: Women's Printing Society, Ltd., 1915.

League of Nations. *International Conference on Traffic in Women and Children.* Provisional Verbatim Report. Geneva. June 30-July 5, 1921.

————. "Report of the Special Body of Experts on the Extent of the International Traffic in Women and Children, II." In *League of Nations IV Social: 1926-27.* (C52) (2) M52 (1) 1927 (IV).

————. "Report of the Special Body of Experts on the Extent of the International Traffic in Women and Children." In *League of Nations Official Journal.* 1927.

————. "Work of the Traffic in Women and Children Committee during its Sixth Session." In *League of Nations Official Journal.* 1927. Doc. C2221.M.60. 1927, IV, annex 971.

National Council of Jewish Women. *Official Report of the Eleventh Triennial Convention:* held in Washington, D.C., November 14-19, 1926. New York: Correct Printing Co., 1927.

————. *The Yearbook:* New York Section, Council of Jewish Women, 1909-1910. New York: Schoen Printing Co., 1910.

Report of the Eighth International Congress for the Suppression of Traffic in Women and Children: held in Warsaw, October 7-10, 1930. London: Harrison & Sons, Ltd., 1930.

Troisième Congrès International pour la Répression de la Traite des Blanches: Paris, 22-25 Octobre, 1906. Rapport du Comité Allemand.

————. Rapport sur la troisième Question.

Unabhängiger Orden Bne Briss. *Die Wirksamkeit des von der Grossloge für Deutschland U.O.B.B. ernannter Comitees zur Bekämpfung des Mädchenhandels.* Hamburg: Druck von M. Lessmann, 1900.

Reference Works

Encyclopedia Judaica. 1971.
Jüdisches Lexikon. Berlin: Jüdischer Verlag, 1928.

Lexikon des Judentums. Gütersloh and Berlin: Bertelsmann Lexikon. 1971.

Segall, Jacob, and Weinreich, Frieda, eds. *Die Geschlossene und Halboffene Einrichtungen der judischen Wohlfahrtspflege in Deutschland.* Berlin: F.A. Herbig GmbH, 1925.

Sveistrup, Hans, and Zahn-Harnack, Agnes V., eds. *Die Frauenfrage in Deutschland: Strömungen und Gegenströmungen 1790-1930.* Burg b.M.: Hopfer-Verlag, 1934; reprint ed., Tübingen, 1961.

Volkszählung: Die Bevölkerung des Deutschen Reichs nach dem Volkszählung 1933. Berlin: Verlag für Sozialpolitik, Wirtschaft, und Statistik, Paul Schmidt, 1936.

Zentralwohlfahrtsstelle der deutschen Juden. *Führer durch die jüdische Gemeindeverwaltung und Wohlfahrtspflege in Deutschland, 1932-33.* Berlin: Zentralwohlfahrtsstelle der deutschen Juden, 1933.

Books

Adler-Rudel, S. *Jüdische Selbsthilfe unter dem Naziregime: 1933-1939.* Tübingen: J.C.B. Mohr, 1974.

————. *Ostjuden in Deutschland: 1880-1940.* Schriftenreihe Wissenschaftlicher Abhandlungen des Leo Baeck Instituts. Tübingen: J.C.B. Mohr, 1959.

Anthony, Katherine. *Feminism in Germany and Scandinavia.* New York: Henry Holt and Company, 1915.

Arendt, Hannah. *The Origins of Totalitarianism.* New York: World Publishing Co., 1966.

Badt-Strauss, Bertha. *Jüdinnen.* Berlin: J. Goldstein, Jüdischer Buchverlag, 1937.

Ball-Kaduri, Kurt Jacob. *Das Leben der Juden in Deutschland im Jahre 1933—Ein Zeitbericht.* Frankfurt/M: Europäische Verlagsanstalt, 1963.

Banéth, Noëmi. *Soziale Hilfsarbeit der Modernen Jüdin.* Berlin: Lamm Verlag, 1907.

Baron, Salo. *The Jewish Community.* Vol. I. Philadelphia: The Jewish Publication Society of America, 1942.

Baum, Charlotte; Hyman, Paula; and Michel, Sonya. *The Jewish Woman in America.* New York: Dial Press, 1976.

Bäumer, Gertrud. *Helene Lange.* Berlin: W. Moeser Buchhandlung, 1918.

Beard, Mary R. *Woman as Force in History.* 3d printing. New York: Collier Books, 1973.

Beauvoir, Simone de. *The Second Sex.* New York: Modern Library, 1968.

Behr, Stefan. *Der Bevölkerungsrückgang der deutschen Juden.* Frankfurt/M: J. Kauffmann Verlag, 1932.

Bernstein, Reiner. *Zwischen Emancipation und Antisemitismus: Die Publizistik der deutschen Juden am Beispiel der "Central Verein Zeitung" 1924-1933.* Berlin: Dissertationsstelle, 1969.

Berthold, Paul [Bertha Pappenheim]. *Eine Verteidigung der Rechte der* _____. *Frauenrechte Schauspiel in Drei Aufzügen.* Dresden: Verlag Pierson, 1899.

_____. *In der Trödelbude: Geschichten.* Lahr: Druck und Verlag von Moritz Schauenburg, 1890.

_____. *Zur Judenfrage in Galizien.* Frankfurt/M: Knauer, 1900.

Bracher, Karl Dietrich. *The German Dictatorship.* Translated by Jean Steinberg. New York: Praeger Publishers, 1970.

Bramsted, Ernest K. *Aristocracy and the Middle-Classes in Germany: Social Types in German Literature, 1830-1900.* Rev. ed. Chicago: University of Chicago Press, 1964.

Braun, Lily [Lily von Gizycki]. *Frauenfrage und Sozialdemokratie:* Reden anlässlich des Internationalen Frauenkongresses zu Berlin. Berlin: Expedition der Buchhandlung Vorwärts, 1896.

_____. *Die Frau und die Politik.* Berlin: Expedition der Buchhandlung Vorwärts, 1903.

Bullogh, Vern L. *The History of Prostitution.* New York: University Books, Inc., 1964.

Carroll, Berenice A. *Liberating Women's History: Theoretical and Critical Essays.* Urbana: University of Illinois Press, 1976.

Caspary, Gerda. *Die Entwicklungsgrundlagen für die Soziale und Psychische Verselbstandigung der bürgerlichen deutschen Frau um die Jahrhundertwende.* Heidelberger Studien, Vol. 3, Heft. 5. Heidelberg: Verlag der Weiss'schen Universitätsbuchhandlung, 1933.

Chafe, William. *The American Woman: Her Changing Social, Economic and Political Roles, 1920-1970.* New York: Oxford University Press, 1958.

Cromer, Else. *Die Moderne Jüdin.* Berlin: Axel Juncker Verlag, 1913.

Crow, Duncan. *The Victorian Woman.* New York: Stein and Day, 1972.

Deutsch Nationalkomitee zu internationaler Bekämpfung des Mädchenhandels. *Der Mädchenhandel und Seine Bekämpfung. Denkschrift.* Berlin: Deutsch Nationalkomitee, 1903.

Edinger, Dora. *Bertha Pappenheim: Freud's Anna O.* Highland Park, Ill.: Congregation Solel, 1968.

_____. *Bertha Pappenheim, Leben und Schriften.* Frankfurt/M: Ner Tamid Verlag, 1963.

Elbogen, Ismar. *Geschichte der Juden in Deutschland.* Berlin: Erich Lichtenstein Verlag, 1935.

Ellenberger, Henri F. *The Discovery of the Unconscious*. New York: Basic Books, Inc., 1970.

Evans, Richard. *The Feminist Movement in Germany, 1894-1933*. Beverly Hills, Calif.: Sage, 1976.

Fischell, Elizabeth. *Untersuchungen über die Entwicklung weiblichen Interessen auf Grund von Selbstdarstellungen*. Paderborn: Druck von Ferdinand Schöningh, 1932.

Freeman, Lucy. *The Story of Anna O*. New York: Walker and Company, 1972.

Freud, Sigmund, and Breuer, Josef. *Studies on Hysteria*. Translated by James Strachey. New York: Avon Books, 1966.

Fürth, Henriette. *Der Haushalt vor und nach dem Krieg*. Jena: G. Fischer 1922.

Gay, Peter. *Freud, Jews and Other Germans: Masters and Victims in Modernist Culture*. New York: Oxford University Press, 1978.

Gersdorff, Ursula von. *Frauen im Kriegsdienst 1914-1945*. Beiträge zur Militär-und Kriegsgeschichte, Vol. 11. Hrsg. Militärgeschichtliches Forschungsamt. Stuttgart: Deutsche Verlags-Antstalt, 1969.

Giese, Wilhelm. *Die Juden und die deutsche Kriminalstatistik*. Leipzig: Verlag von Fr. Wilhelm Grunow, 1893.

Glanz, Rudolf. *The Jewish Woman in America: The Eastern European Jewish Woman*. New York: Ktav Publishing House, Inc., 1976.

Goetz, F. *Die Stellung der Frau im Judentum*. Riga: Tipographie "Splendid," n.d.

Goldman, Emma. *The Traffic in Women and Other Essays on Feminism*. New York: Times Change Press, 1970.

Gräfe, H. *Nachrichten von Wohlthatigen Frauenvereinen in Deutschland*. Cassel: Verlag und Druck der Hotop'schen Officin, 1844.

Grossmann, Kurt, and Strauss, Herbert, eds. *Gegenwart im Rückblick*. Heidelberg: Lothar Stiehm Verlag, 1970.

Holborn, Hajo. *A History of Modern Germany: 1840-1945*. New York: Alfred A. Knopf, 1964.

Imle, Fanny. *Die Frau in der Politik: Einführung in das Staats und Wirtschaftsleben für Frauen und Jungfrauen*. Freiburg/B: Buchdruckerei von Herder, 1920.

Jewish Resistance during the Holocaust: Proceedings of the Conference on Manifestations of Jewish Resistance. Jerusalem, April 7-11, 1968. Jerusalem: Yad Vashem, 1971.

Jung, Leo, ed. *Jewish Leaders*. New York: Bloch Publishing Co., 1953.

_____, ed. *Jewish Library*. 3d series. New York: The Jewish Library Publishing Co., 1934.

Katz, Jacob. *Out of the Ghetto*. Càmbridge: Harvard University Press, 1973.

Kern, Elga. *Fuhrende Frauen Europas*. Munich: Verlag Ernst Reinhardt, 1929.

Key, Ellen. *Die Frauenbewegung*. Die Gesellschaft, Vols. 28-29. Edited by Martin Buber. Frankfurt/M: Rütten & Loening, 1909.

Knodel, John. *The Decline of Fertility in Germany, 1871-1939*. Princeton: Princeton University Press, 1974.

Koltun, Elisabeth, ed. *The Jewish Woman: New Perspectives*. New York: Schocken, 1976.

Kraditor, Aileen S., ed. *Up from the Pedestal: Selected Writings in the History of American Feminism*. Introduction by A.S. Kraditor. Chicago: Quadrangle, 1968.

Krohn, Helga. *Die Juden in Hamburg*. Hamburg: Hans Christians, 1974.

Lange, Helene. *Lebenserinnerungen*. Berlin: F.A. Herbig, 1921.

Lange, Helene, and Bäumer, Gertrud, eds. *Handbuch der Frauenbewegung*, 5 vols. Berlin: W. Moeser Buchhandlung, 1901-1906.

Lemons, J. Stanley. *The Woman Citizen: Social Feminism in the 1920s*. Urbana and Chicago: University of Illinois Press, 1973.

Levy, Richard S. *The Downfall of the Anti-Semitic Political Parties in Imperial Germany*. New Haven: Yale University Press, 1975.

Lewald, Fanny. *Für und Wider die Frauen*. 2d ed. Berlin: Verlag von Otto Janke, 1875.

Lowenthal, E.G., ed. *Bewährung im Untergang: ein Gedenkbuch*. Stuttgart: Deutsche Verlags-Anstalt, 1965.

Lowenthal, Marvin. *The Jews of Germany: A Story of Sixteen Centuries*. New York: Longmans, Green & Co., 1936.

_____, trans. *The Memoirs of Glückel of Hameln*. New York: Schocken, 1977.

Mack, Gudrun. *Wandlungen in der Gesellschaftlichen Stellung der Frau, abgelesen am Auflagenvergleich der Brockhaus Enzyklopädie und anderer Lexika*. Dissertation der Philosophischen Fakultät der Friedrich Alexander Universität, Erlangen-Nürnberg, 1970.

Marcus, Jacob R. *Rise and Destiny of the German Jew*. n.p.: Dept. of Synagogue and School Extension of the Union of American Hebrew Congregations, 1934.

Massing, Paul W. *Rehearsal for Destruction: A Study of Political Anti-Semitism in Imperial Germany*. New York: Harper, 1949.

Mill, John Stuart. *The Subjection of Women*. New York: Frederick A. Stokes Company, 1911.

Millet, Kate. *Sexual Politics*. Garden City, N.Y.: Doubleday & Co., 1970.

Mosse, George. *The Crisis of German Ideology.* New York: Grosset & Dunlap, 1965.

Müthesius, Hans, ed. *Alice Salomon, Die Begründerin Sozialen Frauenberufs in Deutschland, Ihr Leben und Ihr Werk.* Cologne: Carl Heymanns Verlag, K.G., 1958.

O'Neill, William L. *Everyone Was Brave: The Rise and Fall of Feminism in America.* Chicago: Quadrangle, 1969.

Pappenheim, Bertha. *Gebete.* Selected and edited by the Jüdischer Frauenbund. Berlin: Philo Verlag, 1936.

_____. *Kämpfe: Sechs Erzählungen.* Frankfurt/M: J. Kauffmann, 1916.

_____. *Zur Lage der Jüdischen Bevölkerung in Galizien.* Frankfurt/M: Neuer Frankfurter Verlag, 1904.

_____. *Sisyphus-Arbeit: Reisebriefe aus den Jahren 1911 und 1912.* Leipzig: Verlag Paul E. Linder, 1924.

_____. *Sisyphus Arbeit II.* Berlin: Druck und Verlag Berthold Levy, 1929.

_____. *Tragische Momente: Drei Lebensbilder.* Frankfurt/M: J. Kauffmann, 1913.

Pappritz, Anna. *Einführung in das Studium der Prostitutionsfrage.* Leipzig: Verlag von J.A. Barth, 1921.

_____. *Der Mädchenhandel und seine Bekämpfung.* Berlin: F. Herbig, GmbH., 1924.

Paucker, Arnold. *Das jüdische Abwehrkampf gegen Antisemitismus und Nationalsozialismus in den letzten Jahren der Weimarer Republik.* Hamburger Beiträge zur Zeitgeschichte, Vol. 4. Hamburg: Leibniz Verlag, 1968.

Petrie, Glen. *A Singular Iniquity: The Campaigns of Josephine Butler.* New York: Macmillan, 1971.

Philipson, David. *The Reform Movement in Judaism.* New York: Ktav Publishing House, Inc., 1967.

Pivar, David J. *Purity Crusade, Sexual Morality and Social Control, 1868-1900.* Contributions in American History, Vol. 23. Westport, Conn.: Greenwood Press, Inc., 1973.

Pollack, Herman. *Jewish Folkways in Germanic Lands, 1648-1806: Studies in Aspects of Daily Life.* Cambridge, Mass.: MIT Press, 1971.

Puckett, Hugh Wiley. *Germany's Women Go Forward.* New York: Columbia University Press, 1930; reprint ed., New York: AMS Press, 1967.

Pulzer, Peter. *The Rise of Political Anti-Semitism in Germany and Austria.* New York: John Wiley and Sons, 1964.

Reichmann, Eva. *Hostages of Civilization.* Boston: Beacon Press, 1951.

Reicke, Ilse. *Frauenbewegung und Erziehung.* Munich: Rösl und Cie Verlag, 1921.

Reinharz, Jehuda. *Fatherland or Promised Land: The Dilemma of the German Jew, 1898-1914.* Ann Arbor: University of Michigan Press, 1975.

Reuter, Gabriele. *Aus guter Familie: Leidensgeschichte eines Mädchens.* 17th ed. Berlin: S. Fischer Verlag, 1908.

Richarz, Monika, ed. *Jüdisches Leben in Deutschland: Selbstzeugnisse zur Sozialgeschichte, 1780-1871.* Stuttgart: Deutsche Verlags-Anstalt, 1976.

Rudavsky, David. *Emancipation and Adjustment: Contemporary Jewish Religious Movements, Their History and Thought.* New York: Diplomatic Press, Inc., 1967.

Ruether, Rosemary Radford, ed. *Religion and Sexism: Images of Woman in the Jewish and Christian Traditions.* New York: Simon and Schuster, 1974.

Ryan, Mary P. *Womanhood in America: From Colonial Times to the Present.* New York: Franklin Watts, Inc., 1975.

Sachar, Howard Morley. *The Course of Modern Jewish History.* New York: Delta Publishing Co., Inc., 1958.

Salomon, Alice. *Heroische Frauen.* Leipzig: Verlag für Recht und Gesellschaft, 1936.

_____. *Soziale Frauenpflichten.* Berlin: Verlag von Otto Liebmann, 1902.

Schleunes, Karl A. *The Twisted Road to Auschwitz: Nazi Policy toward German Jews, 1933-1939.* Urbana: University of Illinois Press, 1970.

Schorsch, Ismar. *Jewish Reactions to German Anti-Semitism, 1870-1914.* New York: Columbia University Press, 1972.

Siebe, Josephine, and Prüfer, Johannes. *Henriette Goldschmidt: Ihr Leben und ihr Schaffen.* Leipzig: Akademische Verlagsgesellschaft, 1922.

Silbergleit, Heinrich. *Die Bevölkerungs und Berufsverhältnisse der Juden im Deutschen Reich.* Berlin: Akademie Verlag, 1930.

Simon-Friedenberg, Johanna. *Gegenwartsaufgaben der jüdischen Frau.* Berlin: Druck von S. Scholem [1913].

Stephenson, Jill. *Women in Nazi Society.* New York: Barnes & Noble, 1975.

Stern, Fritz. *The Failure of Illiberalism: Essays on the Political Culture of Modern Germany.* New York: Knopf, 1972.

_____. *Gold and Iron: Bismarck, Bleichröder and the Building of the German Empire.* New York: Alfred A. Knopf, 1977.

_____. *The Politics of Cultural Despair: A Study in the Rise of the Germanic Ideology.* New York: Double, 1965.

Straus, Rahel. *Wir Lebten in Deutschland: Erinnerungen einer Deutschen Jüdin, 1880-1933.* Stuttgart: Deutsche Verlags-Anstalt, 1962.

Strecker, Gabriele. *Hundert Jahre Frauenbewegung.* Wiesbaden: Wiesbadener Graphische Betriebe, GmbH., 1951.

Susman, Margarete. *Ich Habe Viele Leben Gelebt.* Stuttgart: Deutsche Verlags-Anstalt, 1966.

Swidler, Leonard. *Women in Judaism: The Status of Women in Formative Judaism.* Metuchen, N.J.: Scarecrow Press, Inc., 1976.

Toury, Jacob. *Die Politische Orientierung der Juden in Deutschland, von Jena bis Weimar.* Tübingen: J.C.B. Mohr, 1966.

Twellman, Margrit. *Die Deutsche Frauenbewegung: Ihre Anfänge und erste Entwicklung, 1843-1889.* Marburger Abhandlungen zur Politischen Wissenschaft, Vols. 17/I-II. Meisenheim am Glan: Verlag Anton Hain, 1972.

Vicinus, Martha, ed. *Suffer and Be Still: Women in the Victorian Age.* Bloomington: Indiana University Press, 1972.

Wachenheim, Hedwig. *Von Grossbürgertum zur Sozialdemokratie.* Berlin: Colloquium Verlag, 1973.

Warburg, G. *Six Years of Hitler: The Jews under the Nazi Regime.* London: George Allen & Unwin, Ltd., 1939.

Weber, Marianne. *Frauenfrage und Frauengedanken.* Tübingen: J.C.B. Mohr, 1919.

Weinryb, Sucher B. *Der Kampf um die Berufsumschichtung: Ein Ausschnitt aus der Geschichte der Juden in Deutschland.* Jüdische Lesehefte, no. 13. Edited by A. Leschnitzer. Berlin: Schocken, 1936.

Wunderlich, Frieda. *Die Frau als Subjekt und Objekt der Sozialpolitik in Deutschland.* Sonderdruck aus der *Kölner Sozialpolitischen Vierteljahresschrift,* Vol. 3. Berlin: Verlag Hans Robert Englemann, 1924.

Zahn-Harnack, Agnes. *Die Frauenbewegung: Geschichte, Probleme, Ziele.* Berlin: Deutsche Buch-Gemeinschaft, 1928.

Zinnecker, Jürgen. *Sozialgeschichte der Mädchenbildung. Zur Kritik der Schulerziehung von Mädchen in bürgerlichen Patriarchalismus.* Weinheim and Basel: Beltz Verlag, 1973.

Dissertations

Hackett, Amy Kathleen. "The Politics of Feminism in Wilhelmine Germany, 1890-1918." Ph.D. dissertation, Columbia University, 1976.

Honeycutt, Karen. "Clara Zetkin: a Left-Wing Socialist and Feminist in Wilhelmian Germany." Ph.D. dissertation, Columbia University, 1975.

Kaplan, Marion A. "German-Jewish Feminism: The Jüdischer Frauenbund, 1904-1938." Ph.D. dissertation, Columbia University, 1977.

Mirelman, Victor A. "The Jews in Argentina, 1890-1930: Assimilation and Particularism." Ph.D. dissertation, Columbia University, 1973.

Pierson, Ruth. "German-Jewish Identity in the Weimar Republic." Ph.D. dissertation, Yale University, 1970.

Articles

Adler-Rudel, S. "Zehn Jahre jüdische Berufsberatung." *Jüdische Wolfahrtspflege und Sozialpolitik* 3 (March 1932): 49-59.
Badt-Strauss, Bertha. "Vom Typenwandel der Jüdin seit Hundertjahren." *Der Morgen* (1936): 459-563.
Baron, E. "Berufsumschichtungbestrebungen innerhalb der jüdischen Bevölkerung Deutschlands." *ZDSJ* 4 (1927): 16-26.
Bridenthal, Renate. "Beyond *Kinder, Küche, Kirche:* Weimar Women at Work." *Central European History* 6 (June 1973): 148-66.
Cahnman, Werner J. "Village and Small-Town Jews in Germany, A Typological Study." *LBIYB* (1974): 107-30.
Cohen, Gerson. "German Jewry as Mirror of Modernity." *LBIYB* (1975): ix-xxxi.
Degler, Carl N. "What Ought to Be and What Was: Women's Sexuality in the Nineteenth Century." *American Historical Review* 79 (December 1974): 1467-90.
Dworkin, Susan. "A Song for Women in Five Questions." *Moment* (May/June 1975): 44-54.
Edinger, Dora. "Bertha Pappenheim: A German-Jewish Feminist." *Jewish Social Studies* 20 (July 1958): 180-86.
Ehrenreich, Barbara, and English, Deirdre. "The Manufacture of Housework." *Socialist Revolution* 26 (October/December 1975): 5-40.
Ellenberger, Henri F. "The Story of Anna O: A Critical Review with New Data." *Journal of the History of the Behavioral Sciences* (July 1972): 267-79.
Fabian, Hans-Erich. "Zur Entstehung der Reichsvereinigung der Juden in Deutschland." In *Gegenwart im Rückblick*, pp. 165-72. Edited by Kurt Grossmann and Herbert Strauss. Heidelberg: Lothar Stiehm Verlag, 1970.
Fürth, Henriette. "Erwerbstätigkeit und Berufswahl der jüdischen Frau." *ZDSJ* 15 (January-March 1919): 1-9.
_____. "Die jüdische Frauen und ihre Aufgaben." *Oest. Wochenschrift* 16 (1899): 257-58.
_____. "Die jüdische Frau in der deutschen Frauenbewegung." *Neue Jüdische Monatshefte* 2 (25 July 1918): 487-96.
Gay, Peter. "The Berlin-Jewish Spirit: A dogma in search of some doubts." *The Leo Baeck Institute Memorial Lecture* 15. New York: 1972.

Glanz, Rudolf. "Das jüdische Element in der Modernen Frauenbewegung." *Ungarländische Jüdische Zeitung* 13 (1912): 197-202.

Grünewald, Max. "Der Anfang der Reichsvertretung." In *Deutsches Judentum: Aufstieg und Krise,* pp. 315-25. Edited by Robert Weltsch. Stuttgart: Deutsche Verlags-Anstalt, 1963.

Hauptman, Judith. "Images of Women in the Talmud." In *Religion and Sexism: Images of Women in the Jewish and Christian Traditions,* pp. 184-212. Edited by Rosemary Radford Ruether. New York: Simon and Schuster, 1974.

Hyman, Paula. "The Other Half: Women in the Jewish Tradition." *Response* 17 (Summer 1973): 67-75.

Jensen, Ellen. "Anna O—A Study of Her Later Life." *The Psychoanalytic Quarterly* 39 (1970), 269-93.

Karminski, Hannah. "Internationale jüdische Frauenarbeit." *Der Morgen* (April 1929): 280-88.

Lerner, Gerda. "New Approaches to the Study of Women in American History." *Journal of Social History* 3 (1969): 53-62.

Lopate, Carol. "The Irony of the Home Economics Movement." *Edcentric: A Journal of Educational Change* 31-32 (November 1974): 40-42, 56-57.

Lotan, Giora. "The Functionary in Jewish Communal LIfe." *LBIYB* (1974): 211-18.

————. "The Zentralwohlfahrtsstelle." *LBIYB* (1959): 185-207.

Pappritz, Anna. "Die Abolitionistische Föderation." In *Einführung in das Studium der Prostitutionsfrage,* pp. 220-60. Edited by Anna Pappritz. Leipzig: Verlag von Johann Ambrosius Barth, 1921.

Prinz, Arthur. "The Role of the Gestapo in Obstructing and Promoting Jewish Emigration." In *Yad Vashem Studies on the European Jewish Catastrophe and Resistance* I: 205-17. Edited by Shaul Esh. Jerusalem: Yad Vashem, 1958.

Richarz, Monika. "Jewish Mobility in Germany during the Time of Emancipation." *LBIYB* (1975): 69-78.

Riley, Glenda Gates. "The Subtle Subversion: Changes in the Traditionist Image of the American Woman." *The Historian* 32 (February 1970): 210-27.

Rosenthal, Erich. "Jewish Population in Germany, 1910-1939," *Jewish Social Studies* 6 (1944): 233-73.

Rürup, Reinhard. "Jewish Emancipation and Bourgeois Society." *LBIYB* (1969): 67-91.

Segal, Phillip. "Elements of Male Chauvinism in Classical Halakhah." *Judaism* 24 (Spring 1975): 226-44.

Segall, Jacob. "Die jüdischen Frauenvereine in Deutschland." *ZDSJ* (January 1914): 2-5; (February 1914): 17-23.

Shorter, Edward. "Female Emancipation, Birth Control and Fertility in European History." *American Historical Review* (June 1973): 605-40.

Stahl, Rudolph. "Vocational Retraining of Jews in Nazi Germany, 1933-1938." *Jewish Social Studies* 2 (1939): 169-94.

Stern, Selma. "Die Entwicklung des jüdischen Frauentypus seit dem Mittelalter." *Der Morgen* (1925): 324-34, 496-516; (1926): 71-81, 648-57.

Uttrachi, Patricia Branca, and Stearns, Peter. "Modernization of Women in the Nineteenth Century." In *Forums in History*. Edited by Peter Stearns. St. Charles, Mo.: Forum Press, 1973.

Walkowitz, Judith R. and Daniel J. "We are not Beasts of the Field: Prostitution and the Poor in Plymouth and Southampton under the Contagious Diseases Acts." In *Clio's Consciousness Raised*, pp. 192-225. Edited by Mary Hartman and Lois W. Banner. New York: Harper & Row, 1974.

Wilhelm, Kurt. "The Jewish Community in the Post-Emancipation Period." *LBIYB* (1957): 47-75.

Wood, Ann Douglas. "The 'Fashionable Diseases': Women's Complaints and their Treatment in Nineteenth Century America." *Journal of Interdisciplinary History* 4 (Summer 1973): 25-52.

Wronsky, Siddy. "Zur Soziologie der jüdischen Frauenbewegung in Deutschland." *Jahrbuch für Jüdische Geschichte und Literatur* (1927): 84-99.

Wunderlich, Frieda. "Deutsch-mann über Alles." *The American Scholar* 7 (1938): 94-105.

Zielenziger, Kurt. "Die Wirtschaftliche Krise der deutschen Juden." *Menorah* (September-October 1931): 439-50.

Interviews

Caro, Klara. Personal interview on the JFB in Cologne. Palisades, N.Y., December 9, 1974.

Edinger, Dora. Many interviews and conversations about the JFB and Bertha Pappenheim. New York, N.Y., 1974-1977.

Liegner, Lilli. Personal interview on the JFB's home economics school in Breslau and the JFB local in that same city. Palisades, N.Y., December 9, 1974.

Mühsam, Margaret Edelheim. Personal interview on the differences between the JFB and the BDF as well as on Jewish career women. New York, N.Y., October 23, 1974.

Pineas, Mrs. Hermann. Conversations about the Berlin JFB after 1938. New York, N.Y., April 28 and May 5, 1976.

Index

Abolitionism, 53 n.26, 105-08, 113-14, 121, 130, 139 n.18, 141 n.49
    See also Butler, Josephine; Pappritz, Anna
Abortion, 69-70, 95 n.36
Acculturation. *See* Assimilation
Addams, Jane, 33, 55 n.64
Agudat Yisroel, 91
Agunah. See Judaism, ritual marriages and divorce
Allgemeiner Deutscher Frauenverein. *See* General German Women's Association
Alliance Israélite Universelle, 154-55, 167 n.27
American Jews, 140 n.39, n.46, 144 n.105
Anna O. *See* Pappenheim, Bertha, as Anna O
Anti-feminism, 60, 64, 74, 170-71, 182, 199
Anti-Semitism, 14-18, 25 n.32, 85
    in the Bund Deutscher Frauenvereine, 83-84
    faced by all Jewish women, regardless of class, 7
    faced by all Jews, regardless of sex, 20, 170-71, 175
    government toleration of, 16, 86, 100 n.106
    and Jewish involvement in white slavery, 113-15, 125.
    Jewish reactions to, 20, 22, 50-51, 175, 199-200

See also Centralverein deutscher Staatsbürger jüdischen Glaubens; Jüdischer Frauenbund; Nazis; Vocational retraining of Jews

Birth rate
    among Germans, 70, 96 n.42
    among Jews, 70, 96 n.42
B'nai B'rith, The Independent Order of, 44, 55n.75, 173, 191 n.18
    women's auxilliary, 91, 207 n.17
    See also Jewish Committee to Combat White Slavery
Breuer, Josef, 31-32, 34-38, 42
Buber, Martin, 55 n.79, 202, 207 n.17
    on Bertha Pappenheim, 37
    Pappenheim's critique of, 47
Bund Deutscher Frauenvereine (Federation of German Women's Associations), 64, 86, 152, 155, 177, 184, 199
    few JFB members belong, 82-83
    goals of, 34, 64, 66, 73, 86, 141 n.49
    membership statistics of, 11-12
    model for JFB, 68-69
    occasional anti-Semitism of, 83-84
    Pappenheim's participation in, 46-47, 82
    and suffrage, 64, 157
    tactics of, 67
Burial societies, Jewish, 10, 67
Butler, Josephine, 33, 53 n.36, 105, 107, 113

Care by Women *(Weibliche Fürsorge)*.
See Pappenheim, Bertha, Care by
Women
Cartel of Women's Employment
Services. *See* Job counseling and
placement services
Catholic Women's Organization, 13,
83-84, 133, 152, 200
Center for the Vocational Guidance of
Jews. *See* Job counseling and place-
ment services
Central Association of Jews in Germany.
See Reichsvertretung der Juden in
Deutschland
Central Association of German Jews. *See*
Reichsvertretung der deutschen
Juden
Central Union of German Citizens of
the Jewish Faith. *See* Centralverein
deutscher Staatsbürger jüdischen
Glaubens
Centralverein deutscher Staatsbürger
jüdischen Glaubens (Central Union
of German Citizens of the Jewish
Faith), 20-21, 157, 167 n.36, 173,
199-201, 206 n.8, n.13
women's auxilliary, 91
Central Welfare Office of German Jews.
See Zentralwohlfahrtsstelle der
deutschen Juden
Civil Code of 1895, 161, 168 n.51
Clubs for Girls. *See* Girls' clubs
Commission for Employment Services.
See Job counseling and placement
services
Contagious Diseases Acts. *See* Regula-
tion
Conversion, 18
Coote, William A., 106
Crystal Night, 136, 187, 204

Depression, 182-83
Dohm, Hedwig, 34, 65
Doppelverdiener, 182
Dormitories for girls. *See* Girls' dormi-
tories and hostels

Early marriage treasury
as prevention against white slavery
and prostitution, 130, 132,
145 n.119
Eastern European Jews, 185
in Eastern Europe, 86, 126, 140 n.32,
142 n.64
emigration from Eastern Europe, 123
German-Jewish philanthropy toward,
127, 129, 175, 188
Education of Jewish women
university, 193 n.31
See also Home economics training;
Pappenheim, Bertha, on the education of women; Vocational
retraining of Jews
Emancipation (of Jews), 8-9, 200
Emigration. *See* Eastern European
Jews; German Jews
Employment of women
German, 124, 170-71, 173-75, 182-84,
190 n.11, 195 n.48
Jewish, 169-77, 184-85, 187-88,
190 n.9, n.12, 191 n.15, n.16,
192 n.20, 195 n.53
Employment services. *See* Job counseling
and placement services

Federation of German Women's Associations. *See* Bund Deutscher Frauenvereine
Feminism
alleged psychological sources of, 32
American, 63-64
English, 63-64
the moderateness of German, 60,
62-63, 65
reflection of liberal heritage, 62-63
result of bourgeois privilege, 63
result of three-class franchise, 63
social feminism and social motherhood, 13-14, 23 n.11, 39-40, 42,
54 n.62, 69-75
mothers of civilization, 72
as related to women's maternal
nature, 45, 62, 154, 173, 177,

197 n.61
social housekeeping, 171, 173, 188
socio-economic and cultural sources
of, 33, 60, 62, 65
See also Bund Deutscher Frauen-
vereine; Home economics training;
Judaism, and feminism; Jüdischer
Frauenbund; Radical feminism;
Socialist feminism
Frankfurt Lehrhaus. *See* Buber, Martin
Freud, Sigmund, 31-32, 42
Freund, Ismar, 159
Fröbel, Friedrich, 61-62
Fürth, Henriette, 82, 111, 154

Geiger, Abraham, 150
Gemeinde (Jewish community)
and anti-Semitism, 148
of Berlin, and women's suffrage, 154
charity work, 67-68, 165 n.1
of Frankfurt, its constitution, 152
as a legal entity, 4, 148
number and size of, 148
women's place in, 147-60
See also Suffrage
General German Women's Association
(Allgemeiner Deutscher Frauenverein), 59, 61, 82
German Association for Women
Suffrage, 64
German Jews
birth control and population decline
among, 10, 130, 176
career attitudes of, 196 n.54
emigration from Germany, 134,
185-86
marriage age of, 130, 132
mobility, social and economic, 10,
169, 175-76
under Nazism, 199-205
social composition of, 24 n.18, 190 n.5
suicide rate of, 176, 193 n.29
urbanization of, 193 n.28
German National Committee for the
Suppression of the White Slave
Traffic, 106, 110, 117-18, 120-21

Gershom, Rabbi, 152
Get. See Judaism, ritual marriages and
divorce
Girls' clubs, 127, 129, 144 n.109
Girls' dormitories and hostels, 127, 129,
133
Goldschmidt, Henriette, 61-62, 82

Hameln, Glückl von, 47
Hausfrau, 72, 78-79
Herzl, Theodor, 48
Hilfsverein, 154-55, 167 n.36
Hilkia, Rabbi, 153
Hirsch, Jenny, 62
Hitler, Adolf, 114, 206 n.14
Hoffmann, Rabbi David, 151-52
Höhere Töchter
Bertha Pappenheim as, 30, 42
Bertha Pappenheim on, 41
Helene Lange on, 30
Home economics training, 173-89, 203
in America, 192 n.26
and domestic service, 173-77, 185,
188, 192 n.22
failure of, 180, 182
"household daughters," 180, 194 n.39
professionalization of housework,
189, 192 n.24
as reflection of class interests, 130,
181-82
to prevent white slavery, 129-30
See also Vocational retraining of Jews
Home Economics Women's School in
the Country (Wolfratshausen),
177-79, 187

Intermarriage, 55 n.80, 176
International Abolitionist Association.
See Abolitionism
International Conferences for the
Suppression of the Traffic in
Women and Children
Second (1902), 111
Fifth (1913), 121-22
Eighth (1930), 125
See also Jewish International Con-
ference on White Slavery

International Council of Women, 44
International Jewish Women's Federa-
   tion, 86
Isenburg, 38, 40, 46, 48, 51, 134, 136

Jewish Association for the Protection of
   Girls, Women, and Children,
   108-10
Jewish Committee to Combat White
   Slavery, 109-10, 113, 117, 154
Jewish community. See Gemeinde
Jewish International Conferences on
   White Slavery
   (1910), 111, 120
   (1927), 124
Jewish Religious Union of England, 163
Jews. See American Jews; Eastern
   European Jews; German Jews
Job counseling and placement services,
   132, 136, 172, 179-80, 185-86
Jones, Ernest, 32
Judaism
   acceptance of female sexuality in, 71,
      97 n.52
   and feminism, 81
   Liberal, 23 n.12, 148-50, 163
   Orthodox, 24 n.12, 148-51, 153, 162,
      163, 166 n.14
   ritual marriages and divorce, 115-16
   as alleged cause of white slavey,
      115-17
   JFB demands modernization of, 117
   women in, 44, 67, 78, 115-16, 130,
      134, 137, 149-50
Jüdischer Frauenbund (League of Jewish
   Women)
   and anti-Semitism, 22, 85, 199-201
   joins Centralverein, 22
   attitudes toward white slavery, 113-17
   on careers, 188-89
   consciousness-raising in, 75-81
   educating women for citizenship, 158
   feminism of, 103, 153
   contradictions of middle-class
      feminism, 171, 174, 180-81, 187

"duties" versus "rights," 59, 73-74,
   93, 159, 162
moderateness of, 14, 88, 132,
   136-37, 173, 177
"mothers of civilizaton," 20, 72,
   97 n.55
founding of, 44, 111
goals of, 6-7, 10, 73, 83, 85-89, 93,
   103, 111, 136-37, 152, 165, 171, 189
on housework, 88-89, 203-04
Jewish identity of, 19, 21, 46, 68, 83-
   85, 114, 129, 177, 179, 202
on marriage, motherhood, and family,
   72-73, 78-80
membership statistics, 10-12, 89-90
traditionalism of members, 75, 79
on menopause, 80
Nazism, reactions to, 22
under Nazism, 88-89, 199-205
organization of, 89-93
   associated organizations, 91
   board of directors, 91-92
   locals and affiliates, 89-90, 100 n.116
   National Commission on Com-
      munity Participation, 158
   National delegate assembly, 158
   regional and provincial associations,
      91, 101 n.119
on Palestine, 87
political neutrality, 77
sense of sisterhood, 75-77, 99 n.85
on sexuality, 70-71, 121
social composition of, 14, 24 n.18, 78,
   85, 130, 174, 180, 189, 197 n.60
social work, 10, 13, 74, 87-88, 154,
   156, 188
strategies and alternatives to power,
   127, 164-65
support of peace movements, 87-88
as volunteer organization, 44-45
See also Abortion; Birth control;
   Early marriage treasury; Feminism;
   Gemeinde; Girls' clubs; Girls'
   dormitories and hostels; Home
   economics training; Railroad
   Station Aid; Suffrage; White slavery

Karminski, Hannah, 36, 78, 92, 205
Ketubah. See Judaism, ritual marriages
    and divorce
Kindergartens. See Fröbel, Friedrich

Lange, Helene, 34, 66-67, 83-84
    on birth control, 71
    on motherhood, 65
    on social motherhood, 40
    See also Höhere Töchter
League of Jewish War Veterans, 157, 183
League of Nations, 116, 123-24
Lenin, Vladimir Illich. See International
    Conferences for the Suppression of
    the Traffic in Women and Children,
    Fifth
Lette Society, 60-62
Levy-Rathenau, Josephine, 82
Lewald, Fanny, 82
Liberal Jews. See Association for Liberal
    Jewry; Judaism, Liberal

Mein Kampf, 114
Meir, Rabbi, 163
Millet, Kate, 107-08
Montagu, Lily, 163
Morality Associations, 141 n.49
Morgenstern, Lina, 61, 82

National Association of Women
    Teachers, 34
National Committees for the Suppression
    of the White Slave Traffic, 106
National Council of Jewish Women
    (U.S.A.), 13
National Socialists. See Hitler, Adolf;
    Mein Kampf; Nazis
National Women's Service, 179
Nazis
    allow JFB to function, 88-89, 133
    anti-female attitudes and legislation,
        183-84
    anti-Semitic legislation, 183-85
    burn Isenburg, 136
    exploit white slavery issue, 125

Newsletter of the Jüdischer Frauenbund,
    81, 179
Nobel, Rabbi Nehemiah A., 152,
    166 n.18
Nuremberg Laws, 51, 88, 185, 202-04

Occupational retraining of Jews, 88
    See also Vocational retraining of Jews
Otto, Louise, 59-60

Pankhurst, Christabel, 107
Pappenheim, Bertha (pseud. Paul
    Berthold)
    on abortion and contraception, 70
    as Anna O, 31-38
        and Breuer, 31-32, 34
        and Freud, 31-32
    and anti-Semitism and Nazism, 50-51
    attitudes toward sex, 37-38
    attitudes toward social work, 44-45,
        55 n.79
    on board of Bund Deutscher Frauen-
        vereine, 46-47
    Care by Women, 43, 154, 172
    death of, 51
    on the education of women, 30,
        40-42, 50, 55 n.64, 115, 127
    family background, 29-30
    on family life, 40, 49
    and Frankfurt Gemeinde, 152
    Jewish identity and religious practice,
        34-35, 37, 46-47
    Jüdischer Frauenbund leader, 12, 35-
        36, 44, 49
    and orphans, 50
    and prostitution, 37-38, 110-12
    as single woman, 39, 78
    travels, 43, 117, 119-20, 127
    Victorian upbringing, 30, 37
    on women's work, 171-72
    works
        The Inheritance, 50
        In the Second Hand Shop, 40
        The Jewish Problem in Galicia, 42
        Mayse Bukh (trans.), 49-50

Memoirs of Gluckl von Hameln
    (trans.), 47
*On the Condition of the Jewish
    Population in Galicia,* 42
Sisyphus Work, 43, 111-12
Tragic Moments, 48
*A Vindication of the Rights of
    Women* (trans.), 41
Women's Rights, 41
Ze'enah U'Ree'nah (trans.), 50
on Zionism, 38, 48-49
Pappenheim, Wilhelm, 30
Pappritz, Anna, 53 n.36, 139 n.18
Paula Ollendorff Home Economics
    School, 178-79
Population decline. *See* German Jews,
    birth control and population decline
    among
Professionalization, 174, 192 n.26
Prostitution
    in Alexandria, 37
    causes of general, 103-05, 107, 122,
        130, 134, 139 n.17, 171
    as degradation of women, 107-08
    from Eastern Europe, 109
    in Eastern Europe and Russia, 109
    in European cities, 104
    Jewish involvement in, 109, 111
    Jewish ritual marriage as cause of, 116
    in Latin America, 105, 108
    during and after World War I, 122-24
Protestant Federation of Women, 13,
    83-84, 133, 152, 155-56, 167 n.35
Prussian Association of Jewish Com-
    munities, 159-60
Prussian General Synod, 167 n.35
Prussian Secession Law of 1876, 148-49

Rabbinical Conference, Breslau (1846),
    150
Radical feminism, 65-66, 151-52
Railroad Station Aid, 132-34, 145 n.120,
    n.121, n.122, n.128
Reform Synagogue of Berlin, 150, 163
Regulation, 100, 105, 113, 138 n.16
Reichstag. *See* Women in politics

Reichsvereinigung der Juden in Deutsch-
    land, 208 n.27
Reichsvertretung der deutschen Juden
    (Central Association of German
    Jews), 100 n.113, 199, 202, 207 n.15
Reichsvertretung der Juden in Deutsch-
    land (Central Association of Jews
    in Germany), 22, 51, 100 n.113,
    157, 185, 202, 205, 208 n.27
Religious equality, 162-64
Rich, Adrienne, 164
Rosenzweig, Franz, 55 n.79, 202

Salomon, Alice, 55 n.77, 82
Schenierer, Sara, 127
Schmidt, Auguste, 59
Schönewald, Ottilie, 75, 92, 157
Schwerin, Jeanette, 82
Singer, Isaac Bashevis, 126
Social feminism. *See* Feminism
Socialist feminism, 66, 69, 177
Social motherhood. *See* Feminism
Soziale Frauenschule, 55 n.77
Stanton, Elizabeth Cady, 33-34, 51 n.1
Stürmer, 114-15
Suffrage
    active and passive, 151-53, 156
    in Germany, 147
    in the Jewish community, 147-49,
        151-52, 155, 157-61, 166 n.18,
        168 n.50
    Jüdischer Frauenbund's National
        Suffrage Week, 159
    in the Protestant community, 147,
        152, 155-56, 167 n.35
    strategies to attain suffrage, 160-61

Talmud, 117, 152-53

Union of Jewish Women (England), 13

Veblen, Thorstein, 206 n.14
Venereal disease, 105, 107
Verband der Deutschen Juden (the
    Association of German Jews), 22
Verband der Vereine für jüdische

Geschichte und Literatur (Union of Associations for Jewish History and Literature), 20-21

Vereinsgesetze (laws of association), 12 64

Victorian age
attitude toward prostitution, 105
cult of the lady, 11, 157
female hysteria, 33
marital sex, 71, 104, 138 n.4
See also Feminism, social feminism and social motherhood; Feminism, mothers of civilization; Pappenheim, Bertha, Victorian upbringing

Vocational retraining of Jews, 175-76, 180, 184-85, 188, 196 n.56, n.59
agricultural retraining of Jewish women, 186-87, 196 n.57

Votes for women. *See Gemeinde,* women's place in; Suffrage

Werner, Sidonie, 111, 120, 154
White slavery
causes of general, 107, 122
causes of Jewish, 108, 110, 118-19, 140 n.32
conditions of, 106, 120
definition of, 103
in and from Eastern Europe, 43, 108-09, 111-12
involvement of German Jews in, 110
Jewish reformers against, 108-13, 124, 127, 129, 172
Jewish white slavery
in Europe, 111
in Latin America, 108-09, 111, 123, 144 n.106
in the Middle East, 108, 112
in South Africa, 108
methods of procuring, 106, 109, 111,

117, 126
organizers against, 106-07, 117-20, 142n.72, 188
Pappenheim on, 118-21, 125
rabbinical reaction to, 126-27
and World War I, 122-23
See also Anti-Semitism; Butler, Josephine; Jewish Association for the Protection of Girls, Women, and Children; Jewish International Conferences on White Slavery; League of Nations; Pappenheim, Bertha; Pappritz, Anna

Winterhilfe. See Winter Welfare
Winter Welfare, 202-04
Wollstonecraft, Mary, 41-42
Woman, The, 34
Woman's "nature," 170
Women in politics, 162
Women's employment. *See* Employment of women
Women's history, 4-7, 23 n.3
Women's International League for Peace and Freedom, 87
World Conference of Jewish Women, 153
World Union of Progressive Judaism, 163

"Year of Duty," 194 n.38

Zahn-Harnack, Agnes von, 200
Zentralausschuss für Hilfe and Aufbau, 202, 207 n.15
Zentralwohlfahrtsstelle der deutschen Juden, 35, 156, 167 n.36
Zetkin, Clara, 69-70, 194 n.33
Zionism, 8, 193 n.30, 196 n.56, 200, 206 n.8
Zionist Union, 157
Zionist women's organizations, 91, 100 n.108

About the Author

Marion A. Kaplan is the Executive Secretary of the Council for European Studies at Columbia University in New York. Her articles have appeared in *Jewish Social Studies* and *New German Critique,* as well as other publications.